Indoor Marijuana Horticulture

by

JORGE CERVANTES

A special thanks to the many anonymous people that provided valuable input and support to make this book possible....THANKS!

First Printing
9 8 7 6 5 4 3 2 1

ISBN: 1-878823-17-5

Editors:	John Bushwell	D. Stanbery	
	Mr. Greengenes	J. Cervantes	
	Barbara Harlequin		
Art work:	D. Turner	Photos:	Jorge Cervantes
	E. Cervantes	Bill Bud	
		Mr. Greengenes	
Cover:	D. B. Turner		

TABLE of CONTENTS

Foreword   5
Legal Considerations   7

SECTION I   22

Chapter One......Indoor Horticulture...22, Indoor vs. Outdoor Horticulture... 27, About Grow Rooms...31, Setting Up the Grow Room...32

Chapter Two......Light, Lamps & Electricity...37, Intensity... 41, Reflective Light...45, Light Balancers...52, The HID Family...55, About Ballasts...58, Mercury Vapor...60, Metal Halide...61, High Pressure (HP) Sodium...66, Incandescents...70, Tungstens...671 Low Pressure (LP) Sodium...72, Fluorescents...73, About Electricity...77, About Electricity Consumption...82, Setting Up the HID...85

Chapter Three......Soil & Containers...89, Soil...90, Soilless Mix...98, Soil Mixes...101, Containers...105, How to Seed a Pot...111

Chapter Four......Water & Fertilizer...113, Application...114, Fertilizer...118, Mixing...132, Application...133, Nutrient Disorders...135

Chapter Five......Hydroponic Gardening...139, Different Kinds of Systems...140, Growing Mediums...142, Nutrient Solutions...146, Nutrient Disorders...148, Building Your Own System...149

Chapter Six......Air...153, Movement...154, Temperature...157, Humidity...160, CO_2 Enrichment...163, Setting Up the Vent Fan...171

Chapter Seven......Bugs & Fungi...174, Bugs...175, Control...176, Fungus...189, Control...191, About Spraying . ..195

Section Two II   199

Chapter Eight......Seed & Seedling...201

Chapter Nine......Vegetative growth...205, Cloning and the Mother Plant...206, Cloning for Sex...210, Cloning Step-by-Step...211, Transplanting...215, Transplanting Step-by-Step...216, Pruning & Bending...218

Chapter Ten......Flowering...222, Male...224, Female...225, Hermaphrodites...228

Chapter Eleven......Harvest...230, Male...230, Sinsemilla...232 Harvest Step-by-Step...236, Seed Crops...239, Second Crops...240, Drying...241

Chapter Twelve......Breeding...244, Breeding Step-by-Step...247,Indoor Cannabis Breeding ... 250

Section III   275

Case Studies......277, Andy...246, Bob...280, Chester and Claire...282, Calendar & Checklist...285

Glossary...298

Index...312

Introduction

I have updated this edition and added the input from two
other authors, Robert Connell Clarke and Ed Rosenthal, both
experts on the subjects that they describe. Clarke has been
breeding *Cannabis* form more than a decade and has traveled
the world in search of new genetic material. He is one of a
handful of serious *cannabis* breeders in the world. Clarke's
milestone work, *Marijuana Botany*, is the only book available
on the subject of *cannabis* breeding. Rosenthal has been
involved with publishing information on *cannabis* since he co-
authored *Marijuana Grower's Guide* with Mel Frank back in the
mid 1970's. Rosenthal's information about the legal aspects of
marijuana cultivation is important reading. The Federal laws
have changed so much that growing is a serious undertaking.
In fact, a conviction for growing more that a thousand plants
carries a sentence more severe than many convicted murders
receive. Working with both of these authors has truly been
fun and exciting. I am sure that you will enjoy their work.

The sections on lighting, hydroponics and nutrients have
been totally updated. These new sections reflect state-of-the-
art changes in indoor gardening. I have also removed most
references to chemical disease and insect control to reflect
the major shift to natural, organic controls.

This Revised Edition will be my last update to this
important work. I am leaving the continent forever. I am
going back to South America to live out my days in the
Amazon before it is destroyed. So to all of my loyal readers, I
bid you a fond farewell.

FOREWORD

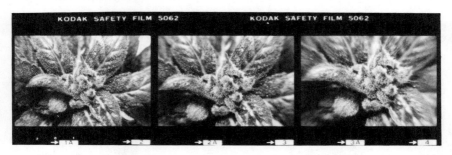

The purpose of this book is to give a simple, complete, description of basic gardening techniques growers use to cultivate marijuana indoors today. Horticulture is the art and science of growing plants. High Intensity Discharge (HID) lamps have made indoor marijuana horticulture grow by leaps and bounds. Today it is possible to grow large quantities of dynamite marijuana in the privacy and security of your own home. All information contained in this book has been tested and proven successful. We do not advocate growing marijuana or breaking the law.

Many factors should be considered when cultivating marijuana indoors. The horticulturist will need to monitor and alter all environmental factors and understand the needs of the plant to have the best possible crop. Which environmental factors have indoor horticulturists found to be most important for a productive crop? What are the most common obstacles faced by indoor gardeners?

These clones were just set under the halide.

This book takes you through a simple, yet intensive, thought provoking, step-by-step process that shows you how people grow marijuana indoors under HID lamps.

 RULES OF THUMB are given for a quick, easy reference. They are an easy-to-remember guide that is somewhere between an educated guess and a scientific formula. The RULES OF THUMB give everyone a for the task or subject.

The same plants on page 13 two weeks later.

Three composite case studies follow the text, so you are able to see, beginning to end, how other successful, and not so successful gardeners, grew super smoke for pennies a day. Of course, nothing can teach like experience. With the help of this book and a capital investment, you will develop your own unique horticultural skill and be growing super smoke in no time, 365 days a year!

A garden "Calendar" and "Checklist" are also in the back of the book to help give additional organization to all indoor horticulturists. This "Calendar" is different from others in that it is only four months long!

Several excellent reference books that all indoor marijuana horticulturists should have on hand include: *The Marijuana Grower's Guide,* by Ed Rosenthal & Mel Frank, and *Marijuana Botany,* by Robert Connell Clark, *Marijuana Insider's Guide,* by Mel Frank and *Marijuana Grower's Handbook,* by Ed Rosenthal.. These books are classics or the of marijuana growing. The *Growers Guide* being the *Old Testament* and *Botany,* the *New Testament.* To keep up-to-date with the newest and the best gardening techniques read such publications as *Organic Gardening, Sunset, Magazine* and the gardening section of the local newspaper for valuable background information.

Legal Considerations

HOW THE POLICE BUST PEOPLE AND WHAT A BUSTED PERSON SHOULD DO

Everyone who has read a detective novel or seen a who-dunit has a good idea of how sleuths work. They examine all the evidence, use tips, hunches and psychology to find the perpetrator. Narcs use these techniques too. They also use lies, extortion, and blackmail to bust and convict people. There are some things one can do to minimize contact with police, and to lower the impact if it does occur.

Most busts occur as the result of an informer, an accident or suspicious activity. Investigations also account for some busts. Many of them can be avoided with a little care and common sense.

People become snitches for a variety of reasons. Anger, self-righteousness and jealousy are three big reasons. In one case in which I appeared as an expert witness, an attorney was charged with cultivation. He and his girlfriend got into a verbal fight and he ordered her out of his house. She dialed 9-1-1. When the police arrived, she said, "The marijuana plants are in the other room." Another grower got into a disagreement with a customer, who called in the police.

A student in San Diego had 51 very small plants in his backyard. Unbeknownst to him, his neighbor could see the plants and held a religious belief that condemned the use of God's herbs. He turned in his neighbor, and got a small monetary reward, too.

A group of workers was at a bar. A few of them went outside to smoke a joint. A co-worker took note of who went outside and reported the stoners to his company because he resented working with "drug abusers".

A grower split up with his flaky partner and they divided the plants and equipment. Flake's plants died and he was very jealous of his successful former partner so he turned him in. One of two best friends started growing. The other one couldn't because of his housing situation. At first the grower gave his friend free pot. After a few months he offered to sell stash at a nominal price. This got the non-grower angry and, as the grower prospered, jealous with a slow burn. The grower was fronting the non-grower stash but had not been paid. The non-grower asked for more stash, but the grower refused and asked his friend to pay the money he owed. The non-grower then turned the grower in.

The number of people busted for personal reasons pales in comparison to people who snitch to save time or counts after being arrested themselves. This is the cops' favorite way of busting people because it takes little time, effort or intelligence on their part to get a good scorecard.

Charges are often reduced if a defendant "cooperates" by turning in friends or associates. Under federal sentencing guidelines a convict's sentence may be reduced if they turn in other people. These are potent weapons used by the state to induce people to snitch. It has caused family members and best friends to betray each other. These laws and policies have turned American morality on its head. Nobody respects a tattle-tale, yet American courts are turning citizens into snitches. Rather than taking responsibility for one's actions, the government is now teaching its citizens that the honorable path is to slough time onto someone else.

K was growing in the hills and lived in a house in the nearby town where he kept his equipment. He invited an underage girl over. She was later picked up for shoplifting and snitched for leniency. L was sentenced to six and a half years for cultivation. After four months in prison he squealed to reduce his sentence by 18 months.

Obviously, smart growers keep their activities as secret as possible and on a "need to know" basis. They never discuss their garden, show it to anyone or even tell people that they own one. A good way to make another suspicious is to "imply" a garden. Talking about them, or how plants grow, or how one used to grow plants is sure to bring an inquiring mind closer to the garden. Grower E was in a bar in August and offered to smoke a joint with two women whom he met there and the boyfriend of one of the women. The boyfriend was a former rip-off turned informer for profit. He figured this guy's leaf joint meant ownership of a garden. He "befriended" the guy and turned him in a month later after gaining his confidence and inducing E to front him most of the harvested crop.

ACCIDENTS

Accidents occur at the most inopportune times. Grower G was growing in a commercial space above a gallery. The day before the gallery was to open a new show the grow room sprang a leak. A rent-a-car stalled and its trunk popped open while it was being towed. There was a fire next door and the fire department broke in to reach the other apartment. Grower H bypassed the meter and circuit breaker to power his system. First there was a small fire, then the electric company investigated.

Although a person cannot always stop accidents from happening, many of them can be prevented or ameliorated. For instance, a passive watering system is less likely to leak than an active one. Smoking a joint in a car while transporting grass could create a disaster. Using an unlicensed car or one that stands out or has mechanical problems is asking for trouble.

SUSPICIOUS ACTIVITY

The U.S. is the most violent industrialized country. As a result it has one of the most paranoid populations in the world. Americans are suspicious of people who look or act differently than themselves. Grower I lived in a suburb in South

Dakota. Other houses in the tract had crew-cut lawns and looked neat. I's house had a lawn overgrown with weeds and messy drapes. J lived in a quiet apartment development rented mostly by young families. There was constant traffic to his apartment.

M was an oil maker. One spring day he went to his town's fair where he got into a conversation with a narc who was in uniform that day. The cop told me later that he smelled pot on M. Several weeks later, M went to city hall to apply for a permit. The cop noticed him and obviously learned his name and address. Later that day, while M was out, there was a 9-1-1 call mysteriously made from his house. The police answered the hang-up call and found some oil.

POLICE INVESTIGATION

The police rarely initiate an investigation on their own. Usually they are given a tip, information from a snitch, or other leads. Once they start, they have many options.

Legally they can do quite a few things to check on an indoor cultivation. They can go to the electric company to see if there is an unusual electric use. They check around the perimeter for grow light leaks, odors or unusual activity such as high traffic. They could also observe growing equipment or activities inside the house. Other investigative techniques are to question neighbors, look through the garbage and to check auto licenses of visitors.

The police can also use thermal imaging, which measures the infrared energy coming from the house. The more heat an object emits, the more it shows up on a thermal image. Electric companies use the technique to show homeowners where they have heat leaks in their homes. Anything emitting heat shows up: warm blooded animals, heaters, hot water pipes and electric lights. Because a high watt lamp emits more heat, it shows up brighter and in greater detail than low energy emitting objects. Thermal imaging can be a potent weapon, however it has its limitations. It works best in one or two story buildings. An inner room of a third story apartment building or the inner portion of a basement is fairly immune to this search.

The police are not allowed to trespass onto the property immediately surrounding the home, nor can they use a ladder to peer over a fence. However, they can ask a neighbor to let them look while on their property. While the police are constrained by the Fourth Amendment, private parties are not. For instance, a private party could use a ladder and binoculars to peer into a house or yard, an action police cannot legally take, and then report the findings to the police, who could apply for a search warrant based on the report.

The police can initiate an investigation and sometimes get a warrant based on an "anonymous" tip or the information of a snitch. Of course this immediately promotes corruption on the part of police, who often make the anonymous calls or who tell a person in trouble who to snitch off. "We know that you know N. He sold you this dope, right? Recorder on, "I bought the dope from N."

In the musical "A Fiddler on the Roof" one character asks, "Is there a blessing for the Czar?" The Rabbi answers, "May God bless and keep the Czar, far away from us." This is the best relationship that an outlaw can have with the government, too. Be inconspicuous, act inconspicuously, and look inconspicuous. The vehicle should be in good working order and be very camouflaged. It should be neither too new nor too old and not too expensive. The home should be kept neat. The garden and lawn should be typical of the neighborhood. Free growers do not brag, show conspicuous wealth or make their friends jealous.

Neighbors can be an outlaw's best friends or worst enemies, since they often are aware of what is going on before the suspect. Smart growers have friendly relations with their neighbors and do not promote suspicion or hostility.

DEA OPERATIONS

In November 1989 the DEA served subpoenas on a number of high tech garden stores. They demanded lists of customers from the stores. In order to give the owners an incentive to cooperate, they seized property and indicted the owners. Most of the establishments in legal difficulties were caught in stings in which the owners or help admitted that the equipment could be used for marijuana cultivation or discussed the subject at greater length. Once armed with the customer lists and UPS logs, the DEA asked UPS to provide lists of deliveries to specific addresses. Most of the time agents arrived at residences without warrants and tried to talk their way in. In same cases they were able to obtain warrants, but most of these appear to have been thrown out by the courts.

More recently the DEA set up its own store and induced customers to talk about illegal activities. The DEA is still putting pressure on the stores. Early this year they tried the "administrative subpoenas", which had no legal authority. Still many stores provided new customer lists. As a result of these government actions, it is risky to purchase from some stores, and it is hard to know exactly which ones.

To check the bona fides of an establishment a customer might ask if they have ever been hassled and whether they have cooperated with government inquiries. If they say they do, or are unwilling to talk about it, the store is a good place not to shop. If the salesperson implies or talks about illegal activities, it is quite possible a sting is in operation.

Smart growers have learned to never purchase goods mail-order from stores since they ship UPS, which keeps logs of all deliveries. They never purchase using credit cards or check since they leave trails. They do not use their vehicle to transport goods since the license plates may be recorded. When they visit the garden store they should look typical of the area.They purchase all the goods that they can from non-suspect garden shops, or even better, used at flea markets or through newspaper classifieds.

WHAT TO DO IF THE COPS COME

Suppose two cops walk up to a door and say to the occupant, "We have reason to believe that you are growing marijuana. we would like to search the place. Either let us in now and we won't bring you to jail. If you don't cooperate, when we come back with the warrant we'll kick the door in." What is a person to do? Tell them to go get a warrant. Here are the reasons: The judge might not grant them a search warrant based on the evidence they present. Even if the police are given one, the courts in later proceedings might find that the warrant was not good. Either there were misrepresentations made in obtaining it, or for other reasons. If a person waives their rights and allows the police to search without a warrant, then there is no chance to fight since there is no warrant.

It will take the police some time to get a warrant. Meanwhile, there might be things which might give the police wrong impression and should never be found at home. Lists of names which might appear to be pay/owe sheets, stray drugs and packaging material. Even if the warrant is not granted, it is still a signal to close up shop. However, one must be very careful during closedown. The police might be curious about boxes being loaded and try to intimidate the suspect at this time.

Suppose the police come in with a warrant, arrest a person and demand cooperation, by which they mean a confession. First they will ask for a waiver of the suspect's Miranda rights. "You have the right to remain silent. Anything you say can and will be used against you in court. You have a right to an attorney. If you can not afford an attorney, one will be appointed to represent you."

These are the rights that say that you do not have to talk to the police, you have a right to an attorney and everything that you say will be held against you. It would also be a good time to call a lawyer if the person has a relationship with one. The attorney might come over to observe the search and protect his client.

If the police knock without a warrant there is no law that one has to open the door or let them in. No matter how they may try to coerce a person to open the door, it should not open. As soon as it does, one cop is likely to say, "I smell marijuana." This simple statement, some courts might find, gives the police the right to search the premises. Opening the door is a no-win decision.

If the police do have a warrant they might knock on the door or bust it in to scare you. In either case the door should and will open. Even after the door is opened the person has some rights.

The Bill of Rights was created for a reason; to protect people from the power of the State. When a person waives their rights they are giving up precious liberties. A person should never agree to talk to the police. They will pervert everything you say, forget to mention or will discount any information a suspect gives them which might be exonerating. Talking with the police gives one no advantage. The police are not permitted to make a deal no matter what they say, "We can't promise anything but we'll put in a good word for you" or "This will make it easier." They may seem sympathetic while they make a bust, but on the stand in court they will try to make things sound as bad as possible. Why should a person talk to his/her enemy? These guys want to put people in jail. Suspects should have nothing to do with them.

It is true that the police have some options and can give a person a hard time if they resist their pleas for cooperation. For instance, in California, they have a choice between citing and arresting the suspect for some offenses, so they might say, "If you cooperate you won't have to go to jail now. We just give you a ticket for a court date. Otherwise we might have to arrest your wife too, and place your kids in foster care." Most of this is bullshit, to try to coerce you to confess and name other people.

So the answer to the question, "Do you waive your rights?" should be a resounding no. The suspect should tell the police, "I don't want to talk to you. I would like to call my attorney." If the person does not have a lawyer, s/he should say. "I don't want to talk to you. I would like to talk to an attorney." The person should try to do this in the presence of other people so there can be no confusing the issue when it gets to court. If they try to coerce a confession, and it is shown that it was not willingly given, but was extorted, the case could get thrown out. No matter how abusive, scary, coercive or bullying the police are, a suspect should never waive rights.

The suspect has been cited or arrested and is arraigned. At the arraignment, the suspect is presented with the charges against him/her. The court informs you of your rights. Bail is set and a date is set for the preliminary hearing.

The preliminary hearing is the time at which the court decides if there is enough evidence to hold a person for trial. The standard for this hearing is just a strong suspicion that you committed a crime. This means that the police just have to prove that it was likely that the suspect committed the offense in order for the suspect to be bound over for trial. This proceeding is very important. It is the time that the defense may make motions (ask the court to consider) to quash illegal warrants and illegally gathered evidence. In some courts, if certain motions are not made at this time, the defendant may lose the right to present evidence or make the motion later even if the motions are valid.

The preliminary hearing is the best time to beat a case. The whole legal proceeding is nipped in the bud so long, drawn-out, expensive legal proceedings may be eliminated. If there is a good case for motions, and the judge is receptive, the opportunity should not be missed and it should be handled by a high quality lawyer. The problem is that the judge often does not follow the law or permits the police to break the law. The court may also reduce the charges at a Preliminary Hearing or pressure the prosecution to plea-bargain a shaky case. Even if the charges are dismissed at a preliminary hearing, the prosecution can refile in some cases. This is usually not done.

CHOOSING A LAWYER

Attorneys are a lot like cars. A person can get one on the road for a few hundred dollars, but one with a smooth ride and reliability costs more, and there is no limit to what one can spend. Lawyer shoppers face the further problem that choosing a lawyer may be more like choosing a used car. Even an expensive lawyer can still be a lemon.

Think of lawyers as if they were surgeons. You want to use them to cut away a disease. Certainly if a person were planning on major surgery to fight a serious disease s/he would get the opinions of several doctors regarding the case. Clients should not be awed because a person has a professional shingle, a well-appointed office or a sharp car. They are humans just like everyone else. Lawyers will have different opinions about the case and suggest different strategies.

The best attorneys are creative, knowledgeable and enthusiastic. They suggest different approaches and tactics. If an attorney lacks any of these abilities, s/he usually should not be considered. No one strategy is necessarily right or wrong and there may be several valid alternatives. It is up to the defendant to decide which strategy suits the case and the budget and with which attorney the person feels most compatible.

Tactical decisions such as when to do motions, when to negotiate are all decisions which are anticipated and discussed, but the final move is best left to the hands of skilled counsel.

Hiring an attorney is an extremely important decision. A lawyer who does not know the law and procedure can do a suspect irreparable damage by waiving rights, not making motions regarding police actions which might cause the case to be dismissed or not representing the defendant with zeal. When shopping around for the right attorney there are some ways to sort through the lists.

It is best to choose an attorney who specializes in marijuana or drug cases, or at least in criminal cases. They can be asked about their record, whether they usually plead people out, turn people into snitches or their general strategies. This may be the most important decision a person can make. The choice of an attorney will determine just how the case is pursued.

Every case has at least one theory, the prosecution's. It sort of reads like the board game "Clue". "He did it in the bedroom with fluorescents and sold the stuff in baggies weighed on the scale." In order to win a case the defense has to prove either that the prosecution cheated or that their theory is wrong. Proving the prosecution cheated, such as a bad warrant or an illegal search usually results in the state's case being severely damaged or dismissed. Proving the state's theory wrong at trial usually results in an acquittal or conviction on lesser charges. To have any chance of winning the defense should have its own theory, "It wasn't his bedroom, there were no sales and the police destroyed the evidence so there is no way of knowing how much was actually there." If the defense has established a theory of the case, then the evidence is manageable.

Most marijuana smokers who are busted do not have a lot of money to spend on defense and are represented by Legal Aid or some other state supported defense program. Usually these lawyers are talented and dedicated. The problem is that they are critically underfunded and horribly overworked. This means that a marijuana case may not get the attention it requires. This is understandable, especially if the overworked public defender or court appointed lawyer is also handling Murder 1, Manslaughter, and/or Assault and Robbery cases, which they consider much more serious. While the Public Defender has many cases, you have only one, and it is very serious to you. An attorney with a practice limited to marijuana or even to drug cases is more likely to treat your case with the seriousness it needs.

Even if there is no recourse but to use a PD, all is not lost. A squeaky wheel may get the most attention. By letting the PD know that s/he is taking the case very seriously and that a certain level of service is expected, the defendant may get much more attention to the case. Helping to prepare the case can save the attorney enormous amounts of time and gives the defendant insight into how the battle is fought. Some things that the client can do is develop a theory of the case, examine and critique the police and prosecution documents, prepare a detailed investigation of crime scene data and find witnesses and experts.

Before hiring a private attorney, inquiries can be made with the State Bar Association, Consumer Affairs Department or local business groups to see if there are complaints or actions against them. The attorney's colleagues can be asked their opinions of the attorney. If they have disparaging remarks they usually couch them in subtleties so one sometimes has to read between the lines. "Jones has a unique style but has not perfected the technique." means he loses cases that could have been won. Former clients can also give a reference. The attorney in question might also be asked to provide references.

I am always suspicious of attorneys who think they know it all and are not interested in input from the client. In my experience, clients often have interesting and useful insights which help make a case. Participate in your defense. Not only will it help, but you will get an education on the law and the judicial system. The best attorneys I have worked with confer closely with their clients in putting the case together.

Your attorney should explain the law to you: you should explain the facts to your attorney. You should reach an understanding of how the law affects the facts, what strategies and tactics are available, what you can afford and will use.

Local attorneys sometimes discourage clients from hiring out of town or well-known attorneys. Their theory is that a high-powered defense would in itself raise suspicions regarding the defendant. My experience watching judges and juries has not borne out that fear. I have found the courts impressed with good quality counsel. They seem to feel that it reflects on the importance of the case, rather than the defendant's guilt.

On the other hand a "big name" does not guarantee vigorous competent representation. A competent specialist gives you a better chance of winning, but be careful not to pay a large fee to a stuffed shirt and end up getting no service. The attorney must be interested and involved in your defense.

During the Vietnam War, the U.S. increased its troop strength incrementally. First a few thousand soldiers, then 50,000 and so on. This gave the enemy time to adjust to the situation and learn how to deal with it. A marginal attorney might say, "Let me do the preliminary hearing and the motions and if you don't win, then get a trial lawyer." I think this is a bad strategy. Rather than increase force gradually, blast them out of the water as soon as possible. It may cost less in the long run since less attorney time is used, the case will end quicker and there will be less pressure on the defendant. A good attorney might be able to quash the government case in the preliminary hearing and thus put an end to the prosecution.

Before hiring someone, the client must talk price and exactly what the attorney will do for that fee. The State Bar requires a written fee agreement and receipt. People who would not think twice about trying to negotiate the price of a stereo in a store, often feel cowed when discussing money with a lawyer. It seems out of place. This works to the lawyer's advantage, and makes it easy for them to set a price. There is no reason that a client should not discuss the price, terms of payment, and how the fees are to be paid. Most important, what these fees are going to purchase: time, attention, motions, experts, expenses, associates - does one fee cover all of these or will they be billed additionally? Attorneys are required by the Feds to report cash payments over $10,000 to the government so they should be paid by credit card, check or money orders.

PRE-TRIAL DEALS

As the date for the trial comes closer,the tension grows. Most courts have a specific hearing to discuss resolution of the case. The vast majority of criminal cases are settled by plea bargaining at the pre-trial conference. Sometime within two weeks before the trial the prosecution may suggest some sort of deal. If you plead to this we will drop that. This removes the uncertainty of the trial, but may leave the defendant, now the convict, in a similar position to the worst case scenario of the trial. Before any plea bargain is made, the defendant should make sure, if possible, that s/he knows exactly what the plea is and what the sentence will be.

Prosecutors sometimes refuse to commit themselves to a particular sentence. Most state cases address the sentencing aspect by an agreement not to impose hard time, which usually means the sentence is a year or less in county jail. Sometimes federal cases are settled with an agreed weight or plant count that forms the basis for the sentence. Be beware, federal judges do not have to follow the recommendation of the prosecutor.

MAKING THE CASE

If every case has a theory, then the proof of the theory usually depends on just a few unanswered questions about which the two sides disagree. In a case in South Dakota, under pre-1988 guidelines, the Feds charged an individual with growing for sale. Their proof was that the grower had 47 female plants. They claimed that each of these plants, which were growing in a total space of 25 square feet, would ultimately produce a pound of bud, or a total of 47 pounds. The defense disagreed, and claimed that only 1 pound or less was involved, clearly personal use. Defense won when the jury agreed with the defense position.

A fellow was charged with possession for sale based on the theory that he intended to plant all the 10,000+ seeds he possessed and the result would be too much for personal use. The defense argument was that there was no indication that there was intention to use the seeds.

A lawyer was growing a few plants on his property. The state contended that the plants were for sale because there was a postage scale and zip-lock bags around. The defense's winning strategy was to show that he had a dis-incentive to sell because he could not have made enough on the few ounces to risk losing his license and was a "pack-rat" who saved baggies from his purchased stash.

The cops said they smelled the growing plants from outside. The defense contended the cops couldn't smell it because the only vent was on the top of the house and the hot air would have gone up into the slight breeze, away from the direction the police were standing.

The 1990 federal sentencing guidelines by statute state that any person growing 100-400 plants must be sentenced to a mandatory minimum of 5 years in prison. In one case, the question was whether newly cut clones were considered a plant. The government claimed the clones had roots and even if they did not, they should still be considered plants. The defense claimed that the clones did not have roots, and were not to be considered plants for this reason, so they should not be counted.

In each of these cases the prosecution had a theory and used an "expert" to expound upon it. These experts may opine on intent (personal use, weight, yield, or quality). In other cases the "witness" to the crime may have the crucial (mis)information. In either case, to win, the defense must discredit the testimony of the key prosecution witness, or to make the witness's testimony irrelevant.

There are several ways to do this. First the defendant and defense lawyer must set realistic goals. If the person was caught in the garden picking plants, they cannot deny involvement, which is often a court's decision. The key question might be limited here to personal use or sale? Other questions at trial might involve weight or yield or consumption.

Police have a tendency to exaggerate and overstate their case and this is often helpful in eventually discrediting them. A classic example of this occurred at a hearing in Woodlake, California. Attorney Logan was cross-examining the state's expert witness, Charlie Stowall (currently head of the marijuana eradication task force of the DEA) regarding yield. At Logan's request Charlie was holding a single stemmed two foot plant in his hand. Charlie admitted that the plant weighed less than an ounce and that it would ripen in six weeks. Charlie then insisted that in that time it would grow large enough to produce a pound of buds. By stubbornly refusing to budge from that position he discredited himself and although his testimony was admitted, his absurd assumptions destroyed his credibility. Ninety outdoor plants were found by the court to be for personal use.

Logically, one would just have to discredit the testimony of the prosecution to convince the court of the innocence or at least reasonable doubt of guilt of a defendant. This is not always the case. The court may need to hear the defense theory.

The defendant may be the best person to explain it. The testimony can be helpful, especially if s/he comes across on the witness stand as believable and sincere. The defendant must tell the truth under threat of perjury and s/he must look like s/he's truthful. Other considerations are whether the prosecution would be able to bring out impeaching or damaging information. The reason for this is that a defendant who takes the stand must answer all the prosecution's questions which the court allows. Even if a defendant has no skeletons in the closet, the court looks upon this testimony as at least self-serving, and possibly of dubious credibility. Common folk theory among lawyers is that for a drug defendant to win, he must testify. This is just not true. There are many good ways to develop a case.

If the defense is believable, then it does help to have the court hear him/her say it was for personal use and explain firsthand the complexities of the evidence.

If it is considered too delicate to have the defendant testify, an expert witness can be used to develop the defense theory and counter the testimony of the police. The police officer's statement might be, "This was the most sophisticated garden we have seen in this area and the 101 indoor plants would have yielded conservatively 101 pounds of bud worth at today's street prices over $1,000,000." The defense expert will give the court a more accurate assessment. "The 76 plants you see in the photograph which are each circled were all growing in an area 8' x 4', an area only 32' square. No matter how many plants were packed in the space the most that could be grown in that area was 1/4-1 ounce per square ft., a total of no more than 2 lbs. However this garden was not very sophisticated and all the indications are that it was being grown for personal use. First of all there was no CO_2, secondly a number of varieties were being grown, which suits home growers. They like to smoke different pot. Commercial growers usually like to stick with a single variety since the harvest is uniform and ripens at the same time. The plants were grown from seed, in soil rather than hydroponically. In addition, the smoking paraphernalia all around the house leads me to believe that he is a heavy user of cannabis."

In a case of medical necessity, all of the prosecution witnesses' testimony regarding the cultivation as well as yield may be irrelevant after the defense educates the court as to the medicinal value of the plant to this particular individual, the defendant. The seemingly large amount of product can also be explained via medical necessity. Therapeutic doses exceed recreational. Cooking rather than smoking requires more material. Making kif, which is a safer way to smoke also requires more material.

Experts can also help the attorney develop a theory of the case and develop cross examination for the prosecution expert. A knowledgeable expert may have been involved in many more marijuana cases than the trial lawyer. A good expert will have lots of information and ideas from prior cases. They are useful from the beginning of the case.

THE TRIAL

Some people think that trials are genteel affairs because there is a certain decorum and many of the players are in suits and ties. In reality, trials are verbal street fights. The lawyers try to beat up each others witnesses, discredit each other's theories and show who is the toughest by winning the case. The sad part is that people's lives are held in the balance for such pettiness.

The burden of proof in a trial is higher than in a preliminary hearing. Instead of "the preponderance of the evidence", it is "guilty beyond a reasonable doubt."

Most cases do not actually go to trial, and most attorneys are afraid to fight jury trials. One reason for this is that the court is likely to impose a harsher sentence if the defendant is found guilty at trial than if s/he pleads. However, federal convicts are sentenced using sentencing guidelines so that the court has little leeway. The best opportunity may be a trial. I have found that most jurors take their responsibilities seriously and try to rend fair verdicts.

There are many strategies for winning at trial. If the facts are on the defendant's side, the object of the defense strategy is to prove those facts to the jury. However, other issues may be importance. Trying the police is one good strategy. If the police messed up their investigation, the defense should let the jurors know about it, so that the jury develops reasonable doubt.

The courts are terribly out of contact with the realities of society and have no idea of the impact of the drug war on peoples lives. At one trial a judge asked me, "Do you mind if we go off the record for a moment?" I replied no. He continued, "So you earn a living legally from marijuana, writing articles and books and photos and testimony?"

I replied, "Yes your honor. But all of us here today are earning a living from cannabis. You, the prosecution and defense attorney, the bailiff, secretary, court reporter, janitor..."

At this point the prosecutor said, "Your honor, I object to this line of reasoning. I don't..."

The judge interrupted him, "I understand Mr. Rosenthal's line of reasoning. This proceeding wouldn't be taking place if marijuana were legal, and none of us would be here. Let's go back on the record."

THE FEDERAL SENTENCING GUIDELINES

LEVEL	POT WEIGHT	HASH WEIGHT	HASH OIL WEIGHT
Level 42	300,000 Kg	60,000 Kg	6,000 Kg
Level 40	100,0000-300,000 Kg	20,000-60,000 K	20,000-6,000 Kg
Level 38	30,000-100,000 Kg	6,000-20,000 Kg	600-2000 Kg
Level 36	10,000 2,000-30,000 Kg	6,000 Kg.	200-600 Kg
Level 34	3,000- 600-10,000 Kg	2,000 Kg	60-200 Kg
Level 32	1,000-3,000 Kg	200-600 Kg	20-60 Kg
Level 30	700-1000 Kg	140-200 Kg	14-20 Kg
Level 28	400-700 Kg	80-140 Kg	8-14 Kg
Level 26	100-400 Kg	20-80 Kg	2-8 Kg
Level 24	80-100 Kg	16-20 Kg	1.6-2 Kg
Level 22	60-80 Kg	12-16 Kg	1.2-1.6 Kg
Level 20	40-60 Kg	8-12 Kg hash,	800 gm-1.2 Kg
Level 18	20-40 Kg	5-8 Kg	500-800 gm
Level 16	10-20 Kg	2-5 Kg	200-500 gm
Level 14	5-10 Kg	1-2 Kg	100-200 gm
Level 12	2.5-5 Kg	500 gm-1 Kg	50-100 gm
Level 10	1-2.5 Kg	200-500 gm	20-50 gm
Level 8	250 gm-1 Kg	50-200 gm	5-20 gm
Level 6	Less than 250 gm	Less than 50 gm	Less than 5 gm

The federal laws regarding sentencing for possession and cultivation of marijuana were drastically changed in 1986 and were amended again in 1988 They were made harsher in 1990. Sentences are based on the weight of dry processed marijuana or the number of plants involved in a cultivation, also allowing for the "criminal history" of the defendant. You can get more time for any prior contact with the law. A first offender gets the usual.

The way the guidelines are written, if the grower has 49 or fewer plants, for sentencing purposes each plant is considered 100 grams, a little more than 3 1/2 ounces a plant or the actual weight if it is more than 100 grams. However, if the grower is responsible for 50 or more plants, for sentencing purposes each plant is considered 1000 grams, or 2.2 lbs. A person with 51 seedlings or rooted clones is sentenced for 51 kilograms, irrespective of the actual weight of the plants or what they would possibly or actually produce.

> ## *Growers should never cultivate more than 49 plants.*

SENTENCING GUIDELINES

Once the Sentencing Guideline level is determined, the court follows another chart which considers the criminal history of the convicted person. The points are calculated as follows:

3 Points- Each prior sentence of more than 13 months.

2 Points- Each prior sentence of more than 60 days.

If the crime was committed while the person was on probation, parole, supervision by the court, imprisoned or escaped.
If the crime was committed less than 2 years after release from imprisonment.

1 Point   For sentences less than 60 days. (Up to 4 points).

As anyone can see these sentences are very harsh and do not fit the crime. The concept behind them was developed by Carleton Turner, President Reagan's first Drug Policy Advisor. In an interview he stated to me, "If marijuana became a capital offense, you know that most of your friends wouldn't touch it with a ten foot pole."

The idea of user responsibility, that the user and not the dealer is the cause of the crime and should be held responsible and be punished is at the heart of this criminal system. Here are some tips that a grower developed to stay out of the system.

SENTENCING TABLE

(Months of Imprisonment)

Offense Level	1 (0-1)	2 (2-3)	3 (4-6)	4 (7-9)	5 (10-12)	6 (13 +)
6	0-6	1-7	2-8	6-12	9-15	12-18
8	2-8	4-10	6-12	10-16	15-21	18-24
10	6-12	8-14	10-16	15-21	21-27	24-30
12	10-16	12-18	16-21	21-27	27-33	30-37
14	15-21	18-24	21-27	27-33	33-41	37-46
16	21-27	24-30	27-33	33-41	41-51	46-57
18	27-33	30-37	33-41	41-51	51-63	57-71
20	33-41	37-46	41-51	51-53	63-78	70-87
22	41-51	46-57	51-63	63-78	77-96	84-105
24	51-63	57-71	63-78	77-96	92-115	100-125
26	63-78	70-87	78-97	92-115	110-137	120-150
28	78-97	87-108	97-121	110-137	130-162	140-175
30	97-121	108-135	121-151	135-168	151-188	168-210
32	121-151	135-168	151-188	168-210	188-235	210-262
34	151-188	188-210	188-235	210-262	235-293	262-327
36	188-235	210-252	235-293	262-327	292-365	324-405
38	235-293	262-327	292-365	324-405	360-LIFE	360-LIFE
40	292-365	324-405	360-LIFE	360-LIFE	360-LIFE	360-LIFE
42	360-LIFE	360-LIFE	360-LIFE	360-LIFE	360-LIFE	360-LIFE

Grower's Tips

1. Keep the garden on a need-to-know basis. Don't tell your friend, neighbor, brother, sister, lover, mother, father, child or any one else. If you have to tell someone, write a letter anonymously if you like. You never know to whom they might let it slip.

2. Loose lips sink ships. Never talk or brag about the garden.
Unreliable, untested anonymous or imaginary information can bring the cops. Mere rumors from friends reaching the wrong ears could bring cops or pirates.

3. Make sure to keep the garden totally hidden and smell proof. Do not throw away anything in the house garbage that you do not want to explain later. Trash is not protected and the cops have a legal right to root through it. Dump it in a secure way where it cannot be connected to you. Get rid of stems, leaf not being used, plant growing material, old lights, equipment you are no longer using and any other material which is extraneous to the present grow.

4. Make sure that you and your space fit into the neighborhood. If everyone else has short hair and suits and ties, so should you. Be unexceptional. Friendly, keep normal hours and don't have constant traffic. Keep your yard clean and groomed like the neighbors', no more or less. Monitor your electric bill and use visible energy hogs such as kilns or welding equipment to explain the electric use increase.

5. Make sure to make the garden as accident proof as possible. Put it away from public areas behind locked doors. Use the simplest systems. Minimize chance of fire using circuit breakers and good wiring, watch for flooding, duplicate safety measures.

6. Don't do the crime if you can't do the time. Talk to some one who knows the rules and punishments. You cannot realistically evaluate risk without information. Go to a library or a lawyer. Read the laws to figure how to minimize your risks and see if you really want to be involved.

7. Keep the project, the property and your house "clean". Be ready for the bust. Proud grower pictures, pay-owe slips, business records, packaging material, scales, fancy electronics or playthings, signs of wealth including checkbooks or keys to a safe deposit box should not be around. There should be no large sums of cash and indications that there is a legal means of income. Signs of prior grows such as large stash, stems, leaves or old growing material should be removed from the premises. On the other hand signs of use such as papers, pipes, roaches or stash, are implications that the occupants of a house are users, indicating at least some personal use. These items should not be kept out in plain view where an officer might see them. However, if they are found in a drawer during a search, their presence might have a favorable bearing on the case. A sterile house could be evidence indicating intent to sell.

CHAPTER ONE

INDOOR HORTICULTURE

One gallon pots contain these 12-18-inch, seven week old clones.

To some, horticulture is just plain gardening, to others, it is agriculture, cultivation, or farming. Regardless of interpretation, we all have the same desire: to grow top quality marijuana quickly, easily and for as little money as possible. The key to successful horticulture is to understand how a plant produces food and grows. Marijuana may be cultivated indoors or out and still have the same requirements for growth. Marijuana needs light, air, water, nutrients, a growing medium, and heat to manufacture food and to grow. Without any one of these essentials, growth will stop and death will result. Of course, the light must be of the proper spectrum and intensity; air must be warm, arid, and rich in carbon dioxide; water abundant, and the growing medium must be warm and contain the proper levels of nutrients for vigorous growth to occur. When all these needs are met consistently, at optimum levels, optimum growth results.

Marijuana is normally grown as an annual plant, completing its life cycle within one year. A seed that is planted in the spring will grow strong and tall through the summer and flower in the fall, producing more seeds. The annual cycle starts all over again, with the new seeds.

The seed has an outside coating, to protect the embryo plant, and a supply of stored food within. Given favorable conditions, including moisture, heat, and air, a healthy seed will normally germinate. The seeds coating splits, a rootlet grows downward, and a sprout with seed leaves pushes upwards in search of light. A seedling is born!

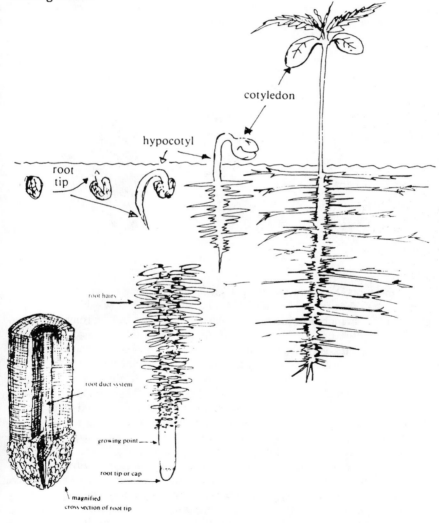

cotyledon

hypocotyl

root tip

root hairs

root duct system

growing point

root tip or cap

magnified
cross section of root tip

The single root from the seed grows down aid branches out, similar to the way the stem branches out above ground. Tiny rootlets draw in water and nutrients (chemical substances needed for life). Roots also serve to anchor a plant in the ground. As the plant matures, the roots take on specialized functions. The center and old mature portions contain a water transport system and may also store food. The tips of the roots produce elongating cells that continue to push farther and farther into the soil in quest of more water and food. The single celled root hairs are the parts of the root that actually absorb water and nutrients. Without water, these frail root hairs will dry up and die. They are very delicate and may easily be damaged by light, air, or klutzie hands if moved or exposed. Because of this, extreme care must be exercised during transplanting.

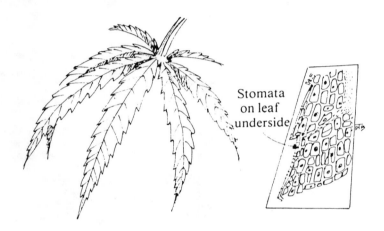

Stomata on leaf underside

Like the roots, the stem grows through elongation, also producing new buds along the stem. The central or terminal bud carries growth upward; side or lateral buds turn into branches or leaves. The stem functions by transmitting water and nutrients from the delicate root hairs to the growing buds, leaves, and flowers. Sugars and starches, manufactured in the leaves, are distributed through the plant via the stem. This fluid flow takes place near the surface of the stem. If the stem is bound too tightly by string or other tie downs, it will cut the flow of life giving fluids, thereby strangling and killing the plant. The stem also supports the plant with stiff cellulose, located within the inner walls. Outdoors, rain and wind push a plant around, causing much stiff cellulose production to keep the plant supported upright. Indoors, with no natural wind or rain present, stiff cellulose production is minimal and plants may need to be staked up, especially during flowering.

Once the leaves expand, they start to manufacture food (carbohydrates).

Chlorophyll, the substance that gives plants their green color, converts carbon dioxide (CO_2) from the air, water (containing nutrients) and light energy into carbohydrates and oxygen. This process is called photosynthesis. It requires water drawn up from the roots, through the stem, into the leaves where it encounters CO_2. Tiny breathing pours located on the underside of the leaf, called stoma, stomatae or stomata, funnel CO_2 into contact with the water. In order for photosynthesis to occur, the leaf's interior tissue must be kept moist. The stomata open and close to regulate the flow of moisture, preventing dehydration. Marijuana leaves are also protected from drying out by an outer skin. The stomata also permit the outflow of water vapor and waste oxygen. The stomata are very important to the plants well-being and must be kept clean at all times to promote vigorous growth. Dirty, clogged stomata breathe about as well as you would with a sack over your head!

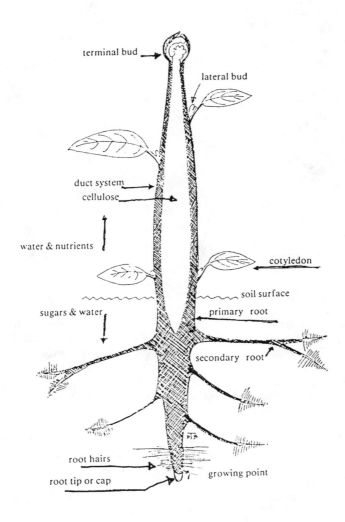

This giant flower top was harvested in February!

Cannabis will flower if conditions are right; the main variable is the photoperiod. In the fall, the days become shorter and plants are signaled that the annual life cycle is coming to an end. The plant's functions change. Leafy growth slows and flowers start to form.

Cannabis has both male and female plants. When both female and male flowers are in bloom, pollen from the male flower lands on the female flower, thereby fertilizing it. The male dies after producing and shedding as much pollen as possible. Seeds form and grow within the female flowers. As the seeds are maturing, the female plant slowly dies. The mature seeds then fall to the ground and germinate naturally or are collected for planting the next spring.

The female *cannabis* flower, left unfertilized, continues to produce larger flowers and more resins while waiting for male pollen to successfully complete her life cycle. After several weeks of heavy flower and resin production, THC production peaks out in the unfertilized, frustrated *Sinsemilla!*

INDOOR vs. OUTDOOR HORTICULTURE

Growing *cannabis* indoors is very different from outdoor cultivation, even though marijuana has standard requirements for growth. The critical factors of the outdoor environment must be totally recreated indoors if *cannabis* is to grow well. Outdoors, a gardener can expend a minimum of effort and Mother Nature will control many of the growth influencing factors. *Indoors, the horticulturist assumes the cherished role of Mother Nature.* The horticulturist is able to wield control over many factors influencing growth. Since few people have ever played Mother Nature before, they usually do not fathom the scope of the job. We must realize that Mother Nature constantly provides the many things plants require to grow. The indoor grower must manufacture the most important factors of the outdoor environment. This requires a general knowledge of the environment about to be created, as well as specific guidelines to follow.

Indoors you are Mother Nature!

Outdoor marijuana gardens are now outdated

Outdoor marijuana cultivation is limited to one season (two in the tropics). Light is most often inadequate, since the marijuana patch must be located in an undetectable place. A friend in the midwest grew a wonderful crop that was camouflaged by several beautiful Sumac trees. This was a great hiding spot for the garden. It was right in the middle of the city and went undetected almost all season. One fine fall day in mid September, there was a freeze, a hard freeze; the Sumac lost all its leaves overnight! The tough marijuana kept all her leaves, but could be seen over a mile away!

Outdoor air is usually fresh, but can become uncontrollably humid, arid, cold or windy. Water and nutrients are usually easy to supply, unless the garden is grown by a guerrilla farmer and located in the middle of nowhere. The beautiful outdoors is also plagued with jerks who steal marijuana and hard nosed policemen, with no sense of humor, who are paid to destroy gardens.

With indoor horticulture, light, air, temperature, humidity, ventilation, CO_2, soil, water and nutrients may be precisely controlled to yield a perfect environment for marijuana growth. Not long ago, with fluorescent tubes, this was not true. An inexpensive artificial light source, providing adequate intensity was the main limiting factor to indoor plant growth.

Technological breakthroughs and scientific research have shed bright light on indoor horticulture, by producing the 1000 watt metal halide and 1000 watt High Pressure (HP) sodium, High Intensity Discharge (HID) lamps. Now, a reasonably priced artificial light source, providing the color spectrum and intensity necessary for marijuana growth, is on the market. With the HID lamps, a gardener may totally control the indoor environment. The 1000 watt metal halide HID lamp provides sufficient intensity, of the proper colors in the spectrum, to grow incredibly potent marijuana. The 1000 watt high pressure sodium lamp is combined with a halide during flowering. It emits a light spectrum similar to the autumn or harvest sun, providing the intense yellows, oranges and reds *cannabis* needs to grow flowers 20% to 100%, larger than if only a single metal halide were used. The HID lamps are essentially a small sun in your basement, spare room or attic. By using a timer, a regular day-night schedule (photoperiod) may be set up. The HID, with a timer, may even be better than the sun! Exact control may be exercised over the hours of light per day, letting the horticulturist create his or her own seasons. Summer and fall are recreated over and over, winter and spring are forgotten and virtually non-existent to the indoor horticulturist!

Outdoors, *cannabis* seeds are normally sown in the spring, grow all summer and flower in the fall. They flower when the fall days grow short. Short days and *long* nights signal marijuana that winter is approaching and it is time to flower. Cold weather slows flowering and below freezing temperatures will result in death. Growers in northern climates are forced to grow plants 6 to 7 months, maybe get ripped-off, and if the weather is freezing, harvest premature flower buds.

Indoors, all growth factors may be individually controlled to give the plant exactly what it needs to promote any stage of growth. A 2 to 12 month old plant may be induced into flowering by shortening the days from 18 hours to 12 hours. This may be done all year round, regardless of the temperature or hours of sunshine outside. When growing clones, 4 to 5 harvests per year are possible, although two grow rooms are necessary for this.

The air outdoors is usually fresh and contains .03 to .04-6 CO_2. Ventilation is usually adequate, but the wind sometimes howls, burning leaves or even blowing plants over. Humidity and temperature are almost impossible to control, except in a greenhouse, which is expensive to build and sticks out like a big neon sign saying "Take Me".

Indoors, AIR may easily be controlled to promote growth and create an unfriendly environment for bugs and fungus. The CO_2 content may be enriched to double or triple plant growth. An open door and/or forced air ventilation system will provide circulation and ventilation necessary to keep air fresh. Humidity is raised by misting the air with water or evaporating water from a bucket. Humidity is lowered by drying the air with heat from the HID system, a heater, furnace or dehumidifier. Circulation, ventilation, humidity and temperature regulation are also fundamental to bug and fungus control. Clones root much faster in a warm, humid, indoor environment. Temperature is easy to keep constant. Usually heat from the HID system provides ample heat for the grow room. An indoor garden will flourish between 70-75° F, but clones root best at 80-85° F. Air temperature may be raised with extra heat and lowered by means of an exhaust fan attached to a thermostat, if outside air is cooler.

Outdoor soil may vary greatly. It could be too acidic or alkaline, have toxic qualities, drain poorly, be full of bad bugs, fungus and bad microorganisms.

Indoor growing mediums may be purchased from a nursery in the form of potting soil or soilless mix. They will contain a minimum of fungus, in sects or weeds. These growing mediums usually have the proper acid-to- alkaline or pH balance. Potting soils usually contain complete, balanced nutrients, while soilless mixes may or may not be fortified with nutrients. Nutrient levels may easily be checked in these growing mediums. Nutrients may then be added or leached (washed) out of containers, providing total soil control. The moisture content of the growing medium may be precisely monitored with a moisture meter and controlled. Potting soil and soilless mixes are blended to retain water evenly, provide good aeration and consistent root growth.

Outdoors, insects and fungi are usually kept in check by Mother Nature and are seldom a problem. Indoors, the grower must take over in Mother Nature's absence. Keep the insects out of the grow room by simple sanitary precautions. It is easy to wash your hands, use clean tools and sweep the floor regularly. If insects and fungus do get started, they are easy to control in an enclosed room, since the grower may control the factors that inhibit their well-being. Organic or chemical sprays may be used in conjunction with humidity, ventilation and temperature regulation to control the pests.

Bandits that would think nothing of ripping-off outdoor plants, are stymied by the concealed indoor grow room. Even if they know the location of a room full of marijuana, breaking and entering your home constitutes a criminal offense, a felony crime in most states. None-the-less, do not tell anyone of the indoor garden and install dead bolt locks on all outside doors. If living in an apartment or rental home, change outside door locks and lock the grow room door with a key. Landlords and managers have legal access to your home.

These maturing plants are safe from bandits indoors.

RULE OF THUMB: Only tell people that are directly involved. Examples: (1) People living in the home (2) another grower you are trading clones with.

In summary, indoor marijuana cultivation is by far superior to outdoor cultivation for many growers. It provides exacting control of all growth inducing factors and bandits are baffled. Not to mention, an indoor garden yields incredible smoke year round!

SURVIVAL OF THE FITTEST

The only factor that can not be easily controlled indoors is the experience of the grower. The gardener, assuming the role of Mother Nature, has control of all the variables that affect the plant's growth. If he or she does not know how to apply this control, it is worthless. The best way to combat inexperience is to take a lesson from Mother Nature. Increase the plants odds of survival by planting 3 to 4 times as many seeds or clones as you plan to harvest. Sound a little pessimistic? It will sound very realistic after your first crop. Look at the following example of what really happens when most growers first try their hand at indoor cultivation.

EXAMPLE:

Sept. 1	100 seeds planted
Sept. 7	80 seeds sprouted
Sept. 21	60 strong healthy seedlings
Dec. 1	30 females (males harvested)
Jan. 25	25 females harvested

100 seeds were sown, 25 mature females were harvested. Look at this example and think about your past experience with plants. Did every seed or clone started grow into a healthy mature adult? We all hate to make mistakes, but experience tells us that mistakes and inexperience will take a toll. It is easy to jerk a sick plant, but it takes forever to grow a new one. If you are worried about what to do with the excess plants in the event of no mistakes, just think what a nice gift they would make for friends that want to start their very own indoor garden. Also, if you smoke the extras and mistakes, you will not be pinching premature leaves and tops off plants before they are ripe.

ABOUT GROW ROOMS

The police may not use the electricity bill alone as grounds for a search warrant. As long as the marijuana grown is not sold, or shown to a tattletale narc, there is no reason for any suspicion. So, all the security needed is a locked door and tight lips!

The best location for a grow room is in the most obscure corner of the basement. The basement is probably the best room in most homes for indoor gardens since the temperature is easy to keep constant year round. The room is well insulated by concrete walls and soil. Basements also remain cool, which helps prevent heat build-up. A room can be enclosed and some old junk can be stacked up around the room for camouflage. Seldom do guests use the basement if uninvited.

Real paranoid people can install a false door in a closet. The grow room is located behind the secret door. Another good secret room, except for the possible heat build-up problems is the attic. Few people venture to an attic that is difficult to get to. One person grew his garden under a trap door in a basement.

Some of the worst places to grow are in out buildings like garages not attached to homes and barns. Often, people do not look at entering a barn or garage as a crime, when they would consider entering the home a crime. Security is much better when the garden is within the home.

There have even been cases of Marijuana on Wheels! That's right, some innovative growers have remodeled trailer houses and busses into grow rooms. Amazing but true. I even saw a grow room made from a tricked out trailer.

The size of grow room determines the wattage of lamp used. The 400 watt lamps are just fine for smaller rooms such as closets or spaces from 9-21 square feet of floor space. A 1000 watt bulb should be employed for 24-100 square feet grow rooms.

The drawings show several common grow room floor plans. As the rooms demonstrate, there are several basic approaches to grow room production. Almost all growers start out with one crop grown in a room. after the crop is harvested, a new batch of clones in introduced. The photoperiod is switched back to 18 hours and the cycle continues.

A second method is very similar to the first, but utilizes two rooms. The first room is for vegetative growth and rooting clones. Since plants are small, the room is about 1/4 the size of the flowering room. The flowering room is harvested and the vegetative crop is moved into flower. A clone crop is transplanted into large pots to start the vegetative cycle.

A third method provides a perpetual crop. Several clones are taken each day or week. The same amount of plants are moved from the vegetative room to the flowering room. Of course the harvest is almost perpetual!

SETTING UP THE GROW ROOM

Before any plants are introduced, the grow room should be set up. Construction requires space and planning. There are just a few things that need to be accomplished before the room is ready for plants.

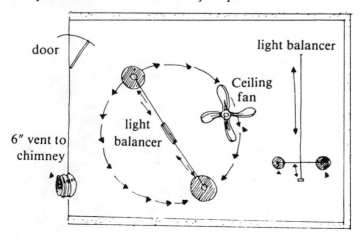

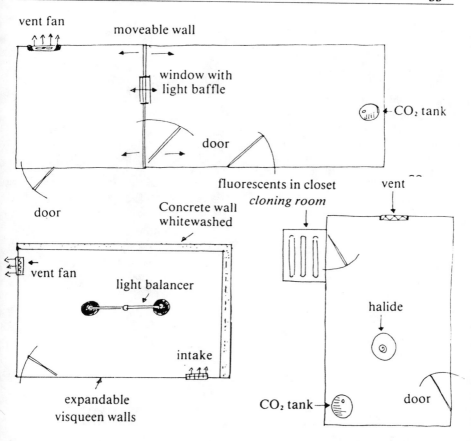

Step One: Choose an out-of-the-way space with little or no traffic. A dark corner in the basement would be perfect. Make sure the room is the right size. A 1000 watt HID, properly set up, will efficiently illuminate up to a 10 x 10 foot room if a light balancer is used. The ceiling should be at least 5 feet high. Remember, plants are set up about one foot off the ground in containers and the lamp needs about a foot of space to hang from the ceiling. This leaves only three feet of space for plants to grow. However, if forced to grow in an attic or basement with a low 4-foot ceiling, much can be done to compensate for the loss of height, including cloning, bending and pruning.

Step Two: Enclose the room, if not already enclosed. Remove everything not having to do with the garden. Furniture and especially drapes or curtains may harbor fungi. A totally enclosed room will permit easy, precise control of everything and everyone that enters, exits and who and what goes on inside. For most growers, enclosing the grow room is simply a matter of tacking up some sheet rock in the basement or attic and painting it flat white. Make sure no light is visible from outside. At night, bright light leaking from a crack in an uncovered window is like a beacon to curious neighbors or bandits.

Step Three: Cover walls, ceiling, floor, everything with a highly reflective material like flat white paint or whitewash. The more reflection, the more light energy that is available to plants. Good reflective light will allow effective coverage of a 1000 watt HID lamp to increase from 36 square feet, with no reflective material, to a maximum of 100 square feet just by putting $10-$20 worth of paint on the walls.

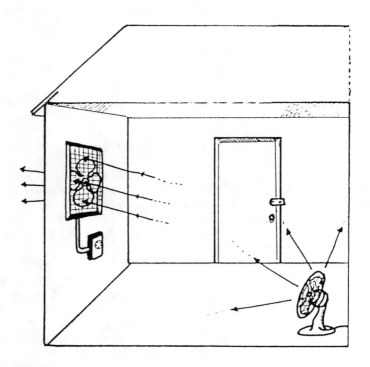

The vent fan on the wall is necessary for a healthy crop.

Step Four: See: "Setting Up the Vent Fan". Constant circulation and a supply of fresh air are essential. There should be at least one fresh air vent in a 10 x 10-foot room, preferably two. Vents may be an open door, window or heat vent. Most growers have found that a small exhaust fan, vented outdoors, pulling new fresh air through an open door will create an ideal air flow. A small oscillating fan works well for circulation. When installing such a fan, make sure it is not set in a fixed position and blows too hard on tender plants. It could cause wind burn, or in the case of young seedlings and clones, dry them out. If the room contains a heat vent, it may be opened to supply extra heat or air circulation.

Step Five: The larger your garden gets, the more water it will need. A 10x10-foot garden may need as much as 30 gallons a week. You may carry water in, container at a time (1 gallon of water weighs 8 pounds). It is much easier to run in a hose with an on/off valve or install a hose bib in the room. A 3-4-foot watering wand may be attached to the hose on/off valve. The wand will save many broken branches, when watering in dense foliage. It is best to hook the hose up to a hot and cold water source, so the water temperature may be easily regulated.

Step Six: Ideally, the floor should be concrete or a smooth surface that can be swept and/or washed down. A floor drain is very handy. In grow rooms with carpet or wood floors, a large, white, painter's dropcloth or thick, white, visqueen plastic, will save floors from moisture. Trays may also be placed beneath each container for added protection and convenience.

Step Seven: Mount a hook, strong enough to support 30 pounds, the center of the growing area to be serviced by the lamp. Attach an adjustable chain or cord and pulley between the ceiling hook and the lamp fixture. This will make it easy to keep the lamp at the proper distance from the growing plants and up out of the way when maintaining them.
CAUTION: A HOT HID MAY EXPLODE IF TOUCHED BY A SINGLE DROP OF COLD WATER. BE VERY CAREFUL AND MAKE SURE TO MOVE THE HID OUT OF THE WAY WHEN SERVICING GARDEN.

Step Eight: There are some tools an indoor gardener must have and a few extra tools that make indoor horticulture much more precise and cost effective. The extra tools help the horticulturist play Mother Nature and make the garden so efficient they pay for themselves within a few weeks. It is best to purchase or find around the house, all tools needed before the plants are brought into the room. If the tools are there when needed, chances are they will be put to use. A good example is a hygrometer. If plants show signs of slow, sickly growth, due to high humidity, most growers will not notice the exact cause right away. They will wait and guess, wait and guess, and maybe figure it out before a fungus attacks and the plant dies. When a hygrometer is installed before plants are in the grow room, the horticulturist will know, from the start, when the humidity is too high and causing sickly growth. See: tool closet and list of tools.

Step Nine: Read and complete: "Setting Up the HID Lamp".

Step Ten: Move the seedlings or rooted clones into room. Huddle them closely together under the lamp. Make sure the HID is not so close to small plants that it burns their leaves. Usually seedlings require the lamp to be at least 24 inches away.

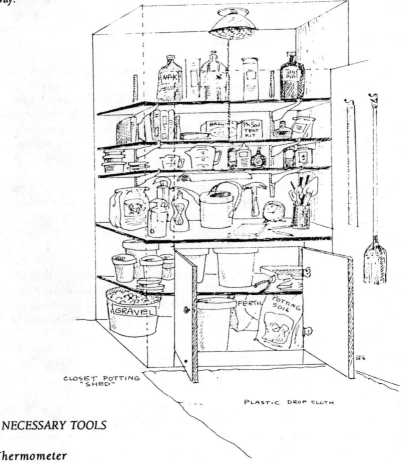

CLOSET POTTING "SHED"

PLASTIC DROP CLOTH

NECESSARY TOOLS

Thermometer

Spray bottle
Liquid biodegradable soap concentrate
Pruner or scissors
Hammer and nails
Pencil or pen
Notebook!
Yardstick (to measure growth)

pH & soil test kit
Hygrometer
Wire (bread sack) ties
Measuring cup
Measuring spoons
Moisture meter

CHAPTER 2 LIGHT, LAMPS & ELECTRICITY

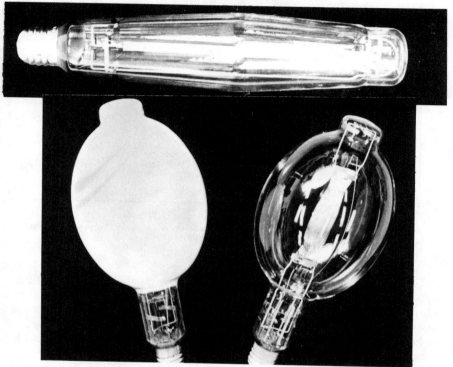

High Presure Sodium Bulb (top), Metal Halide bulbs clear (left) Phosphor coated (Right)

Light is one of the major factors that contribute to plant growth. Indoors, light has been, until recent years, the main limiting factor to plant growth. By understanding how a plant uses light, the indoor horticulturist can use the technology provided by the High Intensity Discharge (HID) lamps to fulfill light requirements and grow spectacular marijuana. The subject of light as used by plants can become very complex. This book will look at the basic ways light affects plant growth.

A plant combines light energy with carbon dioxide (CO_2), water and nutrients to form green chlorophyll and carbohydrates, releasing oxygen as a by product. This process is called photosynthesis. Without light, a plant will not be able to produce green chlorophyll, leaves soon yellow, and eventually death results. With the proper spectrum and intensity of light, chlorophyll is rapidly produced and rapid growth occurs.

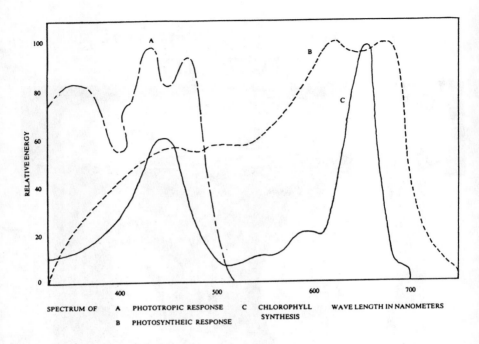

SPECTRUM OF   A   PHOTOTROPIC RESPONSE   C   CHLOROPHYLL   WAVE LENGTH IN NANOMETERS
                                                  SYNTHESIS
                B   PHOTOSYNTHEIC RESPONSE

Outdoors, the sun usually supplies enough light for rapid growth. The sun also supplies much light plants do not use. Scientists have found plants need and use only certain portions of the light spectrum. The most important colors in the spectrum for maximum chlorophyll production and photosynthetic response are in the blue (445 nm) and red (650 nm) range. One nm = .000001 meter. Light is measured in wavelengths, the wavelengths are divided into nm.

Phototropism is the movement of a plant part (foliage) towards illumination. Positive tropism means the foliage moves towards the light. Negative tropism means the plant part moves away from the light. Positive tropism is greatest in the blue end of the spectrum at about 450 nm. At this optimum level, plants lean towards the light, spreading their leaves out horizontally to absorb the maximum amount of light possible.

The photoperiod is the relationship between the length of the light period and dark period. The photoperiod affects the life cycle of all plants. Marijuana will stay in the vegetative growth stage as long as an 18 hour light, 6 hour dark, photoperiod is maintained. 18 hours of light per day will give marijuana all the light it needs to sustain optimum seedling and vegetative growth. The plants will think it is the longest and sunniest day (June 22nd) every day of the year. Marijuana comes from many different parts of the world. Unless the seed was personally collected on location, it's origin is dubious. This is why the 18 hour RULE OF THUMB was developed. Marijuana can use 16-18 hours of light in a 24 hour period before a point of diminishing returns is reached. The light has a minimal effect on growth after 16-18 hours.

This indica has been under a 12 hour photoperiod for 4 1/2 weeks.

Flowering is induced most efficiently with 12 hours of *uninterrupted darkness* in a 24 hour photoperiod. (It is possible to gradually decrease the daylight hours while increasing dark hours to simulate the natural photoperiod. This practice prolongs flowering for several weeks.) Optimum flowering potential is reached when the 12 hour photoperiod is coupled with high levels of intense light from the red end of the spectrum. After plants are 2-12 months old, altering the photoperiod to an even 12 hours, day and night, will induce visible signs of flowering in 1-3 weeks. The older the plant, the more rapidly flowering is induced. The 12 hour photoperiod represents the classic equinox and is the optimum daylight-to-dark relationship for flowering in *cannabis*. Research has proven that less than 12 hours of light will not induce flowering any faster and may substantially reduce flower formation and yield. More than 12 hours of light will prolong flowering; visible signs of flower formation take much longer. Some growers have achieved higher yields by inducing flowering via the 12 hour photoperiod, then changing to 14 hours after 2-4 weeks. However, vegetative growth may be stimulated.

This Thai has been flowering under a HP sodium (right) for 6 weeks.

Some growers, especially if using *sativa* seeds from equatorial regions, give their plants 12 hours of light throughout the life cycle. They -want to replicate the less dynamic photoperiod of the tropics. On the equator, the days and nights are almost exactly the same length year round. Using this method, plants tend to bloom when they are chronologically ready, after thoroughly completing the vegetative growth stage. With shorter 12 hour days, plants will not grow as fast as with 18 hour days and inducing flowering will take longer.

While the photoperiod signals the plant to start flowering, it can also be the signal to stay in (or revert to) vegetative growth. Marijuana must have 12 hours of *uninterrupted, total darkness* to flower properly. Tests have shown that even dim light during the dark period in the pre-flowering and flowering stages will prevent marijuana from blooming. When the 12 hour dark period is interrupted by light, the plant gets confused by the light's signal saying, "it's daytime, start vegetative growth." The plant will try to revert to vegetative growth and flowering will take forever. Make sure to keep flowering plants in *total* darkness, no midnight visits or lit-up open doorways!

Some growers believe it is best to leave the HID on 24 hours a day! Plants can only process 16-18 hours of light per day efficiently. After that, the point of diminishing returns is reached and the electricity is essentially wasted.

INTENSITY

The HID's are incredibly bright. In fact, it is this brightness that makes them so wonderful and useful. However, this intense light must be well managed to get a bumper crop. Intensity is the magnitude of light energy per unit of area. It is greatest near the source of the light and diminishes the further away from the source. The drawing below demonstrates how rapidly light intensity diminishes. Plants that are 4 feet away from the lamp get 4 times less light than plants 1 foot away! The closer plants are to the light source, the better they grow. 6-12 inches is a safe distance for plants to be from the lamp (tender seedlings require 24-36 inches). Any closer and plants run the risk of growing so fast they run into the hot bulb, burning tender growing tips.

SOURCE
(1000 lumens)

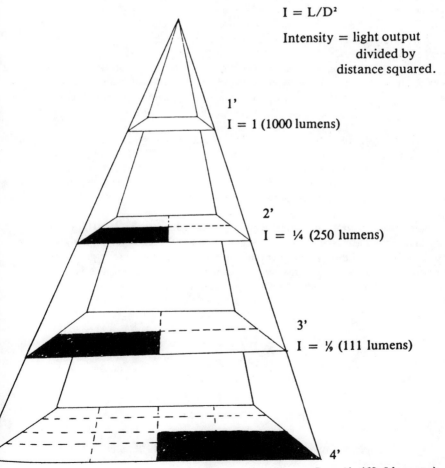

$$I = L/D^2$$

Intensity = light output
divided by
distance squared.

1'
$I = 1$ (1000 lumens)

2'
$I = \frac{1}{4}$ (250 lumens)

3'
$I = \frac{1}{9}$ (111 lumens)

4'
$I = \frac{1}{16}$ (62.5 lumens)

Light Meters

An inexpensive light meter will help you get the most out of your lamp. Try this simple test with a light meter. You will see how rapidly light intensity diminishes.

 RULE of Thumb: Plants with high light requirements but receive less intense or filtered light will yields less and mature later.

A 1000 watt standard metal halide emits 100,000 initial lumens and 88,000 mean lumens. (One lumen is equal to the amount of light emitted by one candle that falls on one square feet of surface one foot away.)

Super halides emit 125,000 initial lumens and 100,000 mean lumens. The HP sodium emits a whopping 140,000 initial lumens! The indoor horticulturist is interested in how much light is emitted by the HID, as well as how much light is received by the plants. Light received is measured by the light and distance chart or in watts-per-square-feet or in foot- candles (f.c.). One foot-candle equals the amount of light that falls on one square feet of surface located one foot away from one candle.

Watts per square feet is easy to calculate, but not very accurate. It measures how many watts are available from a light source in a given area. A 1000 watt HID will emit 10 watts per square feet in a 10 x 10-foot room. Mounting height is not considered in watts per square feet; the lamp could be mounted at any height from 4-8-foot.

Calculating foot-candles is the most accurate way to estimate the amount of light plants receive. Foot-candles may be measured with a light meter reading in foot-candles, or by a photographic light meter, either hand held or built into a camera. The f.c. meter is simply pointed at the light source or reflective surface at any given location, and a read-out in f.c. is given.

When using a photographic light meter, a real pain, set the ASA (film speed) at 200 and the shutter speed at 1/25 second. Focus the camera on a rigid white sheet of paper in the proposed plant location. Hold the paper so it gets maximum illumination. Get close enough so all the camera or light meter sees is the white paper. Adjust the camera lens aperture (f stop) until a correct exposure registers on the light meter. Use the following chart to calculate f.c.

$f4 - 64$ f.c.
$f5.6 - 125$ f.c.
$f8 -- 250$ f.c.
$f11 - 500$ f.c.
$f16 -- 1000$ f.c.
$f22- 2000$ f.c.

Try this simple test above. You will see how rapidly light intensity diminishes.

One of the best ways to demonstrate how light intensity can retard a harvest is found in the outdoor vegetable garden. Have you ever planted 65 day broccoli that took 100 days to mature? Think about it. Did the plants get full sun all day long? It is assumed that the seeds were planted at the peak of the season and perfect temperatures prevailed. Plants that got less light matured slowly and produced less than ones getting full sun all day long.

> RULE OF THUMB - If plants get less intense or filtered light, they will yield less and take longer to mature.

The clone on the left received intense light, while her sister (right) grew up in a distant corner.

SPACING

When light intensity is low, plants s-t-r-e-t-c-h for it. Low intensity is often caused by the lamp being too far away. When the plant is too far away, branches usually form further apart on the stem than if the lamp is close. Simply by keeping the lamp as close as possible, leggy plants are kept to a minimum. If growing naturally leggy *sativa*, the distance between branches is more difficult to deal with.

> RULE OF THUMB: Keep HID 6-12 inches above garden. Tender; clones, seedlings and transplants require 24-36 inches.

Notice plants in background receive less light and are dark.

When light shines on a garden, the leaves near the top of plants get more intense light than the leaves at the bottom. The top leaves shade the bottom leaves, absorbing light energy, making less light energy available to lower leaves. If the lower leaves do not receive enough light, they yellow and die. Do not pick off perfectly good leaves so lower foliage gets more light! Tall 6-8-foot plants take longer to grow and yield more overall then shorter 4-foot plants, but the yield of primo tops will be about the same. The taller plants have large flowers on the top 3-4-foot and spindly buds nearer the bottom, due to lack of light. Tall plants tend to develop flower tops so heavy that the stem cannot support the weight, and they need to be tied up. Short plants support the weight of the tops better and have much more flower weight than leaf weight.

RULE OF THUMB: Any plant that is two months old or older and at least 6 inches tall is ready for inducement of flowering with the 12 hour photoperiod.

Many two week old seedlings or clones may be huddled directly under a single HID. The young plants will need more space as they grow. Plants that are packed too close together sense the shortage of space and do not grow to their maximum potential. Leaves from one plant that shade another plant's leaves slows it's development. It is very important to space young plants just far enough apart so their leaves do not touch. This will keep shading to a minimum and growth to a maximum. Check and alter the spacing every few days. 8-16 mature females, 3-4 months old will completely fill up all the space under one 1000 watt HID.

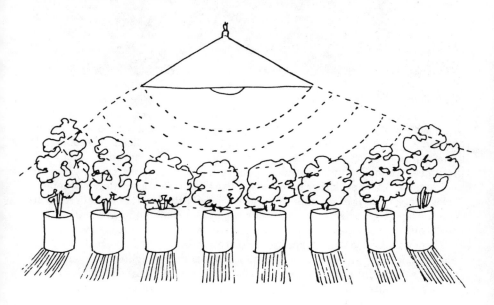

The *stadium* method is a very good way to get the most from an uneven garden profile. Tall plants go on the perimeter, while shorter plants crowd towards the center of the garden. The intensity of light all the plants receive is about the same. See drawing above.

REFLECTIVE LIGHT

Reflective light may also increase light intensity substantially. A large, white, 4-foot reflective hood over the lamp and flat white walls will triple the growing area. EXAMPLE: Using a 1000 watt *super* metal halide with a small, 2-foot hood and ro reflective walls and ceiling, the effective growing area is only 36 square feet When a large, white, 4-foot reflective hood and flat white walls and ceiling are added, effective growing area is increased to 100 square feet

Four foot hoods are inexpensive.

Reflective hoods come in all shapes and sizes. The main things to look for in a hood are the size, the reflective ability, and the specific application. The large, 4-foot hoods work very well. The light has a good chance to spread out and not be reflected around within the walls of the hood. These hoods are very popular because they are inexpensive to manufacture and provide the maximum amount of reflection for the least amount of money. The polished parabolic reflectors are dome shaped. They tend to concentrate the light directly under the source. They work well with light balancers that concentrate intense light directly over plants.

There are many things the hoods may be covered with or constructed from. First and foremost, they should be made of a material that is lightweight, since they will be hanging from the ceiling. The hood should have a heat vent outlet around the bulb so that it will not tend to collect heat. Excessive heat around the bulb could cause premature burn out.

The hoods may be made of sheet metal, polished or painted aluminum, or polished stainless steel. The color is usually flat white, but some companies paint them glossy white (see discussion below on "Flat White"). Sheet metal hoods tend to be much less expensive than aluminum or stainless steel. The other differences are similar to the differences between flat white paint and reflective mylar discussed later. Polished aluminum hoods scratch easily and are expensive. Another type of hood that is increasing in popularity has many triangular facets for the light to bounce off. Here again the hood cost far outweighs the benefits.

The 4-foot hoods are usually manufactured in two, three or four parts. The smaller size facilitates shipping and handling. The customer attaches the pieces together with small screws and nuts.

One option is to remove the reflective hood if the garden is too tall. With no hood, the lamp burns cooler, and the white ceiling provides reflection, but somewhat less than a reflective hood. If the lamp is too close (less than 24 inches) to the ceiling, install a non-flammable heat shield to protect the ceiling. See instruction No. 2 in "Setting Up the Lamp,".

Reflective light also increases light intensity by as much as 30 percent. A large white 4-foot reflective hood over the lamp and flat white walls will triple the growing area.

The farther the light travels from the source, the less intense it is. If this light must be reflected, the closer the reflector is to the bulb, the more intense the light will be when it is reflected. For example, If the reflector is one foot from the bulb, the light that is reflected will be four times more intense than if the reflector were two feet away. Look at the "Light and Distance Chart" on.

To prove all these simple premises, we constructed a black room to measure light. The room is of simple design. It is 10 X 10-foot square and the walls are painted flat black. The floor is covered with black tar paper. On the floor, on 12-inch centers, dots are marked to form a matrix. Each of the four walls has one foot increments marked. The flat black paint and black tar paper floor reflect a maximum of 3 percent light. This small percentage of reflection will facilitate consistent light measurements.

There were two lamps used in this test, a 1000-watt clear super metal halide and a 1000-watt HP sodium. The bottom of each bulb was hung at a distance of 3 feet from the floor. The lamps were warmed up for an hour before any measurements were taken.

A light reading was taken at each square foot of the matrix on the floor. The foot-candle reading was recorded next to a corresponding point on a chart. To complete the charts, a line was drawn connecting all of the dots on the matrix that have a value of 500, 1,000, 1,500 and 2,000 foot-candles. The charts are very interesting and demonstrate where the high-light and low-light plants should be placed.

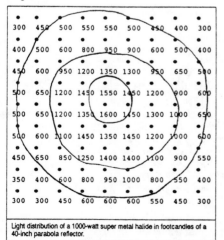

Light distribution of a 1000-watt super metal halide in footcandles of a 40-inch parabola reflector.

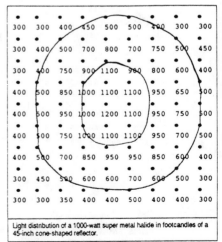

Light distribution of a 1000-watt super metal halide in footcandles of a 45-inch cone-shaped reflector.

The charts show that a 40-inch parabolic reflector delivers 24 percent more light than a 45-inch cone-shaped reflector.

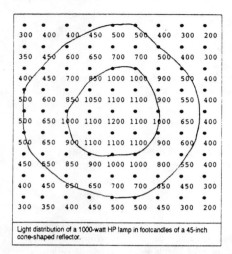

Light distribution of a 1000-watt HP lamp in footcandles of a 45-inch cone-shaped reflector.

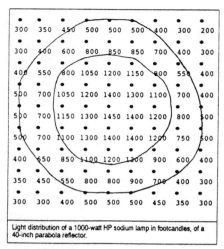

Light distribution of a 1000-watt HP sodium lamp in footcandles, of a 40-inch parabola reflector.

The tests above compare a 45-inch cone-shaped reflector and a 40-inch parabolic dome reflector.

Horizontal reflectors are much more efficient than reflectors requiring the lamp to burn vertically. Turning a lamp horizontally increases light output substantially. By turning the lamp on it's side, the arc tube is parallel with the ground. All of the light comes out of the .arc tube When the tube is already horizontal, half of the light it produces shines directly on plants. Only half of the light needs to be reflected. When the tube is in a vertical position, light is emitted out the sides of the .arc tube This light must be reflected downward before it is of any value to plants.

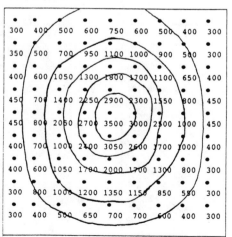

The charts show that a compact horizontal reflector delivers 40 percent more light than a 45-inch cone-shaped reflector. The 40-inch parabolic reflector delivers 19 percent more light than a 45-inch cone-shaped reflector.

The hoods can be covered with white paint or constructed from a reflective. First and foremost, they should be made of a material that is lightweight, since they will be hanging from the ceiling. The hood should have a heat vent outlet around the bulb so that it will not collect heat. Excessive heat around the bulb could cause premature burn-out.

For maximum reflection, paint the inside of the reflector with titanium white paint. Tests we completed showed titanium white reflectors produce 5-10 percent more light.

The 4-foot parabolic hoods are usually manufactured in 9 parts. The smaller size facilitates shipping and handling. The customer assembles the hood with small screws and nuts.

HP sodium lamps mounted horizontally use a small, very effective hood. The hood is mounted just a few inches over the long horizontal HP sodium so that all the light is reflected down toward the plant beds but the small hood creates a minimum shadow. One manufacturer's hood for its HP sodium has a protective glass covering to protect the lamp from water spray when irrigating.

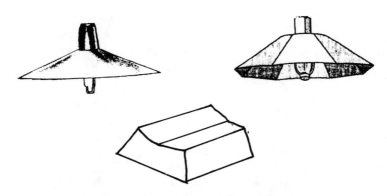

The cone-shaped reflector (above left) is the most inefficient. The dome-shaped hood (right) delivers 24% more light than the cone-shaped hood. The horizontal reflector (bottom) delivers 40% more light than the cone-shaped reflector.

White, reflective walls should be 12 inches or less from the plants for optimum reflection. Ideally, the walls should be taken to the plants. This way, the walls always provide the optimum amount of reflection. The easiest way to install mobile walls is to hang the lamp near the corner of a room. Use the two walls in the corner as reflective walls. The two outside walls are mobile. They will need to be fabricated out of light plywood, sheet rock, or white visqueen plastic.

White Visqueen Plastic is a great way to white out a room. People use it for several reasons: it is inexpensive, expandable, removable and reusable. It may also be used to construct walls. This is very handy when a grower wants to partition off one or several rooms. The walls can expand as the garden grows. The plastic is waterproof, so it may be used on the walls as well as the floor. The white plastic is easy to work with; it may be cut with scissors or a knife, stapled, nailed or taped. Generally, people hang the plastic sheets wrapped around a 1 x 2 inches nailed to the ceiling. The white visqueen actually forms a mobile wall around the garden. It is easy to keep the walls close to the plants for optimum reflection. To make the white walls opaque, just hang black visqueen on the outside. The dead air space between the two visqueens increases insulation.

The only disadvantages of white visqueen plastic are that it is not as reflective as flat white paint, it may get brittle after a year of use under a HID lamp, and it is difficult to find at retail outlets.

Whitewash is an inexpensive alternative to white paint. It is a little messy to apply and thin, so several coats will have to be applied. If fungus or moisture is a problem, like the kind found on wet concrete basement walls, the mess is worth the trouble.

Using flat white paint is one of the simplest, least expensive, most efficient ways to create optimum reflection. Artists white paint is more expensive, but very reflective. It is recommended for reflective hoods. Semi-gloss white is not quite as reflective as the flat white, but it is much easier to wash and keep clean. Regardless of the type of white used, a fungus inhibiting agent should be added before the paint is mixed. A gallon of good flat white paint costs from $15 to $20. One gallon should be enough to white out the average grow room. Use a primer to prevent bleed through of stains or if walls are rough and unpainted. The vent fan should be installed before painting. Fumes can cause headaches.

Why is flat white so reflective? When light shines on a green object, green pigment in the object absorbs all colors but green from the spectrum and the green light is reflected. This is why we see the color green. Flat white contains little or no light absorbing pigment. Flat white essentially absorbs no light, it is almost all reflected, except for a little bit that somehow gets lost. Flat white is whiter and reflects better than glossy white. Glossy white is manufactured with more light absorbing varnish. The glossy surface lends itself to bright spots and glare. Flat white contains less varnish and inhibits the path of reflective light much less. It also has a mat texture, actually providing more reflective surface.

REFLECTIVE CHART

MATERIAL	PERCENT REFLECTED
Reflective mylar	90 - 95
Flat white paint	85 - 93
Semi-gloss white	75-80
Flat yellow	70 - 80
Aluminum foil	70 - 75
Black	less than 10

Reflective mylar provides one of the most reflective surfaces possible. It looks like a very thin mirror. Unlike light absorbing paint, reflective mylar reflects almost all light. It is simply taped or tacked to the wall. Although quite expensive, it is preferred by lots of growers. The trick to setting it up is to get it flat against the wall. When it is loose or wavy, light is reflected poorly.

Aluminum foil is one of the worst reflective surfaces possible. The foil always crinkles up, reflecting light in the wrong directions, actually wasting light. It also reflects more ultraviolet rays than other surfaces. Take a look at the reflective chart. Aluminum foil is not very reflective!

MORE GROWING LIGHT

There are several ways of getting a more even distribution of light in the garden. This can be accomplished by using several 400 watt HID's, installing side lighting or rotating the plants. The most efficient way is to replicate the movement of the sun through the sky. This is done two basic ways. Both methods move the lamp back and forth overhead so it covers more area. The advantages to this are:

(1) The plants get a more even distribution of light and grow more evenly. When the HID is stationary, plants tend to grow towards the lamp. When the lamp is always in the same place, the plants grow up around it, severely shading the rest of the garden. Rotating the plants every few days so they received more even light distribution would solve this problem. It is a back breaking job to muscle around 5 or 10 gallon pots of wet soil. Chances are that when you have a miserable job like this, it will not get done very often. It is much easier to employ one of the following methods to move the lamp rather than the plants.

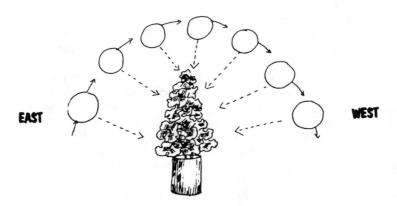

EAST   WEST

When the sun arcs overhead, the plant gets the full benefit of its rays, bottom to top.

(2) A lamp moving overhead increases the intense light that the majority of plants receive. This is not a substitute for more lumens from an additional lamp. It is a more efficient way to use each HID. Since the lamp will be directly overhead more plants, they all will receive more direct, intense light. Young clones and seedlings might s-t-r-e-t-c-h, becoming leggy, to get more light if the lamp travels too far away. Start using the light balancers after the plants are 12 inches tall and have several sets of leaves.

(3) Light is received by the plants from more directions. Total light energy is optimum for all plants, as long as one plant is not shading another. This promotes even growth. In nature, *cannabis* grows into the classic Christmas tree shape. This is the most efficient configuration for the plant to grow. Light gets all the way to the center of the plant as well as to all outside parts.

LIGHT BALANCERS

A light balancer is a device to move a lamp back and forth across the ceiling of a grow room to provide more balanced light coverage. The methods employed to move the lamp across the ceiling may be motorized or manual, fast moving or moving only once or twice a day. The speed at which the lamp moves is of minimal importance. But the more revolutions it travels, the more even the profile of the garden will be and the closer plants can be to the lamp. The unit should not move so fast that the lamp wobbles, making it unstable. It is not necessary for the lamp to move exactly like the sun. Whether the lamp moves from east to west like the sun is of no consequence. The path it takes should be a consistent one that distributes light evenly. That is, if the lamp is allowed to stay in the same position for two or three days before it is moved, plants will get uneven light distribution. The motorized units have an advantage in this respect, since they are moving at a constant rate all the time.

These light balancers may be purchased from an ever increasing number of suppliers and manufacturers or constructed by the grower. There are only two things to be on the lookout for when constructing your own. (1) strength and (2) ease of movement. First and foremost the rigging overhead must be able to support the weight of the lamp and hood. If the system were to come crashing down on the garden it could cause a real problem. Besides wrecking your precious garden, it very well could start a fire. Make sure the thing is secured to the ceiling! The electric cord should not slow down or affect the movement of the light balancer in any way. Second, the system should be easy to move. If it is easy to move, chances are that you will move it. The home made light balancers work best for growers that are able to look after their garden two or three times a day. When looking at the garden, the lamp is moved.

There are two basic kinds of light balancers. (1) The first is a linear system. These systems move in a straight line simulating the sun's path through the heavens. This type of system increases the intense light to plants in a linear oval. The square footage covered by the system depends on the length of the track and the number of lamps employed. The systems use a track that affixes to the ceiling. The lamp moves back and forth across the ceiling, guided by the track. The lamp is hooked to the balancer with an extendible chain or cord so it can be as close as possible to the plants. These units vary as to the length and speed the lamp travels. Some are designed for one lamp, while others are able to move 6 lamps efficiently. A 6-foot linear light balancer increases optimum coverage of light from 36 to 72 square feet

A homemade alternative to the commercial linear unit is the clothesline unit. It is simple to construct. Attach eyebolts at opposite ends of the ceiling or ceiling corners. Pulleys are attached to the eyebolts. Between the pulleys, a small diameter, heavy duty nylon cord is strung in a loop. The HID is attached to the bottom of the loop. This is just like many of the clotheslines that are used in the city, with access from only one side. After the lamp is mounted on the looped cord, it may be moved back and forth as often as desirable. The more often the better. Another variation of the same principle stretches a nylon cord across the ceiling with a single pulley attached to it. Attach the lamp to the pulley, then move the lamp back and forth on the pulley overhead. One industrious person made a balancer out of an old garage door opener. The possibilities are endless! When using these types of units, make sure to watch the plant profile. Try to give the garden the most even distribution of light possible.

The second type is the arc method. It uses a pivoting or hinge motion. The unit swivels from a boom on a wall or the ceiling overhead. The lamp(s) take an arc shaped path, covering a little more area than the linear method.

There are two basic types of arc method: 1) wall mount units that swing back and forth in a partial arc on a motorized hinge. 2) ceiling mount units swivel back and forth on a full or partial arc. The lamp(s) in both types are suspended by an adjustable chain attached to a telescoping boom(s).

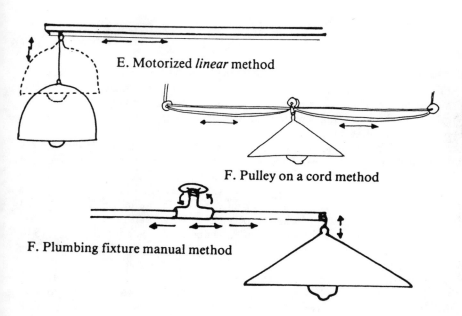

E. Motorized *linear* method

F. Pulley on a cord method

F. Plumbing fixture manual method

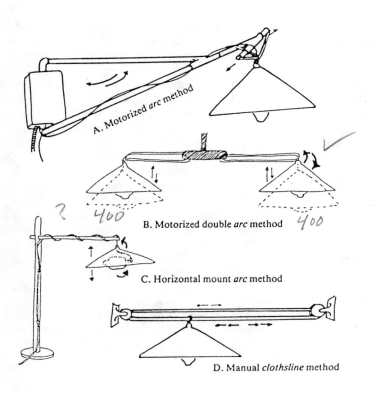

A. Motorized *arc* method

B. Motorized double *arc* method

C. Horizontal mount *arc* method

D. Manual *clothsline* method

Another type of arc method is a home made model employing 1-inch plumbing pipes. It bolts to the ceiling or is mounted on a wooden frame that is in turn affixed to the ceiling. This unit, like the clothesline unit, is non- motorized. The grower simply moves the lamp to a different location daily or as often as necessary to maintain an even garden profile.

Some of the advantages to using the commercial light balancer is that it gives more intense light to more plants for less money. Several growers have reported light balancers make it possible to use fewer lamps and get the same yield. An increase of 25-35% in intense light coverage is afforded by light balancers. Two lamps, mounted on a motorized light balancer will do the job of three lamps. I prefer the motorized light balancers because they keep an even garden profile. Since the HID is already drawing about 9.2 amperes, and is hooked up to a 15 or 20 ampere circuit, it would take another circuit to hang up another HID. The commercial balancer is easily plugged into the same timer and socket as the lamp. Since the motor for the balancer uses about one ampere (75-100 watts) of current it may be attached to the same circuit as the lamp with little risk of overload. This makes it very convenient for the grower and the expense is much less.

Light balancers are used for only part of a plant's life. It would be worthless to use it when the plants are huddled directly under the lamp. Using a balancer on too many seedlings or clones, causes them to s-t-r-e-t-c-h. One of the good things about the home made units is they do not have a particular cycle they must complete. They are operated by hand and may be placed in any location for as long as desired.

Cuttings and young seedlings are huddled below the HID when small and moved into larger containers when they are crowding one another. When they are far enough apart that the light does not afford complete coverage, it is time to employ a light balancer. Before this time, a light balancer might not give them enough intense light and they may get leggy.

Planter boxes or containers on wheels offer a good alternative to the light balancers. The containers are rotated daily. The wheels make this job a snap. The light reaches every corner of the garden without having to move the lamp. This method has essentially the same effect as moving the lamp overhead, but is more work because all plants have to be moved, rather than only one or two lamps.

The 400 watt bulbs offer more even light distribution and the lamp can be closer to the plants since they have less heat build up than 1000 watt HID's. The 400 watt bulbs offer certain advantages, especially if space is a problem. One grower uses two of them in a narrow 4 x 8-foot room with amazing success. Another grower has the brightest closet in town! The 400 watt halides do have a longer life than the 1000 watt lamps, but share the same lumen maintenance curve. For the amount of lumens produced, their initial cost is much higher. However, their life is twice as long, about 20,000 hours. If the 400 watt HID's give you the best value for balanced light several ballasts may be looped together on the same 220 volt circuit. Ask an electrician for help. Do not use a 400 watt lamp in a 1000 watt system! It will work for the first 24 to 48 hours, then BOOM! The lamp and maybe the ballast will blow up, and who-knows-what else!

Side lighting is another way to balance light. Of course this uses more electricity, but increases the amount of light available to the plants. Probably the most efficient lamp to use in this case is the low pressure LP sodium, since its lumen-per-watt conversion is the best there is. The lamps are mounted where light intensity is marginal, along the walls, to provide side light. Fluorescent lamps could also be used, but the lumen-per-watt conversion is much less. Remember the LP sodiums must be used with the halide, which supplies all the blue light the plants need to balance the spectrum. If you are really into getting the most light into the garden possible, you may want to employ all of these methods: side lighting and a light balancer.

THE HID LAMP FAMILY

Incandescent lamps create light by passing electricity through a very fine wire or filament. HID lamps make light by passing electricity through vaporized gas under high pressure. Fluorescent and low pressure (LP) sodium lamps create light by passing electricity through gaseous vapor under low pressure. All of these principles are relatively simple.

All the HID lamps work on the same principle, passing or arcing electricity through gas or vapor, rather than using a tungsten filament, like household incandescent bulbs. The gas is inside a heat resistant glass or ceramic arc tube, sealed under high pressure. The materials contained in the arc tube dictate the colors or spectrum the lamp will produce, except for the effect of the phosphor coating. Passing electricity through vaporized elements is an easy enough principle, but putting it into action requires a little technology.

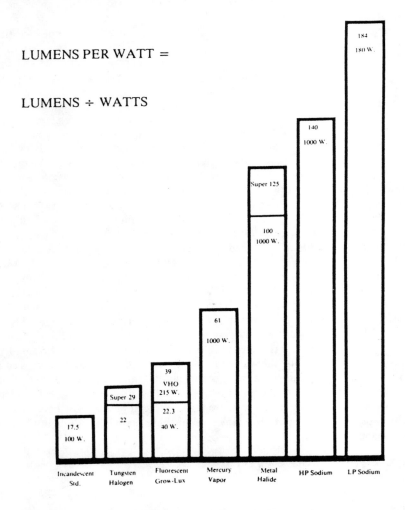

LUMENS PER WATT =

LUMENS ÷ WATTS

						184 180 W.
					140 1000 W.	
				Super 125 100 1000 W.		
			61 1000 W.			
		39 VHO 215 W. 22.3 40 W.				
17.5 100 W.	Super 29 22					
Incandescent Std.	Tungsten Halogen	Fluorescent Grow-Lux	Mercury Vapor	Metal Halide	HP Sodium	LP Sodium

The above chart shows various lamps with their lumen-per-watt conversion. This formula is used to measure the lamps efficiency: the amount of lumens produced for the amount of watts (electricity) consumed. Note the high lumen-per-watt conversion of the halides and sodiums.

Below is a diagram of a HID lamp. They may all work on the same principle, however their starting requirements, line voltage, operating characteristics and physical shape are all unique to each lamp. Remember this; DO NOT TRY TO MIX AND MATCH BALLASTS WITH LAMPS! Just because a lamp fits a socket attached to a ballast, does not mean that it will work properly in it. The wrong lamp plugged into the wrong ballast adds up to a BURN OUT!

RULE OF THUMB - Buy the entire HID system, ballast, lamp, „.: socket, bulb and timer all at the same time from a reputable supplier to ensure the ballast and lamp go together. Make sure to get a written guarantee from the dealer.

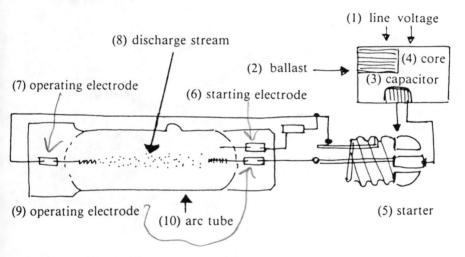

(1) line voltage

(8) discharge stream

(2) ballast

(4) core

(3) capacitor

(7) operating electrode

(6) starting electrode

(9) operating electrode

(10) arc tube

(5) starter

The electricity or line voltage (1) flows through the ballast (2). The ballast is the box that contains a capacitor (3) that provides a high, fast, charge of electricity to start the lamps. Getting the electricity to flow between the electrodes (7) and (9) in the arc tube (10) requires a high voltage, charge or current. This current is sent through the starting mechanism of the lamp (5). In the HP sodium lamps, the starting electrode and the operating electrode are one in the same.

The electricity is then arced or literally shot across the arc tube (10) from the starting electrode (6) to the operating electrode (9) at the other end of the arc tube. As soon as the arc is established and the gasses vaporize, the arc jumps from the starting electrode to the operating electrodes (7) and (9). Once the electricity is flowing across the tube, the elements slowly vaporize into the discharge stream (8).

When the discharge stream (8) is working and the lamp warms up, the line voltage could run out of control, since there is an unrestricted flow of electricity between the two electrodes. The ballast (2) regulates this line voltage by means of a wire coil wrapped around an iron core (4). By employing this core (4) the lamp is assured of having a constant and even supply of electricity.

ABOUT BALLASTS

All HID's require a ballast. It is very important to buy the proper ballast for your HID. Ballast kits may be ordered from G.E., Sylvania, Universal or Westinghouse. Assembly instructions are in the form of a wiring diagram glued to the side of the transformer.

The kits contain a transformer core, cooling capacitor, containing box and sometimes wire. If you wish to purchase the components separately, core manufacturers are Jefferson (Noted as being the quietest, a real concern to apartment dwellers or to people with nosy neighbors) Advance, G.E., Jefferson and Sola. Capacitor manufacturers are Cornell, G.E., Duviler and Dayton. If you are not familiar with electrical component assembly and reading wiring diagrams, it is best to purchase the assembled ballast in a package containing the lamp and hood from one of the many HID distributors.

Do not buy used parts from a junk yard or try to use a ballast if unsure of its capacity. Just because a bulb fits a socket attached to a ballast, does not mean that it is the proper system. The best way to grow a miserable garden is to try to save money on the ballast.

Even though HID's have specific ballasting requirements, the ballasts have a good deal in common. Probably the most common characteristic they all have is noise. This noise could drive some people to great fits of paranoia! The quietest brand of core, the part that makes all the noise, is Jefferson. Ballasts operate at 90-150° F. Touch a strike anywhere kitchen match to the side to check if it is too hot. If the match lights, the ballast is too hot and should be taken into the shop before it creates an accident or burns out. Heat is the number one ballast destroyer! Ballasts are manufactured with a protective metal box. This outer shell safely contains the core, capacitor and wiring. Never build another box around a ballast. It will cause excessive heat and maybe even start a fire!

More expensive ballasts are equipped with ventilation fans to maintain cool operating temperatures. A fan is not necessary unless there are many ballasts in a small room and ventilation is inadequate. Air vents will allow a ballast to run cooler, but are really not necessary. The vents should protect the internal parts and not be prone to letting water splash in.

Some industrial ballasts are sealed in fiber glass or similar material to make them weather proof. These ballasts are not recommended. They were designed for outdoor use where heat buildup is not a problem. Indoors the protection of the sealed unit from weather is not necessary and could create excessive heat.

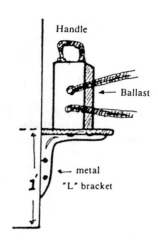

Make sure the ballast has a handle on it. A small 400 watt halide ballast weighs about 30 lbs. and a large 1000 watt HP sodium ballast tips the scales at about 55 lbs. This small, heavy box is very awkward to move with no handle.

Most ballasts sold by HID stores are set up for a 110 volt current found in all homes. Some of them may be ready for 220 volt service. It is usually easiest to use the regular 110 volt system because their outlets are more common. The 220 volt systems are normally used when several lamps are already taking up space on other 110 volt circuits. Changing most ballasts from 110 volts to 220 volts is a simple matter of moving a couple of wires. Consult the wiring diagram in each ballast for specific instructions. There is no difference in the electricity consumed by using either 110 or 220 volt systems. The 110 volt system draws about 9.5 amperes and a HID on a 220 volt current draws about 4.3 amperes. Both use the same amount of electricity! This brings us to OHM's LAW: Volts X Amperes Watts.

220 volt ballasts are easy to loop together. Up to 4 ballasts may be wired in a series circuit on a 220 volt 30 ampere circuit. This is the most efficient way to use HID ballasts. There is less resistance for electricity when ballasts are wired in a series circuit. Less electricity is lost when transmitted. I advise only electricians try this relatively simple procedure. There is a lot more current flowing with more ballasts and grounding requirements increase. Any competent electrician should be able to loop them together.

The ballast has a lot of electricity flowing through it. DO NOT TOUCH THE BALLAST WHEN OPERATING! Do not place the ballast directly on the damp floor, or any floor. Always place it up off the floor and protect it from possible moisture. The ballast should be suspended in the air or on a shelf attached to the wall. It does not have to be very high off the ground, just far enough to keep it dry.

There are remote and attached ballasts. The remote ballast is the best for most indoor situations. It may easily be moved and placed near the floor to radiate heat in a cool portion of the grow room or placed outside if the room is too hot. The attached ballasts are fixed to the hood, require more overhead space, are very heavy and tend to create more heat around the lamp.

Ballasts may be manufactured with an attached timer. These units are very convenient, but the timer should be constructed of heavy duty heat resistant materials. If it is light weight plastic, it could easily melt under the heat of the ballast.

A good ballast manufacturer will place a 10 ampere fuse inside the ballast. This is a double safeguard against anything happening and destroying the lamp or causing a fire.

HIGH INTENSITY DISCHARGE LAMPS

Artificial light from the High Intensity Discharge (HID) lamp family may be used to duplicate growth responses induced in *cannabis* by natural sunlight. This may be seen by comparing charts on HID spectral emission with the chart on photosynthetic response, chlorophyll synthesis and positive tropism.

The HID lamp family contains mercury vapor, metal halide, and High Pressure (HP) sodium lamps.

The two most popular HID wattage's are 400 and 1000. Over 90% of the bulbs sold are the 1000 watt type. Value is the main reason. The 1000 watt system costs about the same as the 400 watt system, but is more efficient in its lumen-per-watt conversion and produces more than twice as much light. By employing a light balancer, uniform light distribution is no longer a problem. The smaller 400 watt systems are great for a closet or a space that is 2-6 feet square. The smaller 400 watt HID's are similar to the larger 1000 watt systems, only smaller, producing less light and heat. Their color spectrum is almost identical to their big brothers. The 400 watt halides last about twice as long as the 1000 watt, but both have the same lumen maintenance curve!

MERCURY VAPOR LAMPS

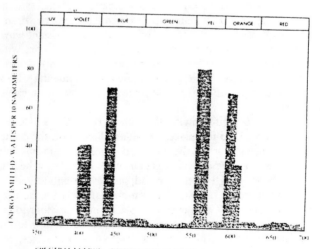

SPECTRAL ENERGY   DISTRIBUTION OF 1000 WATT MERCURY VAPOR LAMP

The mercury vapor lamp is the oldest and best known member of the HID family. The HID principle was first used with the mercury vapor lamp around the turn of the century, but it was not until the mid 1930's that the mercury vapor lamp was really employed commercially.

As the lumen-per-watt chart shows, the mercury vapor lamps produce only 60 lumens-per-watt. A comparison of the spectral energy distribution (above chart) of the mercury vapor and the photosynthetic response chart will show you this is a poor lamp for horticulture. Not only is it expensive to operate, but it produces most of its color in areas that are not helpful to plant growth.

The old mercury vapor lamps produce light by arcing electricity through mercury and a little argon gas which is used for starting. They come in sizes from 40 to 1000 watts. They have fairly good lumen maintenance and a fairly long life. Most wattages last up to three years at 18 hr. daily operation.

The mercury usually requires a separate ballast, however, there are a few low wattage bulbs that have a self contained ballast. All to often these ballasts are scrounged from junk yards or who-knows-where and used in place of halide or HP sodium ballasts. People who used or tried to modify these ballasts for use with another HID, had all kinds of problems and still had to buy the proper ballast in the end. Remember, trying to save money on a ballast usually costs more in produce that was not realized.

In summary, the mercury vapor lamp produces a color spectrum that is not as efficient as the halide or HP sodium for indoor marijuana cultivation. It is NOT the lamp to use if you want any kind of garden at all! Growers that have used them paid more for electricity and their garden yielded much less.

METAL HALIDE SYSTEMS

The metal halide HID lamp is the most efficient source of artificial white light available to the horticulturist today. It comes in 175, 250, 400, 1000 and 1500 watt sizes. They may be either clear or phosphor coated and all require a special ballast. Most growers do not consider using the 175 or 250 watt halides. The 1500 watt halide is also avoided due to its relatively short 2000 to 3000 hour life and incredible heat output. Most growers prefer the 1000 Watt halide and those with small growing areas, the 400 watt.

Three major metal halide manufacturers are General Electric, Sylvania and Westinghouse. Each manufacturer has a super version of the halide. The Super Metalarc, the High-output Multivapor and the Super Metal Halide fit the standard halide ballast and fixture. They produce about 25% more lumens than the standard halides. These super halides cost about $10 more than the standard, but are well worth the money.

The clear halides are the most commonly used by indoor growers. This lamp is the brightest white lamp around. It supplies the most lumens of the best possible spectrum for plant growth. The clear halide works well for seedling, vegetative and flower growth.

The phosphor coated 1000 watt halides emit a more diffused light and are easy on the eyes, emitting less ultraviolet light than the clear halides. They produce the same initial lumens and about 4,000 fewer lumens than the standard halide and have a slightly different color spectrum. The phosphor coated halides have more yellows, less blue and ultraviolet light. Growers using the phosphor coated lamps say: "One (phosphor bulb) seems to even out the color spectrum when more than four clear lamps are used". Some growers prefer the phosphor coated halide to the HP sodium for flowering, saying it is the best all round bulb.

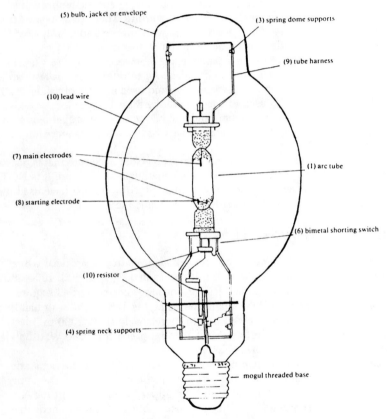

DIAGRAM OF A HID LAMP

The 1000 watt super clear and super phosphor coated halides are the most common halides used to grow marijuana. Compare energy distribution charts and lumen output of all three lamps to decide which lamp offers the most desirable characteristics for your garden. Typically, the home grower starts with the 1000 watt Super Metalarc (Sylvania), High-output Multivapor (G.E.) or Super Metal Halide (Westinghouse).

CONSTRUCTION AND OPERATION

The metal halide lamps produce light by passing or arcing electricity through vaporized argon gas, mercury, thorium iodide, sodium iodide, and scandium iode within the quartz arc tube (1). At the end of the arc tube is a heat reflecting coating (2) to control temperature during operation. Spring supports in the neck (4) and dome (3) of the outer bulb or envelope (5) mount the arc tube frame (9) in place. The bimetal shorting switch (6) closes during lamp operation, preventing voltage drop between the main electrode (7) and the starting electrode (7). Most bulbs are equipped with a resistor (10) that keeps the bulb from shattering under temperature stress. The outer bulb functions as a protective jacket, contains the arc tube and starting mechanism, keeping them in a constant environment as well as absorbing ultraviolet radiation. *Protective goggles that filter out ultraviolet rays are a good idea if you spend much time in the grow room or if you are prone to staring at the HID!*

CAUTION: IF OUTER BULB SHATTERS, TURN OFF (UN-PLUG) LAMP IMMEDIATELY. DO NOT LOOK AT OR GET NEAR THE LAMP UNTIL IT COOLS DOWN. When the outer bulb breaks, it is no longer able to absorb ultraviolet radiation. This radiation is very harmful and will burn skin and eyes if exposed. BE CAREFUL!

Initial vaporization takes place in the gap between the main electrode (7) and the starting electrode (8), when a high starting voltage is applied. When there is enough ionization, electricity will arc between the main electrodes (7). As the lamp warms up, the metal iodide additives begin to enter the arc stream. After they are in their proper concentrations in the arc tube, the characteristic bright white light is emitted. This process takes about 3-5 minutes. NOTE: The metal halide arc system is very complex and requires a seasoning period of 100 hours operation for all of its components to stabilize.

If a power surge occurs and the lamp goes out or the lamp is turned off, it will take 5-15 minutes for the lamp to restart. The gasses inside the arc tube must cool before restarting.

When the lamp is started, incredible voltage is necessary for the initial ionization process to take place. Turning the lamp on and off more than once a day causes UNNECESSARY STRESS on the HID system and WILL SHORTEN ITS LIFE.

A.
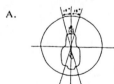

B.
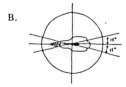

The metal halides operate most efficiently in a vertical +/-15° position (see diagram a.) When operated in positions other than +/- 15° of vertical, lamp wattage, lumen output and life will decrease; the arc bends, creating non-uniform heating of the arc tube wall, resulting in less efficient operation and shorter life. There are special lamps made to B. operate in the horizontal or any other position other than +/- 10° (see diagram b.). These bulbs have *HOR* stamped on the crown or base. *HOR* IS NOT AN ABBREVIATION FOR HORTICULTURE! IT REFERS TO HORIZONTAL!

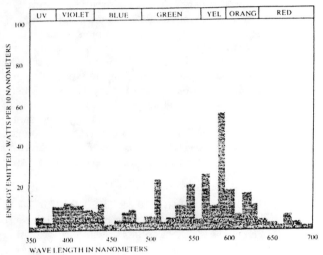

ENERGY DISTRIBUTION OF 1000 - WATT METALARC/C LAMP (PHOSPHOR COATED)

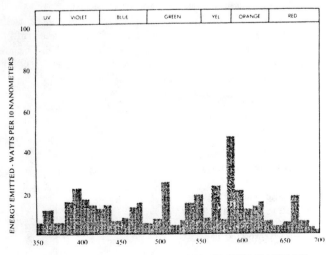

SPECTRAL ENERGY   DISTRIBUTION OF 1000 WATT METAL HALIDE LAMP

LUMEN MAINTENANCE AND LIFE

Metal halides have very good lumen maintenance and a long life. The decline in lumen output over the lamp's life is very gradual. The average life of a halide is about 12,000 hours, almost 2 years of daily operation at 18 hours. Many will last even longer. The lamp reaches the end of its life when it fails to start or come up to full brilliance. This is usually caused by

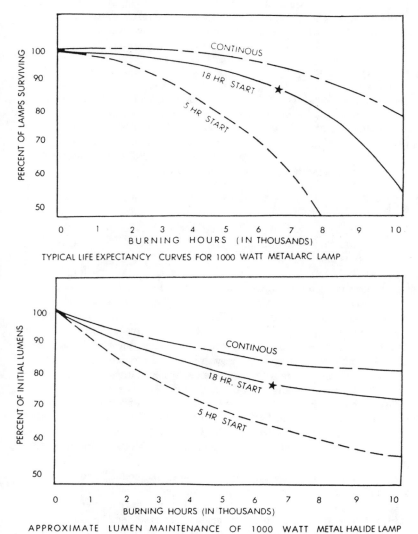

TYPICAL LIFE EXPECTANCY CURVES FOR 1000 WATT METALARC LAMP

APPROXIMATE LUMEN MAINTENANCE OF 1000 WATT METAL HALIDE LAMP

* Successful growers change the bulb before it burns out. This is about every 12-18 months or 6500 hours. This insures maximum light intensity.

deterioration of lamp electrodes over time, loss of transmission of the arc tube from blackening, or shifts in the chemical balance of the metals in the arc tube. I do not advise to wait until the bulb is burned out before it is changed. An old bulb is inefficient and costly. Replace bulbs about every 12-18 months or 6500 hours. Electrode deterioration is greatest during starting and is usually the reason for the end of lamp life. DO NOT START THE HALIDE MORE THAN ONCE A DAY AND USE A TIMER!

The halide may produce a stroboscopic (flashing) effect. The light will appear bright, then dim, bright, dim, etc. This flashing is the result of the arc being extinguished 120 times every second. Illumination usually remains constant, but it may pulsate a little. This is normal and nothing to worry about.

HALIDE BALLASTS

Read "About Ballasts". The ballast for a 1000 watt halide will operate standard, clear and phosphor coated and super, clear and phosphor coated halides on a 110 or 220 volt current. A different ballast is required for the 400 watt halides; it will operate all 400 watt halides: super or standard, clear or phosphor coated. The ballasts must be specifically designed for the 400 or 1000 watt halides, since their starting and operating requirements are unique.

HIGH PRESSURE SODIUM LAMPS

The most impressive fact about the 1000 watt high pressure sodium vapor lamp is that it produces 140,000 initial lumens. That's one heck of a lot of light! The HP sodium is also the most efficient HID lamp available. It comes in 35, 50, 70, 100, 150, 200, 250, 310, 400 and 1000 wattages. All, except for the 200 and 1000 watt bulbs (which are only available in clear) may be either clear or phosphor coated. All HP sodium vapor lamps have their own unique ballast. HP sodium lamps are manufactured by G.E. (Lucalox), Sylvania (Lumalux) and Westinghouse (Ceramalux). As with the halides, most growers find the best value is with the 1000 watt HP sodium rather than the 400 watt. The Unalux comes in 150, 215, 360, and 880 wattages and may only be used in certain 220 volt mercury vapor systems. Sylvania makes a ballast tester that tests mercury vapor sockets and ballasts for Unalux retrofit capabilities. The mercury vapor sockets and ballasts are cheaper, but the largest Unalux (880 watts) has much lower lumen output than the standard 1000 watt HP sodium vapor. If using a Unalux, consult the nearest Sylvania sales office for further information. The Cermalux has a color corrected spectrum. It produces a little more blue than other HP sodiums.

The HP sodium lamp emits an orange-like glow that could be compared to the harvest sun. The color spectrum is highest in the yellow, orange and red end. These colors promote flower production. Marijuana's light needs change when flowering; it no longer needs to produce so many vegetative cells. In fact, vegetative growth slows and eventually stops during blooming. All the plant's energy and attention is focused on flower production so it may complete its annual life cycle. Light from the red end of the spectrum stimulates floral hormones within the plant, promoting more flower production. When using a HP sodium lamp, flower volume and weight may increase 20% or more, depending on strain of seed and growing conditions. Many growers, using a 10 x 10-foot room, will retain the 1000 watt halide and add a 1000 watt sodium during flowering. This not only more than doubles available light, it increases the red end of the spectrum, causing flowers to form and grow like crazy. This 1:1 ratio (1 halide and 1 HP sodium) is a popular combination for flowering.

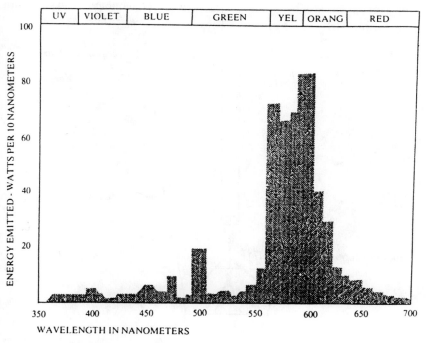

RELATIVE ENERGY EMITTED   HP SODIUM

OPERATION AND CONSTRUCTION

The HP sodium lamp produces light by passing electricity through vaporized sodium and mercury within an arc tube (1). A little bit of xenon gas, used for starting, is also included in the arc tube. The HP sodium lamp is totally different from the metal halide in its physical, electrical, and color spectrum characteristics. An electronic starter works with the magnetic component of the ballast to supply a short, high voltage pulse. This electrical pulse vaporizes the xenon gas and initiates the starting process that takes 3-4 minutes. Electricity passes or arcs between the two main electrodes (6) and (7). If the lamp is turned off, or power surge occurs and the lamp goes out, the gasses in the tube will usually need to cool 3-15 minutes before restarting is possible.

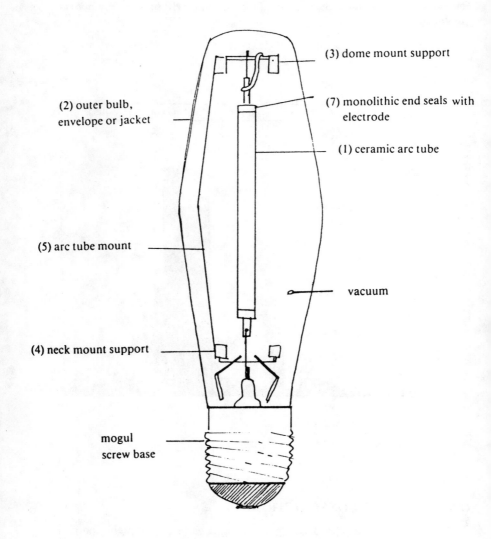

(3) dome mount support

(7) monolithic end seals with electrode

(2) outer bulb, envelope or jacket

(1) ceramic arc tube

(5) arc tube mount

vacuum

(4) neck mount support

mogul screw base

Similar to the metal halide, the HP sodium has a two bulb construction, with an outer protective bulb (2) and inner arc tube (1). The arc tube's frame is mounted (5) by spring supports in the dome (3) and neck (4). The outer bulb or jacket protects the arc tube from damage and contains a vacuum, reducing heat loss from the arc tube. The sodium, mercury and xenon gas are contained within the arc tube and have a constant operating temperature, and the lamp may be operated in any position (360°). However, most prefer to hang the lamp overhead in a vertical operating position.

LIFE AND LUMEN MAINTENANCE

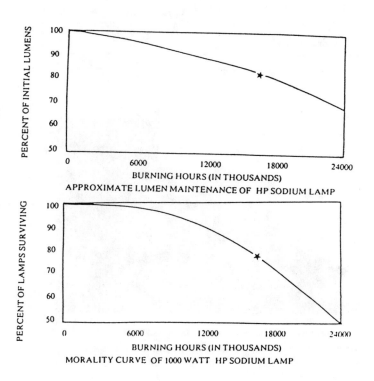

APPROXIMATE LUMEN MAINTENANCE OF HP SODIUM LAMP

MORALITY CURVE OF 1000 WATT HP SODIUM LAMP

The HP sodium lamps have the longest life and best lumen maintenance of all HID lamps. Eventually the sodium bleeds out through the arc tube; over a long period of daily use, the sodium to mercury ratio changes, causing the voltage in the arc to rise. Finally the arc tube's operating voltage will
* For best results, change the HP. Sodium bulb after 15, 000 hours of operation

rise higher than the ballast is able to sustain. At this point, the lamp will start, warm-up to full intensity, then go out. This sequence is then repeated over and over, signaling the end of the lamps life. The life of a 1000 watt HP sodium lamp will be about 24,000 hours, or 5 years, operating at 12 hours per day. As with other HID's, HP sodiums should be replaced before the end of their rated life.

SODIUM BALLASTS

Read "About Ballasts". A special ballast is required specifically for the 400 or the 1000 watt HP sodium lamp. The lamp has unique operating voltages and currents during start-up and operation. These voltages and currents do not correspond to similar wattages of other HID lamps. As with the halide ballast, I recommend purchasing it from a HID lamp store rather than in a component kit.

INCANDESCENT LAMPS

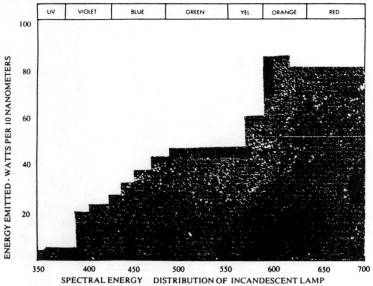

SPECTRAL ENERGY   DISTRIBUTION OF INCANDESCENT LAMP

The incandescent lamp is the electric lamp invented by Thomas Edison. Light is produced by sending electricity through the filament, a super fine wire inside the bulb. The filament resists the flow of electricity, heating it to incandescence (causing it to glow). The incandescent bulbs work on ordinary home current and require no ballast. Filaments may be of many shapes and sizes, but are nearly always made of the tough heat resistant tungsten. They come in a wide range of wattages and constructions for special applications. Most lamps used in homes for Christmas trees, interior lighting and refrigerators are incandescent lamps.

There are many types of incandescent lamps. They usually use a tungsten filament with a glass bulb construction and threaded base that fits household sockets. The bulb is usually under a vacuum or contains some type of gas to minimize wear on the filament.

Most incandescents have a spectrum in the far red end, but there are some incandescent grow lamps that have a more even spectrum. Incandescent lamps are so expensive to operate and produce so few lumens-per-watt, that they are not really worth using. They are most efficiently used as a source of bottom or soil heat for clones rooting under cool fluorescents. A few growers use incandescents during flowering to help promote more and heavier tops.

TUNGSTEN HALOGEN LAMPS

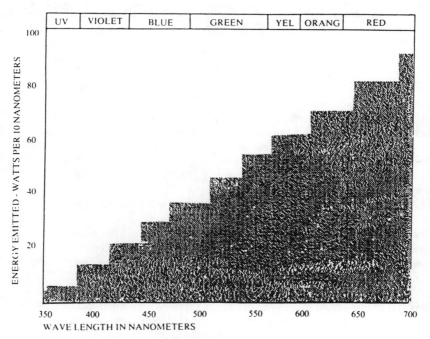

ENERGY DISTRIBUTION OF TUNGSTEN HALOGEN LAMP

The tungsten halogen lamp was originally called Iodine Quartz lamp. This is because the outer tube is made of heat resistant quartz and the main gas inside the quartz tube was iodine, one of the five halogens (fluorine, chlorine, bromine, iodine and astatine).. There are many variations to this quartz halogen or quartz tungsten lamp (See: drawing above). Today, bromine, one of the halogens, is used most often in the lamps, so the name halogen covers all of the gasses in the arc tube. The tungsten lamps are very similar to the incandescents. They use a tungsten wire filament, use a sealed bulb and are very expensive to operate: their lumen-per-watt output is very low. Tungsten halogens, like incandescents, run on a 110 volt current and require no ballast. They are as inefficient to operate as the incandescents (See: Lumen-per-Watt Chart). Their color spectrum is in the far red end with 10-15~o in the visible spectrum.

LP SODIUM LAMPS

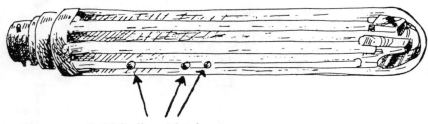

Solid Sodium Metal

Low Pressure (LP) sodium lamps come in 55, 90, 135, and 180 wattages. Their lumen-per-watt conversion is the highest of all lamps on the market today. More Careful inspection of the color spectrum chart above, shows that it is monochromatic or only produces light in one very narrow portion of the spectrum, at 589 nm. The LP sodium lamp emits a yellow glow. Colors are not distinguished and appear as tones.

LP sodium lamps are supplied by Westinghouse. Their main use in industry has been for security or warehouse light.

Each wattage requires its own unique ballast and fixture. The ballast or transformer regulates electric current and is located inside the fixture. The fixture for a 180 watt lamp is just a little larger than a fixture for two 40 watt 4-foot fluorescent tubes.

Westinghouse (Phillips Corp.) is the only supplier of LP sodium lamps. The ballast and fixture for a LP sodium cost about $200. As with other lamps, I advise to purchase the lamp, ballast, and fixture from a reputable supplier and in the same package.

The LP sodium must be used with a metal halide lamp to stimulate photosynthesis and chlorophyll synthesis. LP sodium lamps work well for side lighting or in areas with high electrical rates.

This lamp has the unique quality of maintaining 100% of the lumen output throughout life. There is no gradual decrease in the lumen output over time like with other discharge lamps. The LP sodium lamp will burn out all at once: this happens at about 18,000 hours.

The basic design of the LP sodium lamp is essentially the same as it was when first introduced to the market in 1932. Like HID lamps, the LP sodium has a two bulb construction. The arc tube is made of lime borate glass and contains a mixture of neon, argon, and pure sodium metal. The neon and argon begin to glow after electricity enters the arc tube. As the gas mixture gives off increasing amounts of heat, the sodium metal, which is still in the solid form, begins to vaporize. A yellowish glow is soon emitted from the vaporized sodium.

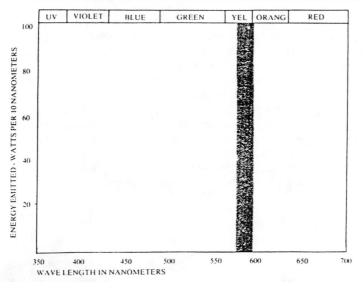

Fixtures can be lightweight plastic due to low outside bulb temperatures. The LP sodium lamp conserves energy by keeping heat inside the lamp. A special reflective coating on the outer tube allows light to pass out while heat remains inside. A vacuum is formed between the outer and inner tubes, conserving heat even more.

To ensure a long life of the lamp, they should be operated horizontally. Do not let them operate at more than 20% + /- of horizontal.

Pure sodium metal will react with air or water and explode. There is about one gram of sodium in a 180 watt LP sodium lamp. Not enough to cause a big explosion, but enough to handle carefully. When disposing of a LP sodium bulb, place it in a dry, plastic garbage can and break it.

FLUORESCENT LIGHT

Until the HID's were developed, fluorescent light was the most efficient and widely used form of artificial light available to the indoor grower. Some fluorescents boast a spectrum almost identical to the sun, but they are just not bright enough to grow marijuana efficiently. Today, these lamps are most efficiently used as a light source to root cuttings. Fluorescent lamps are long glass tubes, and found in many commercial and residential buildings. They come in a wide variety of lengths, from 1 to 12 feet Most growers have found the 4 and 8-foot tubes the easiest to handle and most readily available.

Fluorescent tubes come in several different wattages or outputs and ballast have different wattages. Both tubes and ballasts are made by several companies. The standard or regular tubes use about 10 watts per linear foot. A four foot tube uses about 40 watts, 8 feet: 80 watts, etc. High Output (HO) tubes use about 50-60 more watts per linear foot and emit about 40% more light than the standard. These fluorescents use the standard ballast. Very High Output (VHO) use almost 3 times as much electricity, and produce more than twice as much light as the standard fluorescent. VHO fluorescents are more expensive and more difficult to find. VHO tubes also require a special ballast. They may be ordered from the manufacturer or purchased from the wholesaler.

Fluorescent lamps work very well to root cuttings. They supply cool, diffused light in the proper color spectrum to promote root growth. The VHO are more expensive, but are preferred for their high lumen output. None the less, if low on capital, a grower may use any fluorescent lamp to root cuttings. The only drawback to using the less luminous standard or HO fluorescents is that cuttings may take a few days longer to root. Fluorescents, like HID's, diminish in intensity the further away from the light source. Since fluorescents produce much less light than HID's, they must be very close (2- 4 inches) to the plants for best results.

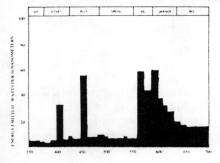

Warm White Fluorescent Lamp

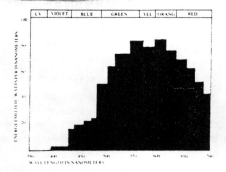

Duro-Lite Fluorescent Lamp

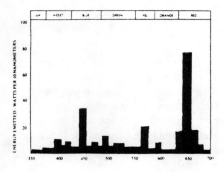

Standard Grow-Lux Fluorescent Lamp

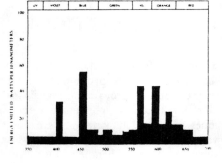

Cool White Fluorescent Lamp

A few growers hang extra fluorescent lamps with HID's to increase light intensity. This works OK, but I have found fluorescents to be more trouble than they are worth for anything but rooting cuttings. When using them in conjunction with HID's, fluorescents must be very close to plants to provide enough intense light to do any good. Fluorescents may also shade plants from HID light and generally get in the way.

Power twist or grove type lamps offer additional lumens in the same amount of linear space. The deep wide groves gives more glass surface area and more light output! Several companies market these power-twist type fluorescents.

Fluorescent bulbs and fixtures are relatively inexpensive. Two, 4-foot bulbs and a fixture will usually cost from $20 to $30. Clones root best with 18 hours of light, but some growers prefer 24 hours. Cloning for sex DOES NOT WORK WELL WITH FLUORESCENT LIGHT.

The fluorescents have a wide variety of spectrums. Sylvania has the GroLux and the Wide Spectrum GroLux. The Standard GroLux is the lamp to use for starting clones or seedlings. It is designed to be used as the only source of light, having the full spectrum necessary for photosynthesis and chlorophyll production. The Wide Spectrum GroLux is designed to supplement natural light and covers the blue to far red regions. Westinghouse has the AgroLight that produces a very similar spectrum to the sun. Warm White and Cool White bulbs used together, make excellent lamps to root clones under, especially if they are VHO.

CONSTRUCTION AND OPERATION

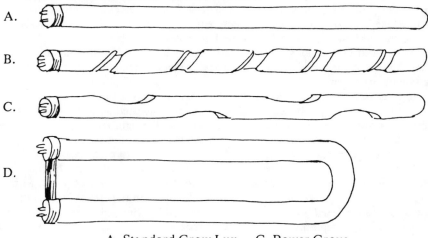

A. Standard Grow Lux   C. Power Grove
B. Power Twist   D. U Shaped Tube

Like the HID family, the fluorescents require an appropriate fixture, containing a ballast (much smaller than the HID ballast) and the ordinary 110-120 volt house current. The fixture is usually integrated into the reflective hood. There are several types of fixtures. Some have one pin on each end while others are two pin types. If purchasing new tubes, make sure the bulb fits the fixture. The fixture may contain 1, 2 or 4 tubes.

The ballast, which is contained in the fixture, radiates almost all of the heat produced by the system. The ballast is located far enough away from standard tubes that plants can actually touch them without being burned. VHO tubes might burn tender plants if they get too close.

The ballast or transformer regulates electricity. Most ballasts and fixtures are for use with standard 40 or 80 watt tubes. Special ballasts are required for VHO fluorescent tubes. The operating requirements of VHO lamps are greater, due to the increase in current, than the standard fluorescents. I advise to order the VHO ballast, fixture and tubes at the same time and from a reputable supplier.

The ballast reduces the current in the tube to the operating voltage required by a particular lamp. The ballast will normally last 10-12 years. Used fluorescent fixtures (unlike used mercury vapor ballasts) are generally acceptable to use. The end of life is usually accompanied by smoke and a miserable chemical odor. When the ballast burns out, simply remove it (or take the entire fixture to the nearest electrical supply store) and buy a new one to replace it. Be very careful if the ballast has brown slime or sludge on or around it. This sludge could possibly contain PCB's. If the ballast contains the sludge, throw it away! Most modern fluorescents are self starting, but older fluorescents require a special starter. This starter may be integrated into the body of the fixture and hidden from view, or be a small metal tube (about 1 inches in diameter and 1/2 inches long), located at the end of the fixture on the underside. The latter starters are replaceable, while the former require a trip to the electrical store.

Most electrical supply stores are able to test starters. If your fluorescent fixture does not work, and you are not well versed on fluorescent troubleshooting, simply take it to the nearest electric store and ask for advice. Make sure they test each component and tell you why it should be replaced.

The tubular glass bulb is coated on the inside with phosphor. The mix of phosphorescent chemicals in the coating and the gasses contained within determine the spectrum of colors emitted by the lamp. The bulb contains a blend of inert gasses: argon, neon or krypton and mercury vapor, sealed under low pressure. Electricity arcs between the two electrodes, located at each end of the tube, stimulating the phosphor to emit light energy. The light emission is strongest near the center of the tube and somewhat less at the ends. If rooting just a few cuttings, place them under the center of the fixture for best results.

Once the fluorescent is turned on, it will take a few seconds for the bulb to warm-up before an arc can be struck through the tube. Fluorescents blacken with age, loosing intensity. I recommend to replace bulbs when they reach 70% of their stated service life listed on the package or label. A flickering light is about to burn out and should be replaced. Life expectancy ranges from 9,000 hours (1 1/4 yrs. at 18 hrs. daily operation) with VHO tubes to 18,000 hours (2 1/2 yrs. at 18 hrs. daily operation) with the standard.

ABOUT BULBS

HID bulbs are tough and durable. They survive being shipped many miles by uncaring carriers. Once the bulb has been used a few hours, the arc tube blackens and the internal parts become somewhat brittle. After a bulb has been used several hundred hours, a good bump will substantially shorten its life and lessen its luminescence.

Never remove a warm lamp. The heat makes them expand within the socket. A hot bulb is more difficult to remove and it must be forced. A special electrical lubricant may be used (Vaseline works too) that is lightly smeared (it only takes a dash) around the mogul socket base to facilitate screwing it in and out.

Always keep the bulb clean. Wait for it to cool and wipe it off every 2-4 weeks with a clean cloth. Dirt will lower lumen output.

Store HID's that are not being used in the same box that they were purchased.

Please read the following rules of disposal before laying a faithful HID to rest.

1) Break the lamp outdoors in a container. Hit it a couple of inches from the base with a hard object. Take care to avoid shattering glass as the bulbs are under vacuum.

2) The lamps contain materials that are harmful to the skin, so contact should be avoided and protective clothing should be used.

3) Once the lamp is broken, place it in a plastic bag, then throw it away.

4) Under no conditions is the bulb to be placed in a fire.

ABOUT ELECTRICITY

The basics of electricity really do not need to be understood to grow indoors, but understanding the basics may save you money, time and the shock of your life. First, simple electrical concepts and terms are defined and briefly discussed. Once these terms are understood, you will be able to see the purpose of fuses, wire thickness (gauge), amperes on a circuit, the importance of ground and the necessity to develop safe habits.

Before anything electrical is touched, please remember the rule below.

 RULE OF THUMB - Work backwards when installing electrical components or doing wiring. Start at the bulb and work towards the plug-in. Always plug in the cord last!

Ampere (amp) - is the measure of electricity in motion. Electricity can be looked at in absolute terms of measurement just as water can. A gallon is an absolute measure of a portion of water, a coulomb is an absolute measure of a portion of electricity. Water in motion is measured in gallons per second and electricity in motion is measured in columbs per second. When an electrical current flows at one columb per second, we say it has one ampere. I guess we could say columb per second, but it would sound a little weird, because everybody uses amperes!

Breaker Box - Electrical circuit box containing breaker switches.

Breaker Switch - ON/OFF safety switch that will turn the electricity OFF when the circuit is OVERLOADED.

Circuit - the circular path that electricity travels. If this path is interrupted, the power will go off. If this circuit is given a chance, it will travel a circular route through your body! Never give it a chance!

Conductor - something that is able to carry electricity easily. Copper, steel and water are good electrical conductors.

Make sure all circuits are grounded.

Fuse - Electrical safety devise consisting of a fusible metal that MELTS and interrupts the circuit when OVERLOADED. NEVER REPLACE FUSES WITH PENNIES OR ALUMINUM FOIL!! THEY WILL NOT MELT
AND INTERRUPT THE CIRCUIT WHEN OVERLOADED. THIS IS
AN EASY WAY TO START A FIRE!

Fuse Box - Electrical circuit box containing fuses.

AMP RATING	AMPS AVAILABLE	OVERLOAD
15	13	14
20	16	17
25	20	21
30	24	25
40	32	33

CAUTION! THE HID LAMP OPERATED ON AN OVERLOADED CIRCUIT WILL BLOW FUSES, SWITCH OFF BREAKERS OR BURN WIRING. IT COULD WRECK THE HID SYSTEM, EVEN START A FIRE. PAY ATTENTION!!

 RULE OF THUMB - use only one 1000 watt HID for each 15/20 ampere circuit.

Ground - means to connect electricity to the ground or earth. Safety is the reason for ground. If a circuit is properly grounded, and the electricity travels somewhere it is not supposed to, it will go via the ground wire into the ground and rendered harmless. Electricity will travel the path of least resistance. This path must be along the ground wire. It is OK to have several ground wires if you are really paranoid!

The ground is formed by a wire (usually green or bare copper) that runs parallel to the circuit and is attached to a metal ground stake. All the circuits in the home are then attached to the ground stake. Metal water and sewer pipes serve as excellent conductors for the ground. They are all attached to one another. Water pipes conduct electricity well and are all in good contact with the ground.

The entire system, pipes, copper wire, and metal ground stake conduct any misplaced electricity safely into the ground.

The ground wire is the third wire with the big round prong. The ground runs through the ballast all the way to the hood.

HID systems must have a ground that runs a continual path from the socket, through the ballast to the main fuse box, then to the house ground. See: drawing above.

Hertz - Irregular fluctuations or cycles in electricity within a conductor (wire). In the United States, electricity runs at 60 HERTZ or cycles per second.

Ohm's Law - A law that expresses the strength of an electric current: Volts x Amperes Watts.

Short Circuit - A side or unintentional circuit formed when conductors (wires) cross. A short circuit will normally blow fuses!

Volts - air, water, gas virtually anything can be put under pressure. Pressure is measured in pounds per square inch (PSI). Electricity is also under pressure or electrical potential; this pressure is measured in volts. Most home wiring is under the pressure of approximately 110 or 220 volts.

Watts - are a measure of work. Watts measure the amount of electricity flowing in a wire. When amperes (units of electricity per second) are multiplied by volts (pressure) we get watts. 1000 watts 1 kilowatt.

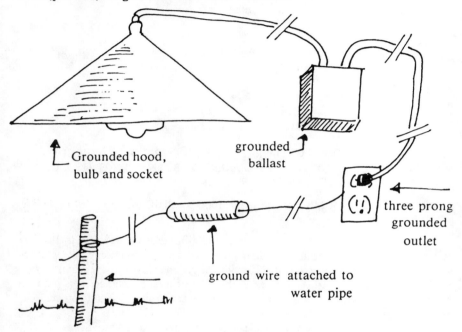

Grounded hood, bulb and socket

grounded ballast

three prong grounded outlet

ground wire attached to water pipe

ground wire attached to ferrous metal stake in earth or ground

A halide lamp that draws about 9.2 amperes x 120 volts 1104 watts. Remember OHM's LAW: Amps X Watts Volts. This is strange, the answer was supposed to be 1000 watts. What is wrong? The electricity flows through the BALLAST, which takes energy to run. The energy drawn by the ballast must then amount to 104 watts.

Watt-hours - measure the amount of watts that are used during an hour. One watt-hour is equal to one watt used for one hour. A kilowatt-hour is 1000 watt-hours. A 1000 watt HID will use one kilowatt per hour and the ballast will use about one watt. Electrical bills are charged out in KWH (See Chart on Cost of Electricity).

Electrical wire comes in all sizes (gauges) and they are indicated by number. In measuring the wire, the higher the number the smaller the wire, and the lower the number the larger the wire (See Drawing Below). 14 gauge wire is found in most homes. Wire size is important for two reasons (1) ampacity (2) Voltage drop. Ampacity is the amount of amperes a wire is able to carry safely. Electricity flowing through wire creates heat. The more amps flowing, the more heat created. This heat is wasted power! To avoid this wasted power, the proper thickness of wire must be used: at least 14 Gauge, be well insulated and have a ground wire.

● ● ● ● ● ●

8   10   12   14   16   18

In addition, forcing too much power (amperes) through a wire, it also creates voltage drop. Voltage (pressure) is lost in the wire. For example: by forcing an 18 gauge wire to carry 9.2 amperes at 120 volts, it would not only heat up, maybe even blowing fuses, but the voltage at the outlet would be 120 volts while the voltage 10 feet away could be as low as 108. This is a loss of 12 volts. Would you like to pay for this? The further the electricity travels, the more heat that is generated and the more voltage drops.

This plug-in connection nearly caused a fire!

Voltage drop is not only wasteful, but causes lamps to function very inefficiently. A lamp that was designed to work at 120 volts, that only receives 108 volts (90% of the power it was intended to operate at) would produce only 70% of the normal light. ALL THIS MEANS: Use at least 14 gauge wire for any extension cords and if the cord is to carry power over 60 feet, use 12 gauge wire.

Wires are usually
BLACK = HOT

WHITE or RED = COMMON
BARE, BLUE or GREEN = GROUND.

When wiring a plug-in or socket:

1) The HOT wire attaches to the BRASS or GOLD screw.
2) The COMMON wire attaches to the ALUMINUM or SILVER screw.
3) The GROUND wire always attaches to the ground prong.
4) TAKE SPECIAL CARE TO KEEP THE WIRES FROM CROSSING AND
FORMING A SHORT CIRCUIT.

Plug-ins and sockets must have a solid connection. If they are jolted around and
the electricity is allowed to jump, the prongs will burn and a fire could result.
Check plug-ins periodically to ensure they have a solid connection.

If a new circuit or breaker box is desired, hire an electrician, or purchase
Wiring Simplified by H.P. Richter and W.C. Schwan. It costs about $3 and is
available at most hardware stores. Installing a new circuit in a breaker box is very
easy, but installing another fuse is more complex. Before trying anything of this
scope, read up on it and discuss it with several professionals. You could be in for
the shock of your life!

ABOUT ELECTRICITY CONSUMPTION

It is not a crime to use electricity that has been legally purchased. No sensible
judge would issue a search warrant on the basis of suspicious electricity
consumption! However, small communities with bored police officers may take it
upon themselves to investigate whatever information they are able to weasel out of
electric company employees. Larger police forces do not have the desire, time nor
the money to look for small time marijuana growers.

Successful indoor growers are good citizens and keep a low profile. The yard
and the home are in excellent repair. The car is street legal and there are no
outstanding warrants on the drivers. Remember, an overdue traffic ticket turns into
a warrant for the violators arrest. Pay bills on time, be nice to neighbors and do
not throw any wild and crazy parties. Loose lips sink ships.

There are many ways to deal with the increase in consumption of electricity.
One friend moved into a home that had all electric heat as well as a fire place.
He installed three HID lamps in the basement that generated quite a bit of heat.
The excess heat was dispersed by using a vent fan attached to a
thermostat/humidistat. He turned off the electric heat, bought a fireplace insert
and started heating with wood. Even running three lamps, consuming three
kilowatts per hour, the electric bill was less than it had been with electric heat! In
Oregon, the electric bills are computerized and the average daily energy
consumption is charted on a bar graph for the previous 12 months. This makes it
easy for a person to see the dynamic increase in electricity consumption.

A 1-3 bedroom home can run 2-3 1000 watt lamps and a 4-5 bedroom home
can operate 3-5 lamps with little or no suspicion. Any more lamps usually require
new incoming circuits or the use of present circuits are severely limited. Besides, 6
or more lamps requires a full time attendant.

Price per

KW hr.	12 Hour Days		18 hour Days	
	Day	Month	Day	Month
$.02	.24	7.20	.36	10.80
$.03	.36	10.80	.54	16.20
$.04	.48	14.40	.72	21.60
$.05	.60	18.00	.90	27.00
$.06	.72	21.60	1.08	32.40
$.07	.84	25.20	1.26	37.80
$.08	.96	28.80	1.44	43.20
$.09	1.08	32.40	1.62	48.60
$.10	1.20	36.00	1.80	54.00

Monthly energy consumption of 1(300 Wall HID lamps al 18 and 12 boor operating cycles.

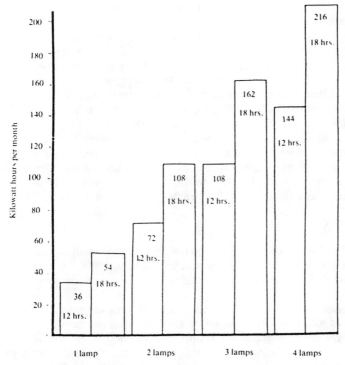

Monthly energy consumption of 1000 watt HID lamps at 18 and 12 hour operating cycles.

The amount of electricity the home normally consumes and the size of the home is considered by electric companies when looking at the amount of electricity consumed. The increase in electric consumption is normal. For example, the electric bill always goes up if there is a baby in the home or more residents. Changing to gas or wood heat and gas stove and water heater will also lower the electricity bill. Some friends bought a new, efficient water heater and saved $17 per month! Just by changing water heaters, they were able to add another halide. Another horticulturist set her water heater for 1300 instead of 1700. This simple procedure saved about 25 KWH per month! DO NOT TURN THE WATER HEATER ANY LOWER THAN 130° F. HARMFUL BACTERIA CAN GROW BELOW THIS SAFE POINT!

The electric company might call to ask if you were aware of your increased electricity bill. This is nothing to worry about. Simply reply that you are aware of the electricity being used. If you like to make excuses, some appliances that draw a lot of electricity are: electric pottery kiln, arc welder and hot tub. If the situation warrants, take showers at a friends house or at a gym, use a laundromat and never use any appliances that use a lot of electricity.

The meter reader may think it is strange to see a meter spinning like a top during the middle of the day, when nobody is home. Change the daylight cycle to be on at night, so the meter reader sees the meter when the lamps are off. One friend had his meter replaced by the power company. The company noticed a major change in electricity consumption at the residence and thought that it could be due to a defective meter, so the meter was changed but no difference was realized. Large electricity consumers may use a heavy duty commercial power meter.

Some people bypass the meter or figure out some other way to steal electricity. This is a bad idea. If you are stealing electricity from a power company, they just might find out. Stealing electricity is a very good way to call unnecessary attention to you, your home, and your growing operation. If you steal electricity, you are making it easy for someone from the power company to investigate you. Of course, some people have stolen electricity for years and gotten away with it, and they might get away with it forever. But the chances are that they will not! One of the main reasons that people steal electricity in the first place is because of security. If conspicuous electricity consumption is a problem, a generator will help.

GENERATORS

Generators work very well in grow rooms that have limited incoming electricity (amps) from the meter or when all of the electricity is being used. Some of the things to consider when purchasing a generator are reliability, ampere output and the noise factor.

Buy the generator new. It should be water cooled and fully automated. Any major brand is OK, but check its noise output and listen to it run before purchasing. Always buy a generator that is big enough to do the job. A little extra cushion will be necessary to allow for power surges. If it fails, the crop fails! Allow about 1300 watts per lamp to be run by the generator. The ballast consumes a few watts as does the wire, etc. A 5500 watt Honda generator will run four lamps with ease.

Honda generators are the most often used because they are the least expensive, dependable and quietist. Any brand will do, One fellow that hooked a generator up to a 6-cylinder gasoline motor. It could run 5 lamps with ease, but used a lot of gas. Diesel motors are more economical to run, but noisy as hell and the fumes could gag a maggot! Always make sure the gasoline powered generator is vented properly. Carbon monoxide which is toxic to plants and humans is produced by the exhaust. The exhaust from the muffler must go outside into the atmosphere.

The gasoline generator motor may be converted to propane which burns much cleaner and the exhaust may be used as a source of CO_2.

SETTING UP THE HID LAMP

Step One: Before setting up the HID system, read - "Setting Up the Grow Room" in Chapter 1 and complete the step-by-step instructions.

Step Two:. Both the lamp and ballast radiate quite a bit of heat. Care must be taken when positioning them so they are not so close 6-12 inches) to plants or flammable walls and ceiling that they become hazardous. If the room is limited in space, with a low ceiling, placing a protective, non-flammable material, like metal or asbestos between the lamp and ceiling will give much more space. If the room is 6 x 6 feet or smaller, an exhaust fan will be necessary to keep things cool. It is most effective to place the remote ballast near the floor to keep things cool. It may also be placed outside the grow room if the temperature is too high, which is unlikely when a good vent fan is used. When hanging the lamp on the overhead chain or pulley system, make sure electrical cords are unencumbered and not too close to any heat source.

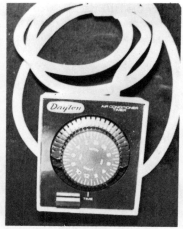

Grounded timer for one lamp   *Grounded timer with gang box*

Step Three: Buy a TIMER! A timer will be necessary for you to play Mother Nature successfully. The reasons for having a timer are obvious. If the HID system is not equipped with a timer, the only way to turn it on and off is to plug and unplug it, a shocking and colorful experience. Mother Nature provides a rigid schedule for plants to count on and live by. When the horticulturist assumes her role, will he or she remember to turn the lamp on and off at exactly the same time each and every day for several months? Or will he or she even be there each and every day, at the same time, twice a day, for several months? This is an expensive system and a lot is at stake. Use a good timer! If the photoperiod bounces around, something Mother Nature would never let happen, there will be a room full of sick, confused plants. These sick plants will produce a minimum of sickly, scrawny plants and a miserable harvest. A decent timer will cost from $20 to $30 and is worth its weight in indica tops...(see: photos of various timers.)

Step Four: To plug-in the HID lamp, it will be necessary to find the proper outlet. A 1000 watt HID lamp will use about 9.5 amperes (amps) of electricity on a regular 110-120 volt house current.

A typical home will have a fuse box or a breaker box. Each fuse or breaker switch controls an electrical circuit in the home. The fuse or breaker switch will be rated for 15, 20, 25, 30, or 40 amp service. These circuits are considered overloaded when more than 80% of the amps are being used. (See: Overload Chart. The fuse will have its amp rating printed on its face and the breaker switch will have its amp rating printed on the switch or on the breaker box. To find out which outlets are controlled by a fuse or breaker switch, remove the fuse or turn the breaker switch off. Test each and every 110 volt outlet in the home to see which ones *do not work. All the outlets that do not work are on the same circuit.* All outlets that work are on another circuit. When you have found a circuit that has few or no lights, radios, TV's, stereos, etc., plugged into it, look a the circuits amp rating. If it is rated for 15 amps, just plug one HID into it. A leeway of 5.5 amps is there to cover any power surges or in congruencies in electricity. If the circuit is rated for 20 or more amps, it may be used for the HID lamp as well as a few other low amp appliances and lights. To find out how many amps are drawn by each appliance, add up the number of watts drawn by each appliance, then divide by 120.

EXAMPLE:
A circuit with a 20 amp fuse containing the following items

> 1400 watt toaster oven
> 100 watt incandescent light bulb + 20 watt radio
> 1520 total watts divided by 120 12.6 amps in use

The above example shows 12.6 amps are being drawn when everything is on. By adding 9.2 amps, drawn by the HID to the circuit, we get 21.8 amps drawn - AN OVERLOADED CIRCUIT. There are three solutions to this problem:(1) Remove one or all of the high amp drawing appliances and plug them into another circuit. (2) Find another circuit that has few or no amps drawn by other appliances. (3)

Install a new circuit. A 220 volt circuit will make more amps available per circuit if using several lamps.

Never put a larger fuse in the fuse box than it is rated for. The fuse is the weakest link in the circuit. If a 20 amp fuse is placed into a 15 amp circuit, the fuse is able to conduct more electricity than the wiring. When this happens, the wires burn, rather than the fuse. An overloaded circuit may result in a house fire. Would you like to explain to the Fire Marshall how the fire started?

Use an extension cord that is at least 14 gauge wire or heavier if the plug will not reach the outlet desired. The thicker 14 gauge extension cord is more difficult to find and may have to be constructed. A smaller 16 or 18 gauge cord will not conduct adequate electricity and will heat up, straining the entire system. Cut the 14 gauge extension cord to the exact length; the further electricity travels, the weaker it gets and the more heat it produces, which also strains the system.

Photo at left shows three prong grounded adapter with 14-gauge extension cord attached. NOTE: screw that forms a ground in wall plug.

Step Five: Always use a *3-prong grounded plug*. If your home is not equipped with working *3-prong grounded outlets*, buy a *3-prong grounded plug and outlet adapter*. Attach the ground wire to a grounded ferrous metal object like a -grounded metal pipe, heavy copper wire, driven into the earth to a form a ground or screw the ground into the plug-in face. You will be working with water under and around the HID system. Water conducts electricity about as well as the human body . . . guaranteed to give you a charge!

Step Six: Once the proper circuit is selected, the socket and hood mounted overhead, the ballast in place on the floor (but not plugged in) screw the HID bulb finger tight into the socket. Make sure the bulb is secured in the socket tightly, but not too tight, and make certain there is a good connection. When secure, wipe off all smudges on the bulb to increase brightness.

Step Seven: Plug the 3-prong plug into the timer that is in the OFF position. Plug the timer into the grounded outlet, set the timer at the desired photoperiod and turn the timer on. *Shazam!* the ballast will hum, the lamp will flicker and slowly warm up, reaching full brilliance in about 5 minutes.

Enclosed grow room is equipped with a CO_2 enrichment system, white walls and a vent fan.

CHAPTER THREE SOIL & CONTAINERS

Large containers grow the best plants.

Marijuana flourishes in rich organic soil as well as soilless mixes. Outdoors, when planted in the earth, *cannabis* roots will branch out and penetrate deep into the soil, in search of water and nutrients. Outdoor *cannabis*, like many plants, tends to grow above ground at the same rate as it grows below the soil's surface. The roots spread out as far as the drip line . If the root system is inhibited from growing and finding water and nutrients, the entire plants growth is inhibited. An outdoor plant will have lateral branches spread out about as far as its roots are able to spread out. It is important to remember how much root space *cannabis* needs and provide adequate soil or growing medium to meet those needs. In the indoor environment, roots must be contained in a pot or planter box. It is virtually impossible to provide an indoor soil environment exactly like that of the great outdoors. This is why extreme care must be taken when selecting soil and containers.

SOIL

Soil is made up of many mineral particles mixed together with living and dead organic matter that incorporates air and water. Three factors contribute to the roots ability to grow in soil: (1) texture (2) pH and (3) nutrient content.

Texture is governed by the size and physical make-up of the mineral particles. The proper soil texture is required for adequate root penetration, water and oxygen retention and drainage, as well as many other complex chemical processes. Clay or adobe soil is made up of very small flat mineral particles. When it gets wet, these minute particles pack tightly together, slowing or stopping root penetration and water drainage. Roots are unable to breathe because very little or no space is left for oxygen. Water has a very difficult time penetrating these tightly packed soils, and once it does penetrate it, drainage is slow. Sandy soils have much larger particles. They permit good aeration (supply of air or oxygen) and drainage. Frequent watering is necessary as the water retention is very low. The soil's water and air holding ability, as well as root penetration, are a function of texture.

wet

dry

soil   air   water

Soil texture is easily checked by picking up a handful of moist (not soggy) soil and gently squeezing it. The soil should barely stay together and have a kind of sponge effect when the hand slowly opens up to release pressure.

Soil Amendments increase the soils air and water retaining ability. Soil amendments fall into two categories: (1) mineral (2) organic.

The amendments in the mineral group are all near neutral on the pH scale and essentially contain no nutrients of their own. Mineral amendments decompose through weathering and erosion, which does not effect soil pH. The amendments are also very lightweight. This is a good point to consider when containers have to be moved much.

Perlite (sand or volcanic glass expanded by heat like popcorn) holds water and nutrients on its many irregular surfaces and works especially well for aerating the soil. This is a good medium for people planning to push plants with heavy fertilization. It drains fast and does not promote salt build-up. Perlite is also a favorite for hydroponics. Perlite comes in three grades, fine, medium and coarse. Medium and coarse are the choice of most growers for a soil amendment.

Pumice (volcanic rock) is very light and holds water, nutrients and air, in its many catacomb-like holes. It is a good amendment for aerating the soil and retaining moisture evenly.

Vermiculite (mica processed and expanded by heat) holds water, nutrients and air within its fiber and gives body to fast draining soils. Fine vermiculite also works very well as a medium in which to root cuttings. This amendment holds more water than perlite or pumice. It works best for water retention in small pots or for people who do not like to water. Vermiculite is used for hydroponic wick systems since it holds so much moisture. Vermiculite comes in three grades, fine, medium and coarse. Always use the fine to root clones. If fine is not available, crush coarse or medium between the hands, rubbing the palms back and forth. As a soil amendment, coarse is the best choice.

Organic soil amendments break down through bacterial activity, slowly yielding humus as an end product. Humus is a soft, spongy material that binds minute soil particles together, improving the soil texture. Young, composting, organic soil amendments require nitrogen to carry on their bacterial decomposition. If they do not contain at least 1.5% nitrogen, the organic amendment will get it from the soil, robbing roots of nitrogen. When using organic amendments, make sure they are thoroughly composted (at least one year) and releasing nitrogen rather than using it from the soil. A good sign of fertility is a dark, rich color.

I prefer to use mineral amendments because there is no bacterial activity that alters nutrient content and pH. Others prefer rich, thoroughly composted organic matter that not only amends texture, but supplies nutrients as well. Leaf mold, garden compost (at least one year old) and many types of thoroughly composted manure, usually contain enough nitrogen for their decomposition needs and are releasing, rather than using, nitrogen. When using organic amendments, it is best to purchase them at a nursery to help control quality. Carefully look over the bag to see if it guarantees it contains no harmful insects, larva, eggs, fungus or bad microorganisms.

Garden compost and leaf mold may be rich and organic, but are usually full of insects and who-knows-what-else. For example, the compost pile is a favorite breeding ground for cutworms. Just one cutworm in a 5 gallon pot means certain death for the defenseless marijuana plant.

Barnyard manure may contain toxic levels of salt and copious quantities of weed seeds and fungus spores. If using manure, it is best to purchase it in bags that guarantee its contents. There are many kinds of manure: cow manure, horse manure, rabbit manure, chicken manure, and the less common pig, and duck manure. All of these manures are bulky and can be used as soil amendments ability. Their nutrient content varies, depending upon the diet of the animal and the decomposition factors.

Peat is the term used to describe partially decomposed vegetation; the decay has been slowed by the wet and cold conditions of the northern U.S. and Canada, where it is found. The most common types of peat are formed from sphagnum and hypnum mosses.

Sphagnum peat moss is light brown and the most common peat found at commercial nurseries. It works well for water retention, absorbing 15 to 30 times its own weight, and giving the soil body. It contains essentially no nutrients of its own and the pH ranges from 3-5. After decomposing several months, the pH could get very acidic. However, fine dolomite lime may be added to compensate and stabilizes pH.

Hypnum peat moss is more decomposed, darker in color, with a higher pH (5-7). This peat moss is less common and contains more nutrients than sphagnum peat moss. This type of peat works well for a soil amendment, however, it can not hold as much water as the sphagnum moss.

Peat moss is very dry and difficult to wet the first time, unless you bought it wet, which is real heavy. When using peat moss as a soil amendment, it is easiest to dry mix all of the components, then wet the mix using a wetting agent like liquid concentrate soap (2-3 drops per gallon). Another trick to mixing peat moss is to squarely kick the sack a few times before opening to break the bale up. This makes for a smooth even mix with less work.

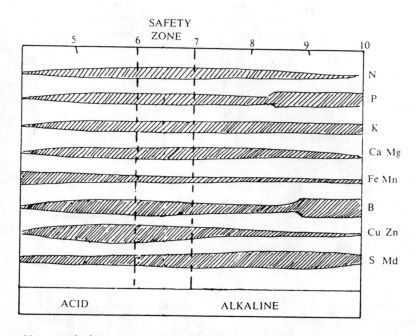

pH is a scale from 1 to 14 that measures acid-to-alkaline balance. 1 is the most acidic, 7 is neutral and 14 is most alkaline. *Cannabis* will grow best in soil with a pH from 6.5 to 7. Within this range, marijuana can properly absorb and process available nutrients. If the pH is too low (acidic) the nutrients are chemically bound by acid salts and the roots are unable to absorb them. An alkaline soil, with a high pH, will cause toxic salt build up and limit water intake by roots. Hydroponic solutions perform best in a pH range a little lower than for soil. The pH range for hydroponics is from 5.8 to 6.8, with 6.3 being ideal.

There are several ways to measure pH. A pH soil test kit, litmus paper or electronic pH tester may be found at most nurseries. When testing pH, take two or three samples and follow soil test kit, litmus paper or electronic pH tester directions to the letter. There are several brands of soil test kits on the market. They cost from $10 to $30 and will measure soil pH and N-P-K content by mixing soil with a chemical solution. Make sure you buy a kit with a good set of understandable directions.

If using litmus paper, collect soil samples that demonstrate an average of the soil. Place the samples in a clean jar and moisten it with distilled water. Place two pieces of the litmus paper in the muddy water. After 10 seconds, remove one of the pieces. Wait a minute and remove the other one. Both pieces of litmus paper should be the same color. The container the paper came in should have a pH color chart on the side. Simply match the color of the litmus paper with the colors on the chart to get a pH reading. The only way litmus paper could give a false reading is if the fertilizer (Peters, RaPid-Gro, Miracle-Gro, etc.) contain a color tracing agent or the water pH used for the test were not a neutral 7.

Electronic pH testers are inexpensive, fairly accurate and very convenient.

There are many brands of electronic soil pH testers. They are inexpensive ($15-$30), very convenient, and fairly accurate. Pay special attention to the soil moisture. Most electronic testers are designed to work in soil that is *very* moist. When checking pH regularly, the electronic tester is much more economical than the test kits and more convenient than litmus paper. The electronic unit will test pH an infinite number of times, while the chemical test kits are good for about a dozen tests. For an accurate test: (1) clean the probes of the pH meter after each test with an abrasive agent that wipes clean any corrosion (2) pack the soil tightly around the probes (3) water soil with distilled or neutral pH water before testing.

Check the pH of the water being used. Sometimes the water pH is too low or too high. After repeated watering, this can substantially alter the pH, especially with soils high in organic amendments. Coastal, rainy climates generally have acidic water, while desert regions are prone to alkaline water. A problem that surfaces in the late autumn, when all the leaves fall and everything is decomposing. This biodegradation process makes for a low pH. The acidic leaves lower the pH of the outside soil and in turn the pH of the water. This problem is most common among smaller municipal and well water systems. Generally larger water facilities carefully monitor and correct pH so there are fewer problems for the gardener. Be on the lookout for any major environmental changes that could affect the water pH. It is very important to keep an eye on the pH at all times. Check pH at least once every two weeks.

Soil pH should be between 6.5 to 7 for maximum growth and nutrient up- take. Marijuana will grow in just about any soil, but it seems to do best within this range. Commercial potting soil almost never has a pH over 7.5. A lower pH is more normal, even as low as 5.5. The ideal range would be between 6.8 and 7. Some potting soils purchased at a nursery are pH balanced and near a neutral 7. However, most potting soils have a tendency to be a bit acidic since they are generally used for indoor, perennial, acid-loving plants. Outdoor marijuana likes a slightly alkaline soil, but indoor crops do best in a neutral medium. The easiest way to maintain and/or raise the pH is to mix in one cup of fine dolomite lime per cubic foot of potting soil. Mix dolomite lime thoroughly into dry soil. Remix the soil in the container after it has been watered. This ensures a thorough, even mix.

Fine dolomite lime keeps the pH perfect.

Fine Dolomite Lime has been a favorite pH stabilizes of gardeners for years. It is virtually impossible to apply too much as long as it is thoroughly mixed in. Since dolomite has a neutral pH of 7, it can never raise the pH above 7. Dolomite works to lower as well as raise the pH. It stabilizes the pH safely. That is, by adding dolomite to the soil when planting, the pH is guaranteed to remain stable, even with changes in the water supply and acidic fertilizers. Dolomite lime is a compound of magnesium (Mg) and calcium (Ca), which accounts for its immense popularity among indoor growers. Both of these secondary nutrients are needed by marijuana, but many fertilizers do not supply adequate amounts of them. Dolomite does not save the soil from excess salt build up, only you, Mother Nature, and regular leaching will take care of toxic salts. When purchasing dolomite, ask for the finest (dust-like) grade available. Since it will be used for only a few months, it should be as fine as possible so it is readily available.

Make sure to mix the fine dolomite thoroughly with the soil when planting. Improperly mixed, the dolomite will form a cake or layer that burns roots and deflects water. Coarse dolomite could take as long as a year before it is even available to the plants.

RULE OF THUMB: When planting, add one cup of fine dolomite lime to each cubic foot (or one ounce per gallon) of planting medium to stabilize the pH and provide Ca & Mg.

Hydrated Lime is very similar to dolomite lime, but as the name hydrated implies, it is very soluble. Hydrated lime works OK to alter pH after planting. Mix it thoroughly with warm water and apply with each watering. Many horticulturists use a mix of 1/4 hydrated lime and 3/4 dolomite lime. This mix provides lime that is immediately available to neutralize the pH and the dolomite lime has a long lasting effect. It is not advisable to use over one cup of hydrated lime per cubic foot of soil. With only hydrated lime in a soil mix, it is released so fast, it might be toxic to plants, and will be washed out within a couple of weeks. Hydrated lime may be mixed with water and applied in solution to, the soil surface to raise the pH rapidly.

Whitewash is made from hydrated lime and table salt. The recipe is printed on sacks of hydrated lime. Whitewash is not as viscous as paint and may require a few coats. I really like whitewash because it sticks to damp concrete basement walls and it is antiseptic against fungus. This is the most effective way to safely white out damp, sweaty walls. The famous *Bordeaux* fungicide mix uses hydrated lime and copper sulfate. Hydrated lime may also be used as a grow room fungicide. Just sprinkle it on the floor and around the room. It will kill fungus on contact.

Do not use quicklime; it is toxic to plants. Calcic lime contains only calcium and is not a good choice for marijuana growth. It does not have the buffering qualities of dolomite, nor does it contain any magnesium (Mg).

There are several ways to raise the pH. They require putting some form of alkali in the growing medium or water such as: calcium carbonate, potassium hydroxide, sodium hydroxide, or several other compounds. Both hydroxides are caustic and require special care when handling. They are normally used to raise the pH of hydroponic nutrient solutions. The easiest and most convenient way to raise the pH and/or stabilizes it, is to add fine dolomite lime and hydrated lime before planting.

RULE OF THUMB: to raise the pH one point is to add 3 cups of fine dolomite lime to one cubic foot of soil. An alternate fast acting mix would be to add 2 1/2 cups of dolomite and 1/2 cup of hydrated lime to one cubic feet of soil.

There are many ways to lower the pH. The simplest and easiest for soil is to add dolomite lime. If the water has a high pH, distilled white vinegar will solve the problem. Calcium nitrate or nitric acid, used mainly in hydroponic units, and sulfur also work very well to lower pH. If using fertilizers containing these nutrients, keep close watch on the pH, they could lower it substantially.

RULE OF THUMB: to lower the pH one point, add three cups of fine dolomite lime to one cubic feet of potting soil before planting.

One cup of hydrated lime may be substituted for one cup of dolomite. An alternative mix to lower the pH of the water adds one teaspoon of white distilled vinegar per gallon of water to lower the pH one point. Check pH of the solution before watering because the pH of vinegar varies according to type and manufacturer.

After altering the pH, check it, then check it again several days later, and once or twice the following weeks to make sure it remains stable.

RULE OF THUMB - If soil pH is under 6 or over 8, it is easiest, and less expensive in the long run, to change soil rather than experimenting with changing the pH.

Pulverized eggshells, clam or oyster shells and wood ashes have a high pH and work to raise pH. It takes many, many eggshells to fill a cup and it takes a long time for the shells to break down and effect the pH; wood ashes usually have a pH of about 11 and are easy to over apply. Many times ashes come from fireplaces or wood stoves that have been burning all kinds of trash and are, therefore, unsafe. Do not use wood ashes!

Potting soil, fresh out of the bag, generally supplies the plant with enough N-P-K for the first month of growth, before supplemental fertilization is necessary. Secondary and trace elements are usually found in sufficient quantities and unnecessary to add, except for fine dolomite lime. If you are totally into organic horticulture, supplemental fertilization may be replaced by organic soil amendments and fertilizer. See Chapter 4: "Gradual Release Organic Fertilizers".

Potting soil from the nursery is the easiest soil to use for indoor cultivation. It is usually pH balanced, contains adequate levels of most all nutrients, retains water and air evenly, drains well, and allows easy root growth. Most potting soils, except those containing exceptional amounts of organic fertilizer amendments, will be depleted of nutrients within 3-4 weeks. After this time, supplemental fertilization will usually be necessary. Potting soils tend to be very localized, since they are so heavy and shipping costs prohibitive. There are many good brands to choose from. Ask your nurseryperson for help in selecting one. None-the-less, make a point of checking the pH yourself.

NOTE: Potting soils containing over 50% vermiculite, pumice, or perlite may tend to stratify when heavily saturated with water before planting. The light mineral amendments tend to float, with the heavier organic matter settling to the bottom. If this happens, mix the water-saturated soil thoroughly with your hands until it is evenly mixed before planting or transplanting.

Mushroom Compost is an inexpensive potting soil that is high in organic amendments. Frequently mushroom compost has been sterilized chemically for several years so mushrooms would grow in it. After the mushroom growers discard the rich compost, the law usually requires that it sit fallow for two or more years before it is able to be used. The fallow time is for all the harmful sterilints to leach out. The compost is very fertile since it has been allowed to decompose for many years. Check at your local nursery or extension service for a good source of mushroom compost. Some of the most abundant harvests I have seen used mushroom compost for the growing medium.

Potting soil can get somewhat expensive when used only once, then discarded. If used for more than one crop, undesirable microorganisms and insects may have time to get started, nutrients are depleted, water and air retention are poor and compaction leads to poor drainage. There is an inexpensive alternative to potting soil: soilless mix.

SOILLESS MIX

Soilless Mix is a very popular, inexpensive, lightweight sterile growing medium, that has been used in nurseries for many years. It is generally made from one or all of the following: pumice, vermiculite, perlite, sand, and sphagnum peat moss. Soilless mix is my favorite. It allows for good, even root growth. It can be pushed to amazing lengths with total control and best of all, it is very inexpensive!

Soilless mix is preferred by commercial nurserypeople and indoor growers alike. It has good texture. It contains essentially no nutrients of its own, unless fortified with nutrients, and is generally at or near 7 on the pH scale. The soilless mix works very well for growers that tend to overwater, overfertilize or like to push plants with heavy fertilization. It drains fairly rapidly, may be leached efficiently and there is little build up of nutrients to toxic levels. Soilless mix may be purchased ready-mixed in bags of Jiffy Mix, Ortho Mix or Terra-lite. Some growers say these mixes hold moisture too long and they add 10-50% perlite for better drainage. These commercial soilless mixes are fortified with small amounts of all necessary nutrients. The fortified nutrients generally last for about a month. None-the-less, it is a good idea to use a fertilizer containing trace elements. After that, supplemental fertilization will be necessary to sustain vigorous growth.

Soilless components may be purchased separately and mixed to the desired consistency. Mix small amounts right in the bag. Larger batches should be mixed in a wheel barrow or on a concrete slab. NOTE: Mixing soil or soilless mix is a dusty, messy, miserable job; it is best to do outdoors and wear a respirator.

 RULE OF THUMB: Mix soilless amendments outdoors and when they are dry. Use a respirator to avoid dust.

Vermiculite, coarse sand, and a little steer manure is a popular inexpensive mix.

Coarse sand, fine vermiculite, or perlite work well for rooting cuttings. Sand and perlite are fast draining which helps prevent damping-off. Vermiculite holds water longer and makes cloning easier. Soilless mix also allows for complete control of critical nutrient and root stimulating hormone additives, essential to asexual propagation.

Texture of soilless mix should be coarse, light and spongy. This allows drainage with sufficient moisture and air retention, as well as providing good root penetration qualities. Fine soilless mix holds more moisture and works well with smaller containers. Soilless mixes using more perlite and sand drain faster, making it easier to push with fertilizer and not lead to excessive salt buildup. Vermiculite and mosses (10-15%) hold water longer and are great for small pots, rooting clones or situations that require good water retention.

pH is generally a neutral 7. If using more than 15% moss in your mix, add appropriate dolomite or hydrated lime to correct and stabilizes pH. Check the pH every 2-4 weeks; continued watering will promote a lower pH. Soilless mix tends to maintain a neutral pH easily. It is mainly composed of mineral particles that are not affected by organic decomposition, which could change pH. The pH is affected very little by acidic fertilizers or by water with a high or low pH.

Nutrients are not contained in the soilless mix unless they are fortified or added by the grower. Regular frequent feeding with a soluble N-P-K fertilizer, containing trace and secondary elements like Miracle-Gro, RaPidGro, or Peters, is necessary, even if fortified! (See: "Trace Element Fertilizers".)

Here are a few examples of the many soilless mixes:

1. *1/8 peat moss*   2. *1/4 coarse sand*
    1/8 coarse sand   *1/4 perlite*
    1/4 vermiculite   *1/2 vermiculite*
    1/2 perlite

3. *1/3 peat*   4. *1/2 peat*
    1/3 perlite   *1/2 perlite* *
    1/3 vermiculite *

*amount of dolomite or hydrated lime to bring pH up to neutral.

SOIL TEMPERATURE

Raising the soil temperature makes the chemical process faster and hastens nutrient uptake. Ideally, the soil temperature should range from 65 to 75° F. The soil may be heated by means of heat tape which is placed in, or under, soil. Heat tape may be purchased at most nurseries. Some friends use a waterbed heating pad to heat a large bed. It is an inexpensive alternative to heating the air. Soil may also be heated by placing the container up off the floor on blocks to allow the flow of warm air underneath. Using this method, an additional heat source may not be needed. Do not heat the soil or nutrient solution over 75° F. It will dehydrate and cook the roots!

Root cubes or Jiffy 7 Pellets and Oasis cubes are the neatest invention since the crutch. These root cubes and peat pots are very convenient and lend themselves to clones or seedlings with a strong root system. Peat pots are small compressed peat moss containers with an outside expandable wall. The flat pellets pop-up into a seedling pot when watered. They work very well for sowing seeds or even rooting cuttings. Just place the seed or cutting in the wet peat pot or root cube and keep it evenly moist. For clones, make sure to crimp the top in around the stem so constant contact is made between the stem and the root cube or peat pot. When roots show through the side, slit the side and remove the expandable nylon shell of the peat pot. Set pot or cube into a larger pot. There will be virtually no transplant shock. They do tend to dry out and contract which exposes stems. Be sure to check peat pots or root cubes daily, keeping them evenly moist, but not drenched. Root cubes and peat pots do not have any nutrients within them. Seedlings do not really require any nutrients for the first few weeks. After that, they tend to run out. Remember to feed seedlings after the first week or so and clones as soon as they are rooted. I like to feed clones and seedlings Up Start when planted and with each watering for the first two weeks.

A seedling emerges from a peat pot. Remember to remove the nylon mesh before transplanting!

SOIL MIXES

Some gardeners like to mix their own soil. Many of them go out to the back yard and dig up some good looking DIRT that drains poorly and retains water and air unevenly. This DIRT is then mixed with garden compost, full of microorganisms and bugs. They think this unique organic soil mix will grow the best dope possible and besides, it is much cheaper than buying it! The truth of the matter is, by saving $10 on soil, they will pay for it many times over in marijuana that was not produced. If you choose to mix your own soil, buy all of the components at the nursery. Alternatives

that require more work are to sterilize them by baking in the oven at 160° F for 30 to 45 minutes, or follow the solarizing technique below. This bakes all the bad bugs, but leaves most of the good ones. The stench is horrible, not to mention the mess. If using garden soil, be sure to find the richest, darkest soil with a good texture. 30 to 60% perlite and/or vermiculite will probably be necessary as a soil amendment. Even well draining garden soils tend to compact and need more fluff for good drainage and water and air retention. Check the pH before digging soil to make sure it is within the acceptable 6.5 to 7 range. Add fine dolomite regardless of the pH. Check it two or three times after mixing to ensure the pH has stabilized.

COMPOST

Many growers have no trouble with organic composts, but some of them loose their entire crop or have poor yields due to disease in the soil. Many good compost recipes are available from monthly publications such as *Sunset, Organic Gardening, Mother Earth News* or from the companies specializing in organic composts.

A good compost pile would have cow manure, the older, the better; or any kind of manure that is handy. (See: Box below). Manure from horse stalls or feed lots are mixed with straw or bedding. Make sure the bedding is not saw dust. The saw dust is very acidic and will leach all of the nitrogen out of the pile as well. The best kind of manure to acquire is the oldest, rottenest possible. It is less prone to have any weed seeds that are still alive. Fresh grass clippings are one of my favorites to use in a compost pile. The clippings are full of nitrogen and want to get rid of it. Put your hand down deep into a pile of grass clippings that has been in the sun for a couple of hours... Now that's hot! This chemical activity breaks down the clippings and liberates the nutrients.

Horse and sheep manures are hot because they contain little water and lots of air. They heat up readily in a compost pile. Cow and swine manures are cold because they hold a lot of water and can be compacted easily, squeezing out the air. Worm castings and bat guano are considered sweet because their nutrients are immediately available to plants and they will not burn. Most city zoos offer the manure and bedding from the animals at the zoo. This Zoo Doo as it is called in Portland, is full of nutrients, but should be composted for at least a year before it is used indoors.

The best way to build a compost pile is high, and keep turning it. Good compost pile recipes include the addition of organic trace elements, enzymes and the primary nutrients. The organic matter used should be ground up and in the form of shredded leaves and grass. Do not use large woody branches that could take years to decompose.

Probably the easiest and most effective way to rid soil and compost of bad bugs, larva, weed seeds and fungi is to let the sun do it for you. This technique is called solarizing (see drawing above). The principle is simple: just place a piece of clear plastic (black plastic will retain the heat and not let it pass into in the compost pile) over the compost pile or soil. The heat from the sun will cook all the bad stuff out. Use a piece of plastic 2-6 mils thick; the thicker the plastic, the longer it will last under the sun's destroying rays. The compost pile should be in a sunny location. The more sun it gets, the more heat that is generated. The sun's rays pass through the clear plastic, heating up the interior of the pile. This heat is then trapped below the plastic. This trapped heat develops 100% humidity and the temperatures often reach 140°! The plastic must completely cover the pile. Hold it down with a continuous pile of dirt around the entire outside perimeter. The soil or compost will be clean of all harmful bugs, larva, weed seeds, and fungi in one to three months, depending on the intensity and the amount of sun the pile receives. Remember, the sun is the most intense when it is near or directly overhead. So, the best time for the pile to receive sunlight is from 10 am to 3 p.m. If the pile is located on a slab of concrete, or a platform that is able to heat up, the heat builds up from both directions rapidly.

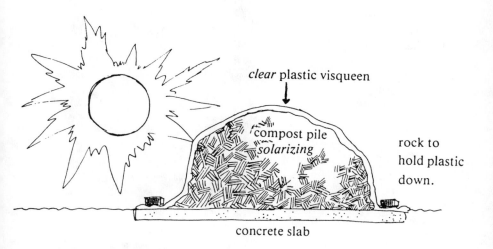

clear plastic visqueen

compost pile *solarizing*

rock to hold plastic down.

concrete slab

One of the few pests that can make it through the intense heat of the plastic coated compost pile is the cutworm. They are most common in compost piles with a dirt foundation. There are several different cutworms. They all live in the soil, flourish in compost piles and curl up for protection when exposed. Cutworms are 1/4 to l-inch in length and may easily be spotted with the naked eye. If these pests make it to the soil where the crops are growing, just one cutworm per pot could destroy the entire garden.

Before using compost, pour it through 1/4-inch mesh hardware cloth (screen). Place a heavy duty framed screen over a large garbage can or a wheel barrow to catch the sifted compost. This will break the humus up well before mixing it with the soil. After mixing with soil, the mix may be resifted for additional mixing. Earthworms found on the screen may be returned to the medium, while cutworms are promptly squished.

Growers using 1/3 worm castings A perlite and 1/3 organic matter have had best results. The perlite lets the plants breathe. Many growers mix 1/3 to 1/2 perlite to a bag of rich potting soil that has lots of worm castings. Worm castings are heavy, compacting the roots and leave little or no space for air to the roots. Adding perlite aerates the soil.

Here are just 3 examples of the many possible combinations of soil mixes.

1. *1/3 worm castings*
   1/3 manure
   1/3   coarse sand

2. *1/3 worm castings*
   1/3 perlite
   1/3 vermiculite

3. *1/3 peat*
   1/3 vermiculite
   1/3 worm castings

Add fine dolomite lime
to each one of these soil
mixes, regardless if the pH
is off.

CONTAINERS

Grow bags are becoming very popular.

Containers come in all shapes and sizes. They may be constructed of almost anything; clay, metal, plastic, wood, and fiber are the most common. Just about any kind of container will do, as long as it is thoroughly clean and has not been used for any petroleum products. See Chart on "Potting". Clay, fiber, and wood containers breathe better than plastic or metal ones. Clay pots are heavy and notorious for absorbing moisture from soil inside, causing soil to dry out quickly. The type of container is usually a matter of cost and availability.

Grow bags are a good, inexpensive, long lasting alternative to rigid containers. In fact some people use the sack the potting soil came in as a container. Once the soil is inside and moist, the bag holds its shape well. The bags tend to expand and contract with the soil, lessening the chance of burned root tips that grow down the side of the pot.

Fiber or pulp pots are very popular and inexpensive, but their bottoms habitually rot out. Painting the inside of the fiber container with latex paint will keep the bottom from rotting for several crops.

Other than making sure containers are clean, there are two important factors to consider: (1) drainage holes (2) size.

Drainage holes should let the excess water drain easily, but not be so big that soil in the bottom of the container washes out onto the floor. Pots may be lined with newspaper if drainage is too fast or soil washes out drain holes. This will slow drainage, so be wary!

 RULE OF THUMB: have at least two 1/2-inch holes per square foot of bottom. When using a tray under pot, do not let excess water sit in the tray for over 3 days. This stagnant water could cause root rot and fungus.

Both clones came from the same mother. The six gallon grow bag produced 2.8 ounces of dried tops. The two gallon container produced less than one ounce!

The size of container is of utmost importance. *Cannabis,* being an annual plant, grows very rapidly, requiring a lot of root space for vigorous growth. If the roots are confined, growth slows to a crawl. A good example of this may be found at most retail nurseries about midsummer. Tomato plants, that are still in small 4-inch or gallon pots, will be fully mature and have a few ripe tomatoes. Notice the branches do not extend much beyond the sides of the container and drip line; the plants are tall and leggy with curled down leaves. They have an overall stunted sickly appearance. These plants are pot or root-bound. Sure, they could be kept alive or maybe even made to grow a little by I fertilizing with the exact balance of necessary nutrients. This is a lot of work, it is easy to overfertilize, and the plant might always be a runt.

Marijuana roots develop and elongate quickly, growing down and out, away from the main tap root. When roots reach the sides of the pot, they grow straight down. I'm sure you have seen soil contract and separate from the container wall. When this happens, the root hairs that are responsible for absorbing water and nutrients are helpless to dry this contraction problem, is to run your finger around the inside lip of the pot, cultivating the soil, filling the crack between the pot and soil. Check this every few days. Also maintaining evenly moist soil will help keep root hairs on soil perimeter from drying out.

It is important to transplant before the plant is pot bound and stunted. Once a plant is stunted, it will take several weeks to grow enough new roots and root hairs to resume normal growth.

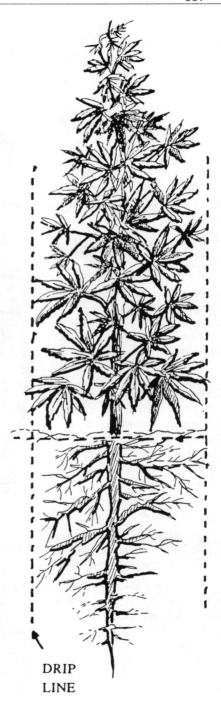

DRIP
LINE

MINIMUM CONTAINER SIZE

PLANT AGE IN MONTHS   CONTAINER SIZE

0-1	*4 inches*
1-2	*1 gallon*
2-3	*2 gallon*
3-4	*3 gallon*
4-5	*5 gallon*
4-6	*10 gallon*

This chart shows the minimum size container a plant should be in at various ages.

The best way to solve the pot bound problem is to plant seedlings or clones directly into a 5 or 10 gallon pot. This method requires fewer containers, less work and is less stressful to both plants and transplanter. This works well for clones grown in a short crop. The clone is moved into the large pot after it is well rooted. It is left in the vegetative growth stage for 4 to 8 weeks, then flowering is induced. Roots tend to grow less during flowering. By the time it is potbound, the harvest is ready.

Soil can hardly be seen.

RULE OF THUMB: allow 1 1/2-2 gallons of soil for every month the plant will spend in the container. A 3-6 gallon pot will support a seedling or clone for 3-4 months.

Another way of solving this pot bound problem is to repot the plant every month or so into the next largest size pot. This transplanting could easily stress out both you and the plants.

Pots are the most common containers for indoor use. They are inexpensive and readily available. Complete individual water and nutrient control may be exercised with pots. An individual plant may be quarantined from the rest of the garden or dipped in a medicinal solution. When plants are small, they may be huddled tightly together under the HID lamp and moved further apart as needed.

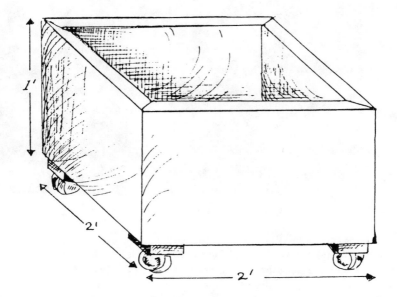

Planter box on casters

Large planters may be placed on the ground or set up on blocks or casters to allow air circulation underneath. This lessens the chance of fungus growth and keeps the soil warmer than if it were sitting on a cold floor. The planters range in size from 2 x 2 x 1 feet to 10 x 10 x 2 feet. The roots have 2-3 times as much soil to grow in and much less side surface for roots to run in- to and grow down. Roots are able to intertwine and grow like crazy.

Generally plants or clones are left in one gallon pots until they are 1 to 1 1/2 months old, then transplanted to the large planter box before they are root bound. This allows young plants to be bunched together under the lamp and receive maximum light intensity. As many as 20 plants may be placed in a 2 x 2 x 1 feet planter, but 4 to 6 plants are much more reasonable. Once plants start crowding and shading one another, they may be bent outwards and tied down to a trellis that is nailed to the sides of the planter. The large planters work very well and are highly recommended because they require less maintenance. Since there is a larger mass of soil, water and nutrients are retained much longer and more evenly.

One gallon plants are transplanted into the raised bed.

Raised beds can be installed right on the earthen floor of a garage or basement. If drainage is poor, a layer of gravel or a dry well is laid under 12-24 inches of soil, with a 2 x 12 inches as a border for the raised bed. If the bed is subterranean, it may be very close to the water table. When it rains, the water may collect underneath. The garden seldom needs watering! Plants are kept a little bit too wet and there may be a build-up of salts (nutrients) in the soil, since it can not be leached effectively.

If drainage does not present a problem and you are able to grow in a raised bed, by all means do so! The large soil mass gives a chance to build up a good organic base after several crops. There will need to be organic activity within the soil. Your job is to make sure it is the good, not the bad, microorganisms that live in the bed. When mixing soil or adding amendments, use the best possible organic components and follow organic principles. There should be good drainage and the soil should be as deep (12-24 inches) as possible. The more organic matter present, the more fertile the soil will be.

A good deal of heat may be generated by the organic activity. This not only speeds nutrient uptake, but helps heat the room as well. Ventilation is necessary to lower heat, humidity and keep the room free of fungus and bad bugs. The organic garden may sound great, but it is one hell of a lot of work to replicate the great outdoors. Another drawback to the raised bed is that the crop will take a few days to a couple of weeks longer to mature than if it were grown in containers. However this longer wait is offset by a larger harvest. When marijuana is grown in a container, with its roots restricted from growing, the plant will mature and flower faster.

HOW TO SEED A POT

In this example we will use a one gallon plastic pot, which is readily available and reusable.

1.   Acquire the desired number of clean pots.

2.   Fill the pot with well-mixed growing medium to about 1 from the top.

3.   Water with 1-2 quarts of warm water or until soil is completely saturated and excess water runs out the drain holes. Wait 15 minutes and repeat watering to ensure soil saturation.

4.   With your finger, make 1 to 10 small holes 1/2 inches deep in the surface. Place one to three seeds per hole and cover with soil. Pack it gently, but firmly in place. Place a paper towel over the seeds to maintain soil surface moist and to keep soil from washing.

5.   Sprinkle water on the surface. Make sure seeds remain at proper depth and do not wash out.

6.   Maintain soil surface evenly moist until seeds sprout.

7.   Thin to one pot per plant

8.   Grow a strong, healthy plant.

9.   See: "Cloning for Sex".

10.   Clone desirable females, save males for breeding.

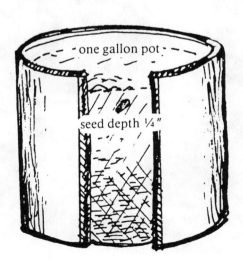

one gallon pot

seed depth ¼"

Both seedlings are 7 weeks old. One gallon plant is stunted and overfertilized. Five gallon plant received the same treatment but is healthy. Use large pots, 6 gallons of container one cubic foot of soil.

CHAPTER FOUR WATER & FERTILIZER

Water and fertilizer work hand in hand. The nutrients in fertilizer dissolve in water. Water carries nutrients through the plant. Water is essential to plant growth, making up over 75% of a plant's weight.

The root hairs absorb water, nutrients (fertilizer) and oxygen in the soil and carry them up the stem to the leaves. This flow of water from the soil through the plant is called the transpiration stream. A fraction of the water is processed and used in photosynthesis. The water evaporates into the air, carrying waste products along with it, via the stomata in the leaves. This process is called transpiration. Some of the water also returns manufactured sugars and starches to the roots.

Unfortunately, common tap water may contain high levels of alkaline salts, sulfur or chlorine, and may have a pH out of the acceptable 6.5 to 7 range. Water containing sulfur is easily smelled and tasted. Saline water is a little more difficult to detect. Water in coastal areas is generally full of salt, because it washes inland from the ocean. This problem is worst in southern California and other coastal areas.

Chlorine and salt are added to many household water systems. Chlorine does not seem to affect marijuana growth, but salt softened water should be avoided. Enough salt will kill any plant! Chlorine does tend to make soil acidic after repeated use. The best way to get chlorine out of water is to let it sit one or two days in an open container. The chlorine will evaporate as a gas when it comes in contact with the air. If chlorine noticeably alters soil pH, it may be adjusted with hydrated lime. Salts, from saline water or fertilizer residue can build up to toxic levels quickly in container gardens. Excessive salts inhibit seed germination, burn the root hairs and tips or edges of leaves, and stunt the plant. Excess salt built up in the soil can easily be leached out by pouring 2 gallons of water per gallon of growing medium. Repeat leaching once or twice if burn is severe. This will wash out any toxic build up of salts. If you use soft water, saline water, or have any unwanted substances in the soil, it is a good idea to leach containers every month or two. Hard or well water may be alkaline and usually contains notable amounts of calcium (Ca) and magnesium (Mg). Both of these micronutrients will be put to good use by marijuana. It is doubtful that hard water could contain enough Ca or Mg to toxify the soil. It is still a good idea to leach the soil at least every two months. Generally, water that is OK to drink, is OK for plants.

APPLICATION

Large plants use much more water than small plants, but there are many more variables than size that dictate a plant's water consumption. The age of the plant, container size, soil texture, temperature, humidity and ventilation all contribute to water needs. Change any one of these variables and water consumption will change. Good ventilation is essential to promote transpiration, water consumption and rapid growth. Generally, the healthier a plant, the faster it grows and the more water it consumes.

 RULES OF THUMB - (1) Apply tepid (70- 80° F) water. Plants are able to process tepid, or room temperature water rapidly and it better penetrates the soil. Tepid water does not shock tender root hairs or leaves. Would you rather jump into a warm or a cold swimming pool? What happens to your body when you dive into a cold swimming pool? (2) Water early in the day so excess water will evaporate from soil surface and leaves. Leaving leaves and soil wet leads to fungus attack.

Many growers irrigate on a wet and dry cycle. They water, then let the soil dry out to about 2 inches below the soil surface before the next watering. Other growers keep moisture more consistent by irrigating more often. A fertilizer solution is often added with each watering.

Marijuana does not like soggy soil. Soil kept too wet essentially drowns roots, making it impossible for them to breathe. This causes slow growth and possible fungus attack. Tiny root hairs dry up and die, if the soil dries out, even in pockets. It seems to take forever for the roots to grow new hairs.

RULES OF THUMB about irrigation: (1) Irrigate small seedlings and clones when the soil surface is dry. For clones rooting in sand or vermiculite with good drainage and no humidity tent, the surface is dry almost daily. (2) Irrigate larger plants in the vegetative and flowering stages when soil is dry 2 inches below the surface. Contrary to popular belief, flowering marijuana uses high levels of water to carry on rapid floral formation. Letting a flowering plant wilt between waterings actually stunts flower formation. (3) Line pots up so they are easy to keep track of.

A moisture meter makes watering very exact.

A moisture meter takes most of the guess work out of watering. They can be purchased for $10 to $30 and are well worth the money. The meter can tell exactly how much water the soil contains at any level or point. Many times, soil will develop dry pockets and/or not hold water evenly. Checking moisture with a finger is, at best, an educated guess and disturbs the root system. A moisture meter will give an exact moisture reading without bothering the roots as much.

Cultivating the soil surface allows water to penetrate evenly and guards against dry soil pockets. It also keeps water from running down the crack between the inside of the pot and the soil and out the drain holes. Gently break up and cultivate the top 1/2-inch of soil with your fingers or a salad fork. Make sure tiny surface roots are not disturbed much.

The trick is to apply enough water so all of the soil gets wet and not let too much run out the drain holes, which will cause a leaching effect, carrying away nutrients. None the less, a little drip (about 10%) out the drain holes is beneficial.

Overwatering is a common problem, especially with small plants. Too much water drowns roots by cutting off their supply of oxygen. If you have symptoms of overwatering, buy a moisture meter! It will let both you and your garden breathe easier. Sometimes, parts of the soil are overwatered and other soil pockets remain bone dry. Cultivating the soil surface, allowing even water penetration and using a moisture meter will overcome this problem. One of the main causes of overwatering is poor air ventilation! The plant needs to transpire and water needs to evaporate into the air. If there is nowhere for this wet, humid air to go, literally gallons of water may be locked in the grow room. Well ventilated air carries the wet air away, replacing it with new dry air. If using trays to catch runoff water, use a turkey baster (large syringe) or sponge to draw the excess water from the tray. Signs of overwatering are: leaves curl and yellow, constant soggy soil, fungus, and slow growth. Overwatering may affect a plant and the inexperienced gardener may not see any blatant symptoms for a long time.

 RULES OF THUMB - about watering (1) large plants transpire more than small ones, (2) maintain good ventilation and (3) check the soil of each plant for moisture. This will be a base to work from in developing your watering skill.

Underwatering is less of a problem. However, it fairly common if small (1-2 gallon) pots are used, or if small pots are used by growers that do that do not realize the water needs of plants for rapid growth. Small containers dry out quickly and may need daily watering. If this is forgotten, the poor water starved plant is stunted. Once tender root hairs dry out, they die; the plant is stunted. Most growers panic when they see their prize marijuana plants wilted in bone dry soil.

If the soil is nearly or completely dry, take the following steps: Add a few drops (one drop per pint) of a biodegradable, concentrated liquid soap like Castille or Ivory concentrate to the water. It will act as a wetting agent, helping the water penetrate soil more efficiently and guard against dry soil pockets. Most soluble fertilizers contain a wetting agent. Apply about 1/4 to 1/2 as much water/fertilizer as the plant is expected to need, wait 10 to 15 minutes for it to totally soak in, then apply more water/fertilizer until the soil is evenly moist. If trays are underneath the pots, let excess water remain in the trays a few hours or even overnight before removing it with a large turkey baster.

Having a readily accessible water source is very convenient; it saves time and labor. A 10 x 10 garden, containing 24 healthy plants in 6 gallon pots, could need

10 to 30 gallons of water per week. Water weighs eight lbs. a gallon. 30 gallons x 8 lbs. 240 pounds! That-foots a lot of containers to fill, lift and spill. Carrying water in containers from the bathroom sink to the garden is OK when plants are small, but when they get large, it is a big, sloppy, regular job. Running a hose into the garden saves much labor and mess. A lightweight 1/2-inch hose is easy to handle and is less prone to damage plants. If the water source has hot and cold water running out the same tap and is equipped with threads, a hose may easily be attached and tepid water used to water the garden. A dishwasher coupling may be used if the faucet has no threads. The hose should have an on/off valve at the outlet, so water flow may be controlled while watering. A rigid watering wand will save many broken branches while leaning over to water in tight quarters. The wand may be found at the nursery or constructed from plastic PVC pipe. Do not leave water under pressure in the hose. Garden hoses are meant to transport water, not hold it under pressure, which may cause it to rupture.

To make a siphon or gravity fed watering system, place a barrel at least 4 feet high in the grow room. If humidity is a problem, put a lid on the can or move it to another room. The attic is a good place because it warms the water and promotes good pressure. Place a siphon hose in the top of the tank or install a PVC on/off valve near the bottom of the barrel. An inexpensive device that measures the gallons of water added to the barrel may be purchased at most hardware stores. It is easy to walk off and let the barrel overflow. A float valve may also be installed in the barrel so there is a constant supply of water.

A drip watering system may be employed. These systems use low pressure plastic pipe with friction fittings. Water flows down the pipe and out the emitters, one drop at a time. The emitters are attached to the main hose and may be either spaghetti strap or nipple type. There are several kits on the market or you can construct your own system from component parts.

The drip system does offer certain advantages. Once set up, it seems to cut watering maintenance. Fertilizer may also be injected into the system. This facilitates fertilization, but gives the same amount of nutrient to each plant. If growing clones that are all the same age and size, a drip system would work very well. This may or may not be desirable, depending on the nutrient requirements of each plant. One grower loves the convenience and constant feeding ability of the system. She injects a fertilizer solution into the system with each watering. She notes that plants grown using a drip system are able to survive in smaller containers and root growth is minimal, since the nutrients and water are in constant supply. In fact, using soilless mix and a drip system is essentially a non-recovery hydroponic system.

Drip Water Emitter

The drip system may also be attached to a timer so it irrigates when Mother Nature is on vacation. This is very convenient, but may be expensive, not only in monetary terms but in yield as well. The automated system may promote negligence! The garden needs daily care! If it is automated, it may discourage you from actually checking the moisture with a meter or looking at each and every plant daily. Automation is great, but is not a substitute for good gardening practices.

FERTILIZER

Marijuana grows so fast under HID lamps that ordinary potting soil can not supply all necessary nutrients for rapid, healthy growth. Fertilizing is necessary to make extra nutrients available for sustained vigorous growth.

There are about 16 known elements necessary for plant life. Carbon, hydrogen, and oxygen are absorbed from the air and water. The rest of the elements, called nutrients, are absorbed mainly from the soil or fertilizer. The primary nutrients (Nitrogen (N), Phosphorus (P), and Potassium (K)) are the elements a plant uses the most. Almost all fertilizers show the N-P-K percentages in big numbers on the front of the package. They are always listed in the same N-P-K order. For example a 23-19-17 fertilizer has 23% nitrogen, 19% phosphorus and 17% potassium.

Calcium (Ca) and magnesium (Mg) are secondary nutrients or elements,. Iron (Fe), sulfur (S), manganese (Mn), boron (B), molybdenum (Mb), zinc (Zn), and copper (Cu) are micro-nutrients or trace elements. Marijuana uses more magnesium than most general purpose fertilizers supply. Mg and Ca are usually added in the form of fine dolomite lime when soil is mixed. Trace elements are usually found in sufficient quantities in potting soil and in complete fertilizers like Peters and Eco-Grow for healthy plant growth and do not need to be added. Unless fortified, soilless mixes may be severely lacking in secondary and trace elements. It is still a good idea to use a fertilizer containing trace elements. Secondary and trace elements are usually not listed on fertilizer labels.

PRIMARY NUTRIENTS

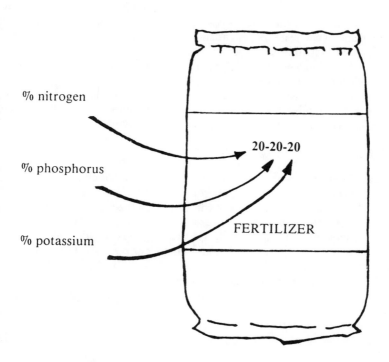

% nitrogen

% phosphorus

20-20-20

% potassium

FERTILIZER

Nitrogen (N) is the most important nutrient. It regulates the plant's ability to make proteins essential to new protoplasm in the cells. N is essential to the production of chlorophyll and is mainly responsible for leaf and stem growth as well as overall size and vigor. Nitrogen is most active in young buds, shoots and leaves. Marijuana loves N and requires high levels during vegetative growth. Calcium and Magnesium are also classified with N-P-K as Macro-nutrients.

Phosphorus (P) is necessary for photosynthesis and provides a mechanism for energy transfer within the plant. P is associated with overall vigor as well as resin and seed production. *Cannabis* uses highest levels of P during the germination, seedling, cloning and flowering stages of growth.

Potassium or potash (K) is essential to the manufacture and movement of sugars and starches, as well as growth by cell division. K increases chlorophyll in foliage and helps regulate stomata openings so plants make better use of light and air. Potash encourages strong root growth and is associated with disease resistance and water intake. K is necessary during all stages of growth.

SECONDARY ELEMENTS

Magnesium (Mg) is found as a central atom in every chlorophyll molecule and is essential to the absorption of light energy. Mg aids in the utilization of nutrients. It also neutralizes soil acids and toxic compounds produced by the plant. It is the only secondary nutrient that is commonly found deficient. Adding dolomite lime before planting will stabilize pH and add Mg and Ca to the soil. Add Epsom salts with each watering if no dolomite was added when planting.

Calcium (Ca) is fundamental to cell manufacture and growth. Marijuana must have some calcium at the growing tip of each root.

Trace Elements are essential to chlorophyll formation and must be present in minute amounts, but little is known about the exact amounts that are needed. They function mainly as catalysts to plant processes and utilization.

FERTILIZERS

The goal of fertilizing is to supply the plant with proper amounts of nutrients for vigorous growth without toxifying the soil by over-fertilizing. A 5-6 gallon container, full of rich, fertile potting soil will supply all the necessary nutrients for a month or longer. After the roots have absorbed most of the available N-P-K nutrients, they must be added to the soil to sustain vigorous growth. Unless fortified, soilless mixes require N-P-K fertilization from the start. I like to start fertilizing fortified soilless mixes after the first week or two of growth. Most commercial soilless mixes are fortified with secondary and trace elements. Use a N-P-K fertilizer containing secondary and trace elements in mixes that are not fortified.

A plant has different fertilizer needs as its metabolism changes throughout life. During germination and seedling growth, intake of phosphorus (P) is high. The vegetative growth stage requires high amounts of Nitrogen (N) for green leaf growth. P and K are also necessary in substantial levels; a general purpose N-P-K fertilizer is recommended. In the flowering stage, the marijuana is no longer concerned with vegetative growth. P intake is highest; N and K are less important. Using a super bloom fertilizer, low in N and K, and high in P will promote larger flower growth. However, some growers use an N-P-K, general purpose fertilizer and get OK results. A high N content fertilizer usually promotes greener, leafy growth during flowering. *Cannabis* does need some N during flowering. Without N, older foliage may yellow and die prematurely.

Fertilizers may be either (water) soluble or gradual release. Both soluble and gradual release fertilizers can be organic or chemical.

SOLUBLE fertilizers lend themselves to indoor container cultivation and are preferred by commercial nurserypersons, as well as many indoor growers. Soluble fertilizers dissolve in water and may be added or washed (leached) out of the soil easily. It is easy to control the exact amount of nutrients available to plants in a soluble form. Versatile soluble fertilizer may be applied in a water solution to the soil or misted directly on the leaves. Foliar feeding supplies nutrients directly to the leaves where they are used.

CHEMICAL SOLUBLE FERTILIZERS

Chemical granular fertilizers can easily be over applied, creating toxic soil. They are almost impossible to leach out fast enough to save the plant.

Osmocote™ chemical fertilizers are essentially time release. They are used by many nurseries because they are easy to apply and only require one application every few months. Using this type of fertilizer may be convenient, but exacting control is lost. They are best suited for ornamental containerized plants where labor costs and uniform growth are the main concerns.

General Purpose

Blossom Booster

PETERS™ fertilizer has been the choice of professional nurserypersons for many years. Indoor growers love it because the salts are so pure and easy to work with. It is formulated with chelating agents to prevent settling out of elements, contains necessary secondary and trace elements, and has no chloride carbonates or excess sulfates, preventing build up of excess salts. It is excellent for use with both soil and soilless mixes. Peters comes in many different N-P-K formulas. Those most commonly used indoors are listed.

The following formulas are mixed from 1/2 to 1 tablespoon per gallon of water and applied with each watering.

1. General Purpose (20-20-20) is most readily available and used during the seedling and vegetative stages. 2 Trace element content: Mg .O5-6, Fe .05%, Mn .0031%, B .0068%, Zn .0025%, Cu .0036%, Mo .0009%

2. Peat-Lite Special (20-10-20) works very well during vegetative growth in both soil and soilless mixes. Less P helps contain roots. It contains high levels of secondary and trace nutrients. Trace element content: Mg .15%, Fe .10%, Mn .056%, E .02%, Zn .0162%, Cu .01%, Mo .01%

3. Geranium Special (15-15-15) also used during vegetative growth works very well for low pH situations. Geranium Special has a non-acidic source of N and reduced ammonium toxicity potential. Trace element content: Mg .15%, Fe .10%, Mn .056%, E .02%, Zn .0162%, Cu .01%, Mo .01%

4. Blossom Booster (10-30-20) contains a high level of P, which is necessary during flowering. It increases bud set, count and size. Trace element content: Mg .15%, Fe .10%, Mn .056%, E .02%, Zn .0162%, Cu .01%, Mo .01%

Eco GRow   Ra-Pid-Gro

ECO-GROW™ is produced in Seattle, WA by Eco Enterprises. Its various formulas are made with the hydroponic horticulturist in mind, but can be used with soil as well. ECO-GROW is a balanced formula that gives plants all of the nutrients necessary for strong, healthy growth. All the elements in ECO-GROW are derived from natural minerals and nothing artificial is added. One of the interesting qualities of ECO-GROW is it does not totally dissolve in the nutrient solution. There are enough nutrients in the solution that plants get properly nourished, so do not worry about a little sediment in the solution. The pH is balanced at 6.3 when mixed with neutral tap water.

Eco-Grow - Secondary and trace element analysis: Ca 6%, S 2.6%, Mg 2.0%, Fe .2%, Mn .1%, Cl .1%, Cu .005%, Zn .05%, B .045%, Mo .002% .001% Co.

1. Standard (10-8-14) - is a general purpose fertilizer formulated for vegetative growth.

2. Monstera (20-6-12) - This formula is for plants needing high N intake for rapid vegetative growth.

3. Bloom (3-35-10) - A blossom boosting formula low in N and high in P. Great for fat, healthy, strong buds.

RA-PID-GRO™ is a favorite of some professionals and marijuana growers. The Multi-Use (23-19-17) formula will dissolve easily in water, is readily available, and contains a few trace elements. Supplemental trace element fertilization is necessary. Ra-Pid-Gro is used during the seedling and vegetative growth stages. It may be used during flowering, but supplies high levels of unnecessary N, which could promote undesired green vegetative growth.

MIRACLE-GROW is the old, reliable houseplant and vegetable food. It comes in several formulas and may be found at just about any store with a gardening section.

Miracle-Gro lists secondary and trace elements on the guaranteed analysis panel: Copper .05%, chelated Iron .10%, Manganese .05%, and Zinc .05%.

1. The tomato formula (18-18-21) also contains Magnesium (Mg) .05%. Tomatoes and marijuana have very similar nutrient requirements. This formula is great for seedling and vegetative growth.

2. The All-Purpose (15-30-15) formula is preferred by growers during flowering. The high concentration of Phosphorus (P) helps rapid bud formation.

GRADUAL RELEASE ORGANIC FERTILIZERS

Organic *cannabis* boasts a sweeter taste, but implementing an organic indoor garden requires horticultural know how. The limited soil, space and the necessity for sanitation must be considered when growing organically. Outdoors, organic gardening is easy because all the forces of nature are there for you to seek out and harness. Indoors, essentially none of the natural phenomena are at play. Remember you are Mother Nature and must create everything! The nature of growing indoors does not lend itself to long term organic gardens, but some organic techniques have been practiced with amazing success.

Most indoor organic gardens use potting soil, high in worm castings, peat, sand, manure, leaf mold, compost and fine dolomite lime. In a container, there is really no space to build the soil by mixing all kinds of neat composts and organic nutrients to cook down. Even if it were possible to build soil in a container, it would take months of valuable growing time and could foster bad bugs, fungi, etc. It is easiest and safest to throw old depleted soil outdoors and start new plants with fresh organic soil.

Organic nutrients, manure, worm castings, blood and bone meal, etc., work very well to increase the soil nutrient content, but nutrients are released and available at different rates. The nutrient availability may be difficult to calculate, but it is hard to over-apply organic fertilizers. Organic nutrients seem to work best when used in combination with one another. This gives a more consistent availability of nutrients. Usually growers use a mix of 20-40% worm castings with other organic agents to get a strong, readily available nitrogen base. They fertilize later with bat guano during flowering.

An indoor garden using raised beds allows true organic methods. The raised beds have enough soil to hold nutrients, promote organic, chemical activity and ensure a constant supply of nutrients. The raised bed has enough soil mass to promote heat and all kinds of fundamental organic activity.

Alfalfa Meal is rich in nitrogen, containing about 2.5 percent and .5 percent phosphorus and about 2 percent potash.

Blood (dried or meal) is collected at slaughterhouses, dried and ground into a powder or meal. It is an excellent source of fast-acting soluble nitrogen (12 to 15 percent by weight), about 1.2 percent phosphorus and under one percent potash. Apply just before planting or as a side dressing to stimulate green leafy growth. It can burn plants if set on foliage or applied to heavily. Blood meal attracts meat-eating animals, so always cultivate it into the soil if using as a side dressing.

Bone meal is an old time fertilizer that is rich in phosphorus and nitrogen. The age and type of bone determine the nutrient content of this pulverized slaughterhouse product. Older bones have a higher phosphorus content than young bones. Use bone meal in conjunction with other organic fertilizers for best results. It's lime content helps reduce soil acidity and acts fastest in well-aerated soil.

Material	N	P	K	Notes
Blood (dried or meal)	12-15	1.2	1	soluble
Bone meal(unsteamed	2-4	15	25	calcium, TE
Bone meal(steamed)	2-3	18-25	.2	20% Ca, TE
Canola meal	0	1.2	1.3	iron, TE
Cottonseed meal 2	2	acidic		
Poultry manure(dry)	3-4	2-4	1-2	soluble, TE
Compost	1-2	1	1	TE
Cow (steer) manure.	6-2	.3	.5-1	excess salts
Coffee grounds	2	.3	.7	acidic
Feathers (dry or meal)	12-15	0	0	some TE
Fish meal	8	7	2	soluble
Goat manure.	5	.4	.4	TE
Granite dust0	0	4-5	some TE	
Potash rock	0	6-8	0	some TE
Greensand(glauconite)	-	1	5-7	iron, Mg., TE
Guano(bat)	2-5	8-10	1-2	soluble, TE
Guano(seabird)	10-15	5	2	soluble, TE
Hoof & horn meal	6-15	2	0	TE
Horse manure.6	.4	.4	TE	
Paper ash	0	.1	2-3	high pH
Soft phosphate	0	18-24	0	calcium, TE
Seaweed (liquid)	5	.5	.3	soluble, TE
Seaweed (meal)	1	1	1	soluble, TE
Sheep manure	.8	.4	.5	TE
Swine manure.	6	.4	.2	TE
Wood ash (hardwood)	0	1.5	7-10	soluble
Wood ash (softwood)	0	.8	5	soluble
Worm castings3.5	1	1	TE	

TE = Trace elements

The nutrients in organic fertilizers may vary greatly depending upon source, age, erosion, climate, etc. The above figures are only approximate. For exact nutrient content, consult the vendor's specifications.

Raw, unsteamed bone meal contains 2 to 4 percent nitrogen and 15 to 25 percent phosphorus. Fatty acids in raw bone meal requires longer to decompose.

This meal is most commonly used as a phosphorus source when planting fall bulbs.

Steamed or cooked bone meal is made from fresh animal bones that have been boiled or steamed under pressure to render out fats. The pressure treatment causes a little nitrogen loss and an increase in phosphorus. Steamed bones are easier to grind into a fine powder and the process helps nutrients become available sooner. It contains up to 30 percent phosphorus and about 1.5 percent nitrogen. The finer bone meal is ground, the faster acting. Apply as a seasonal source of phosphorus to the soil when planting or to enhance flowers and fruit set as a mid summer top dressing that is lightly cultivated into the soil and covered with mulch.

Cottonseed meal is made from shelled cotton seed that has had the oil extracted. Virtually all chemical residues from commercial cotton production are dissolved in the oil. This acidic fertilizer contains about 7 percent nitrogen, 2.5 percent phosphorus and 1.5 percent potash. It should be supplemented with rock phosphate or bone meal to form a balanced fertilizer blend.

Cottonseed meal is an excellent food for acid-loving plants.

Chicken manure is a favorite of many gardeners because it is so high in nitrogen. If you can find a good source of chicken ,manure get as much as you can. Pile it up next to the compost pile, let it rot for a couple of months then cover it with a tarp to slow decomposition. Use it as a compost activator, a top or side dressing as often as possible. If the manure comes from a commercial chicken ranch that uses growth hormones, let it compost at least a year so the hormones are washed out or "fixed". Many times chicken manure is full of feathers that contain as much as 17 percent nitrogen which is an added bonus.

The average nutrient content of wet chicken manure is: N - 1.5%, P - 1.5%, K - 0.5% and dry: N - 4%, P - 4%, K - 1.5% and both have a full range of trace elements.

Compost tea is used by numerous organic gardeners as the only source of fertilizer. Comfrey is packed with nutrients and many gardeners grow it just to make a compost tea.

Cow manure is sold as "steer "manure but it is collected from dairy herds. Gardeners have used cow manure for centuries and this has led to the belief that it is a good fertilizer as well as a soil amendment.

Steer manure is most valuable as a mulch and a soil amendment holds water well and maintains fertility for a long time. The nutrient value is quite low and should not be relied upon for the main source of nitrogen.

The average nutrient content of cow manure is N - .0.6%, P - 0.3%, K - 0.3% and a full range of trace elements. Apply at the rate of 25-30 pounds per square yard.

Coffee grounds are acidic and encourage acetic-acid-bacteria in the soil. Drip coffee grounds are the richest containing about 2 percent nitrogen and traces of other .nutrients Add to the compost pile or scatter and cultivate in as a top dressing around acid loving azaleas, blueberries, camellias and rhododendrons.

Diatomaceous earth, the fossilized skeletal remains of fresh and salt water algae, contains a full range of trace elements and is a good insecticide. Apply to the soil when cultivating or as a top dressing.

Dolomite lime adjusts and balances the pH and makes phosphates more available. Generally applied to "sweeten" or de-acidify soil. It consists of calcium and magnesium, sometimes listed as primary nutrients but generally referred to as the secondary .nutrients

Feathers and feather meal contain from 12 to 15 percent nitrogen that is released slowly. Feathers included in barnyard chicken manure or obtained from slaughterhouses, are an excellent addition to the compost pile or as a fertilizer. Feathers are steamed under pressure, dried, then ground into a powdery feather meal. Feather meal contains a slow-release nitrogen of about 12.5 percent. Apply in the fall with cover crops for nitrogen-rich soil the following spring.

Fish meal is made from dried fish that is ground into a meal. It is rich in nitrogen (about 8 percent) and contains around 7 percent phosphoric acid and many trace elements. It has an unpleasant odor and should not be used indoors. A great compost activator. Apply to the soil as a relatively fast-acting side or top dressing make sure to cultivate it into the soil or cover with mulch after applying. Always store in an air tight container so it will not attract cats, dogs and flies.

Fish meal and fish emulsion can contain up to 10 percent nitrogen. The liquid generally contains less nitrogen than the meal. Even when deodorized, the liquid form has an unpleasant odor.

Inorganic potash is added by some manufacturers and is "semi-organic."

Fish emulsion, an inexpensive soluble liquid, is high in organic nitrogen, trace elements and some phosphorus and potassium. This natural fertilizer is difficult to over-apply and is immediately available to plants. Fish emulsion may be diluted with water and used as a foliar spray, but may clog small nozzles if mixed too rich. Even deodorized fish emulsion smells. Use only on outdoor plants.

Goat manure is much like horse manure but more potent. Compost this manure and treat it as you would horse .manure

Granite dust or granite stone meal contains up to 5 percent potash and several trace elements. Releasing nutrients slowly over several years, granite dust is an inexpensive source of potash and does not affect soil pH. Apply as a top dressing or at the rate of ten to fifteen pounds per 100 square feet. Combine granite dust with phosphate rock and manure for a complete fertilizer mix to start crops in the spring.

Potash rock supplies up to 8 percent potassium and may contain many trace elements.

Greensand (glaucomite) is an iron potassium silicate that gives the minerals in which it occurs a green tent. It is mined from an ancient New Jersey sea bed deposits of shells and organic material rich in iron phosphorus, potash (5 to 7 percent) and numerous micronutrients. Some organic gardeners do not use greensand because it is such a limited resource. Greensand does not burn plants, slowly releasing its treasures in about four years. Apply liberal amounts of greensand as a top dressing or blend with soil at the rate of 15 to 25 pounds per 100 square feet any time of year as a long-term source of potassium and trace elements.

Guano (bat) consists of the droppings and remains of bats. It is rich in soluble nitrogen, phosphorus and trace elements. The limited supply of this fertilizer, known as the soluble organic super bloom, makes it somewhat expensive. Mined in sheltered caves, guano dries with minimal decomposition. Bat guano can be thousands of years old. Newer deposits contain high levels of nitrogen and are capable of burning if applied too heavily. The more popular older deposits are high in phosphorus and make an excellent flowering fertilizer. Bat guano is usually powdery and used any time of year as a top dressing or diluted in a tea and used as a foliar spray. Do not breathe the dust when handling it can cause nausea and irritation. Bats are too often associated with rabies and horror movies. Only ten cases of rabies have been reported in the U.S. from bat bites. Some bats eat thousands of insects nightly, others rotting fruit. These prehistoric descendants are invaluable to the ecosystem and should be protected as our friends. Bat guano may be difficult to find at retail stores however, several suppliers listed in The Growing Edge Magazine stock bat .guano

Guano(sea bird) is high in nitrogen and other .nutrients The Humboldt Current along the coast of Peru and northern Chile keeps the rain from falling, and decomposition of the guano is minimal. South American guano is among the world's best. The guano is scraped off the rocks of arid sea islands. The average dose is one tablespoon per gallon of water. Guano is also collected from many coastlines around the world.

Gypsum, hydrated calcium sulfate, is used to lower soil pH and improve drainage and aeration. It is also used to hold or slow the rapid decomposition of nitrogen.

Hoof and horn meal is a coarse granular substance that is an excellent source of slow-release nitrogen. The drawback of meal is that it draws flies and encourages maggots. Soil bacteria must break it down before it is available to roots. Apply two to three weeks before planting. It remains in soil for six months or longer. Hoof and horn meal contains from 6 to 15 percent nitrogen and about 2 percent phosphoric acid. Finely ground horn meal, on the other hand, makes the nitrogen available quicker and has few problems with fly maggots.

Horse manure is readily available from horse stables and race tracks. Use horse manure that has straw or peat for bedding wood shavings could be a source of plant disease.

Compost horse manure for two months or more before adding to the garden. The composting process kills weed seeds and it will make better use of the .nutrients Straw bedding may also use up much of the available nitrogen. But the straw makes a lot of air space within the manure so it can be piled quite high without adding other materials to provide ventilation. In fact, stomping the manure down as you stack it will drive out extra air spaces so that it will hold more water necessary for composting.

Nutrient content of horse manure N - 0.6%, P - 0.6%, K - 0.4% and a full range of trace elements.

Kelp is the "Cadillac of trace minerals." Kelp should be deep green, fresh and smell like the ocean. Seaweed contains 60 to 70 trace minerals that are already chelated (existing in a form that's water-soluble and mobile in the soil).

Oyster shells are ground and normally used as a calcium source for poultry. They contain up to 55 percent calcium and traces of many other nutrients that release slowly. Add ground oyster shells to compost or in small amounts with other fertilizers when cultivating to ensure adequate calcium content.

Paper ash contains about 5% phosphorus and over 2% potash. It is an excellent water soluble fertilizer, but do not apply in large doses because the pH is quite high.

Pigeon manure has a very high concentration of nitrogen but is more difficult to find. It can be used in the same fashion as chicken manure.

Rabbit manure is also excellent fertilizer but is difficult to find in large quantities. Use rabbit manure as you would chicken or pigeon manure.

Rock phosphate (hard) is a calcium or lime based phosphate rock that is finely ground to the consistency of talcum powder. This rock powder contains over 30 percent phosphate and a menagerie of trace elements. It does not leach out of the soil, remaining unchanged until taken up by roots. Apply at the rate of ten pounds per 100 square feet of soil or turf grass every four or five years a couple of months after applying annual manure

Colloidal phosphate, also called powdered or soft phosphate, which is a natural clay phosphate deposit that contains just over 20 percent phosphorus (P_2O_5), calcium and many trace elements. Colloidal phosphate is an excellent value in organic fertilizers. It yields 2 percent phosphate by weight the first season and a total of 18 percent over the next several years. Soft phosphate will not burn and is available to plants as they needed. It is also a good soil builder that encourages earthworms and beneficial soil microbes. Cultivate soft phosphate into the soil annually at the rate of five pounds per 100 square feet of soil or turf grass piles in conjunction with lime and nitrogen-rich manures and seaweed meal. Or till in 15 to 20 pounds of soft phosphate per 100 square feet along with lime every four years.

Rock potash is an important source of potassium. It releases very slowly and stays in the soil for several years.

Seaweed meal or kelp meal is harvested from the ocean or picked up along beaches, cleansed of salty water, dried and ground into a powdery meal. It is packed full of potassium (potash) numerous trace elements, vitamins, amino acids and plant hormones. The nutrient content varies according to the type of kelp and its growing conditions. Seaweed meal is easily assimilated by plants and contributes to soil life, structure and nitrogen fixation. It may also help plants resist many diseases and withstand light frosts. Apply the dry powder at the rate of one or two pounds per 100 square feet of garden soil or lawn in the spring for best results, but it can be applied any time. Allow several weeks for soil bacteria to make nutrients available. Kelp meal is also speeds compost decomposition and eases transplant shock.

Seaweed (liquid) contains nitrogen, phosphorus, potash, all necessary trace elements that are chelated (existing in a form that's water-soluble and mobile in the soil) and plant hormones. Apply dilute solution to the soil or use as a foliar spray for a quick cure of nutrient deficiencies. Liquid seaweed is also great for soaking seeds and dipping cuttings or bare roots before planting.

Sheep manure is normally found indoors in the sheep pens. It is high in nutrient sand makes a wonderful tea. The average nutrient content is: N - 0.8%, P - 0.5%, K - 0.4% and a full range of trace elements.

Sheep manures are hot because they contain little water and lots of air. They heat up readily in a compost pile. Cow and pig manures are cold because they hold a lot of water and can be compacted easily, squeezing out the air.

Shrimp & crab wastes contain relatively high levels of phosphorus.

Sulfate of potash is normally produced chemically by treating rock powders with sulfuric acid, but one company, Great Salt Lake Minerals and Chemicals Company produces a concentrated natural form. The sulfate of potash is extracted from the Great Salt Lake.

Swine manure has a high nutrient content but is slower acting and wetter than cow and horse manure. The average nutrient content of pig manure is: N - 0.6%, P - 0.6%, K - 0.4% and a full range of trace elements.

Wood ashes (hardwood) supply up to 10 percent potash and softwood ashes contain about 5 percent. Potash leaches rapidly, so collect ash soon after burning and store in a dry place. Apply in a mix with other fertilizers at the rate of five or ten pounds per 100 square feet. The potash washes out of heavy layers of wood ash quickly and cause compacted, sticky soil. Avoid using wood ashes, which are highly alkaline, around azaleas, blueberries, camellias, rhododendrons and other acid-loving plants. Wood ash makes an excellent addition to compost piles.

Worm castings are digested humus and other organic matter that contain varying amounts of N-P-K. They are an excellent source of non-burning soluble nitrogen that is available immediately. Worm castings are also an excellent soil additive that promote fertility and soil structure. Mix with potting soil to form a rich, fertile blend. Worm castings, when pure, look like coarse graphite powder. They are high in available nitrogen as well as many other .nutrients Worm castings are used as an organic fertilizer and soil amendment. Earthworms eat and digest decomposing organic matter. The castings are this excreted organic matter. Worm castings are heavy and very dense. When mixing with soil, use no more than 30 percent .worm castings They are so heavy, root growth can be impaired. Worm castings vary in the amount of nitrogen they contain. Most nurseries do not stock worm castings. However, there are many people making their own. Check the newspaper and ask at the nursery for possible sources.

Note: The nutrients in organic fertilizers may vary greatly depending upon source, age, erosion, climate, etc. For exact nutrient content, consult the vendor's specifications.

Trace Element Fertilizers

Seaweed, either liquid or powdered, is packed with trace elements that are immediately available to plants. Seaweed is the number one trace element fertilizer of environmentally conscious gardeners.

THE TEA BAG

Five or ten gallon pots do not contain enough soil to hold all the organic nutrients a plant will need throughout life. This dilemma is solved by using organic tea. The tea is a bit messy, even stinky, but very effective. These tea concoctions may contain just about any organic nutrient diluted in water. Fish emulsion is the most readily available commercial organic tea. You can even pour old goldfish water on the plants! Worm castings high in nitrogen, and bat guano high in phosphorus are the most common ingredients in U-mix organic teas because their soluble nutrients are immediately available to plants. If bringing bat guano, cow manure or any kind of feces into the home, then mixing it with water, and pouring it on plants is repulsive to you, do not garden organically!

There are many different mixtures of organic tea and they are all generally safe to use. Just mix the organic nutrient(s) with water, let it sit over night, mix it again, then strain out the heavy stuff by pouring the solution through an old nylon before applying. The tea may be applied as often as each watering.

TRANSPLANTING, SEEDLING & CLONING FERTILIZERS

Ortho Up-Start(R) is recommended for a smooth move of clones and transplants, as well as seedling growth. There are many similar products that work just as well as this one. Up-Start is a liquid that will readily dissolve in water. The 3-10-3 nutrient formula provides 10% available P, just what young roots need for vigorous growth. Vitamin B_1 helps ease transplant wilt and shock: The root hormone 1-naphthalene-acetic acid (.015% by weight) stimulates root formation and growth. When cloned or transplanted, the roots are the first part a plant must develop in order to supply water and nutrients to stems and leaves.

Vitamin B_1, available under many brand names, is an organic vitamin that helps ease transplant shock and wilt. Using vitamin B_1 makes transplanting fast and easy.

Superthinve™ is a vitamin-hormone (listed ingredients: vitamin B_1: .09% and 1-naphthylactic acid: 048%) liquid concentrate that many growers claim to be a universal elixir. Who knows, it just might help. Everything that I can find out about it shows that it does not hurt plant growth.

Superthrive is used to induce root growth. First, dip the cutting in full strength Superthrive 2-5 minutes before planting. Next, plant the clone in a rooting medium and water the rooting clone with a solution of about 25 drops Superthrive to one gallon of water. This is a one time application!

It is also used as a fertilizer additive. Along with the first dose of fertilizer, add up to 25 drops per gallon of solution. This (25 drops per gallon) is a one time only application. Subsequent dosage is one drop per gallon with each watering.

TRACE ELEMENT FERTILIZERS

Compound 111, S.T.E.M. and FTE are all Peters™ products. Many other companies, both local and national, produce excellent products that are similar to Peters. These trace element formulas are used by many indoor growers and nurserypeople alike. They work well to alleviate any trace element deficiency except for magnesium (Mg). None of the formulations have any Mg.

Compound Ill is a supplemental formula containing trace elements (Fe 1.5%, Mn .12%, Zn .0754%, Cu .11362%, B .23242%, Mo .10757%) chelating agents, penetrating agents and color tracers. This formula is highly recommended if you mix your own fertilizer out of single elements or are using a fertilizer that does not contain trace elements. Compound 111 is the easiest trace element formula to use and the safest. It has less of each element to toxify the soil, and unlike the S.T.E.M. formula, does not contain sulfur. Compound 111 works well to treat any mysterious trace element deficiency. Often trace elements are suspected of being deficient, but the exact deficiency is not known for sure. By applying Compound 111, the problem will be solved and you will not have to know the exact cause of the deficiency.

The S.T.E.M. (Soluble Trace Element Mix) was developed to furnish trace elements immediately, in large doses. This is the hottest or most potent trace element formula around. Be very careful when using it. The S.T.E.M. formula was developed for a one time application in treating trace element deficiencies. Note the percent concentrations of the trace elements. The guaranteed analysis of Peters S.T.E.M. formula is: S 15.0%, B_1 45%, Cu 3.20%, Fe 7.5%, Mn 8.15%, Mo .046%, Zn 4.5%

FTE (Fruited Trace Elements) are mixed with the soil or soilless mix for a long lasting, slow release application of 6-12 months. The elements are en- cased in a pulverized glass complex that resists heavy leaching. The nutrients are available at a more constant rate throughout life. This is a form of gradual release fertilizer, and is the only one that I recommend. The FTE formula is a safer one to use than the soluble ones, but may be overdone also. Once overdone, FTE may not be leached out. Apply only 1/2 teaspoon per cubic foot of soil. The guaranteed analysis of Peters FTE is: Mn 5.0%, Fe 14.0%, Cu 1.5%, Zn 5.0%, B 0.8%, Mo 0.07%

MIXING

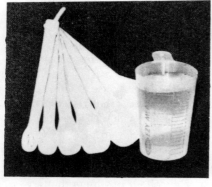

To mix, dissolve powder, crystals, or liquid into a little warm (90-100° F) water; make sure it is totally dissolved, then add the balance of the tepid water. This will ensure that the fertilizer and water mix evenly.

Containers have very little soil in which to hold nutrients and toxic salt build-up may become a problem. Follow dosage instructions to the letter. Adding too much fertilizer will not make plants grow faster. It may change the chemical balance of the soil and supply too much of

Measuring cup and spoons

a nutrient or lock in other nutrients, making them unavailable to the plant.

APPLICATION

The first thing that must be determined is: do plants need fertilization? This may be determined by visual inspection, taking an N-P-K soil test, or experimenting on a test plant(s). No matter which method is used, remember: plants in small containers use available nutrients quickly and need frequent fertilizing, while plants in large planters have more soil, supply more nutrients, and require less frequent fertilizing.

Visual Inspection - If plants are growing well and have deep green healthy leaves, they are probably getting all necessary nutrients from the soil. The moment growth slows, or leaves begin to turn pale green, it is time to fertilize. Do not confuse yellow leaves caused by a lack of light and yellow leaves caused by a nutrient deficiency.

Taking an N-P-K soil test will reveal exactly how much of each major nutrient is available to the plant. The test kits mix a soil sample with a chemical. After the soil settles, a color reading is taken from the liquid, then matched to a color chart. The appropriate percent of fertilizer is then added. This method is very exact, but more trouble than it is worth.

Many gardeners prefer to experiment on two or three test plants. This method yields experience and develops horticultural skills. Clones work especially well for this type of experiment. Give the test plants some fertilizer and see if they green up and grow faster. If it is good for one, it should be good for all.

Now it has been determined the plants need fertilizer, but how much? The answer is simple. Just mix fertilizer as per instructions and water as normal, or dilute fertilizer and apply more often. Remember, small plants use much less fertilizer than large ones. Fertilize early in the day, so plants have all day to absorb and process the fertilizer.

It is almost impossible to explain how often to apply fertilizer. We know that large plants use more nutrients than small plants. The more often fertilizer is applied, the less concentrated it should be. Frequency of fertilization is one of the most widely disagreed upon subjects in the horticultural industry. Indoor, containerized marijuana may be pushed to incredible lengths; it will absorb amazing amounts of fertilizer and grow well. Lots of growers add as much as one tablespoon per gallon (Peters (20-20-20) or (10-30-20)) with each watering! This works best with growing mediums, especially soilless mix that drain readily and are easy to leach. Other growers use only rich organic potting soil with fine dolomite lime added. No supplemental fertilizer is applied until a super bloom formula is needed for flowering.

A siphon applicator found at most nurseries will mix soluble fertilizers with water. The applicator is simply attached to the faucet with the siphon submerged in the concentrated fertilizer solution, and the hose attached to the other end. Often applicators are set at 1:15 ratio. That is, for every 1 unit of liquid concentrate fertilizer, 15 units of water will be mixed with it. Sufficient water flow is necessary for the suction to work properly. Misting nozzles restrict this flow. When the water is turned on, the fertilizer is siphoned into the system and flows out the hose. Fertilizer is generally applied with each watering, since a small percentage of fertilizer is metered in.

A garbage can, set 3-4 feet off the floor with a garden hose fitting at the bottom will act as a gravity flow source for fertilizer solution. The container is filled with water and fertilizer. With this system, the water temperature is easy to keep warm and fertilization is much easier.

I've found, when it comes to fertilization, experience will tell more than anything else. There are hundreds of N-P-K mixes and they all work! When choosing a fertilizer, make sure to read the entire label and know what the fertilizer claims it can do. Do not be afraid to try a few test plants.

Once you have an idea of how often to fertilize, put the garden on a regular bi-weekly, weekly, bi-monthly, every watering, every other watering or every third watering feeding schedule. A schedule usually works very well, but it must be combined with a vigilant, caring eye that looks for over- fertilization and nutrient deficiency signs.

 RULE of THUMB - leach soil with 1-2 gallons of fresh water per gallon of soil every 1-2 months. This is the best form of preventive maintenance against toxic salt build-up in the soil. Leaching too often, say weekly, would essentially wash everything out.

FOLIAR FEEDING

Foliar feeding (misting the leaves with fertilizer solution) makes some nutrients available and usable immediately. Food is absorbed directly into the leaves. Foliar feeding is a good way to keep toxic nutrient levels from building up in the soil, but like soil fertilization, may be over done. Daily foliar feeding with a weak solution, for example, leaches the nutrients from the leaves, just as excessive watering leaches nutrients from the soil. A good foliar feeding program would start after the plant's first month of growth. Apply fertilizer solution with a fine spray. See: "About Spraying".

Foliar feeding is more work, but creates almost instant results. Nitrogen deficient plants have turned from a pale yellow to a lime green in 12 short hours! In the case of nutrient deficient soil, foliar feeding is a simple quick cure. The nutrients are supplied directly and used immediately. Soil condition or pH are not affected, but root absorption may improve. A combination of soil and foliar feeding is common. Good organic foliar fertilizers are fish emulsion and bat guano. Of course, it must be strained through a tea bag and the sprayer should not be prone to clogging. There are many chemical foliar fertilizers; Peters, Ra-Pid-Gro, Miracle-Gro and Eco-Gro. Dilute them the same as for regular fertilization for foliar feeding.

OVER-FERTILIZING can become one of the biggest problems for indoor growers. Too much fertilizer causes a build up of nutrients (salts) to toxic levels and changes soil chemistry. When over-fertilized, growth is rapid and super lush green, until the toxic levels are reached. When the toxic salt (fertilizer) level is reached, leaf tips burn (turn yellow, then black) and if the problem is severe, the leaves will curl under like a bighorn sheep's horns.

Fertilizer Burn   *Severe over fertilization*

Chance of over-fertilization is greater in a small amount of soil; it can only hold a small amount of nutrients. While a large pot or planter can hold much more soil and nutrients safely, it will take longer to flush if overdone. It is very easy to add too much fertilizer to a small container. Large containers have good nutrient holding ability.

To treat severely over-fertilized plants, leach soil with 2 gallons of water per gallon of soil, so as to wash all the excess nutrients out. The plant should start new growth and be looking better in one or two weeks. If the problem is severe, and leaves are curled, the soil may need to be leached several times. After the plant appears to have leveled off to normal growth, start foliar feeding or apply diluted fertilizer solution.

NUTRIENT DISORDERS

There are many things that could go wrong indoors that are confused with a lack of fertilizer. The pH of both the growing medium and water is of prime importance. If the pH is not between 6.5 and 7 (6-6.5 for hydroponic units) some nutrients will be locked in the soil, even if the nutrient is in supply. The plant is not able to absorb it chemically because the pH will not let it. For example, a full point movement in pH represents a tenfold increase in either alkalinity or acidity.

This means that a pH of 5.5 would be ten times more acidic than a pH of 6.5. A pH below 6.5 may cause a deficiency in calcium. If this happens, root tips could burn and leaves could get fungus (leaf spot). A pH over 7 could slow down the plant's iron intake, and chlorotic leaves with yellowing veins could result.

Incorrect pH contributes to most serious nutrient disorders. It has always amazed me that so many people worry about fertilizer application and do not pay attention to the pH! See: "pH Chart,".

Besides the pH problem, there are the basic elements of the environment that must be checked. Marijuana is a weed outdoors and has little problem thriving. Since you are Mother Nature indoors, you are responsible for creating a perfect climate for this weed to grow. Check each of the vital signs and fine tune the environment, especially ventilation, before deciding that plants are nutrient deficient. See: "Checklist".

Nutrient Deficiencies will normally not occur in fresh potting soil containing dolomite lime or in soilless mix fortified by the grower, containing all necessary trace elements and dolomite lime. This fresh planting mix is coupled with a regular fertilization schedule. There are two basic things that go wrong regarding nutrients: 1) not enough, indicated by lime green leaves. This is treated by applying a general purpose fertilizer. N-P-K are all used at similar rates and a single nutrient seldom builds to toxic levels. 2) Too much, indicated by super dark green leaves and/or burnt tips. Treat by leaching the soil of excess nutrients.

PRIMARY NUTRIENT DISORDERS

Nitrogen is the most common nutrient found deficient. Growth slows, lower leaves turn yellow and eventually die. Remedy by fertilizing with N or N-P-K fertilizer. For fast results, foliar feed. An overdose of N will cause soft, weak growth and even delay flower production if it is allowed to accumulate.

Phosphorus deficiency is less common. Leaves will get deep green, be uniformly smaller and the plant will be stunted. Lower leaves will yellow and die. Treat with P or N-P-K fertilizer. Toxic signs of P will take a long time to surface. Marijuana uses a lot of phosphorus throughout life and may tolerate even higher levels. Toxic signs are an overall smaller plant with very dark green foliage. Treat by leaching the soil heavily.

Potassium deficiency occurs occasionally. Many times K deficient plants are the tallest and appear healthy. But the lower leaf tips turn yellow, followed by whole leaves that turn dark yellow and die. The K is usually present in the soil, but locked in by high salinity. First, leach the toxic salt out of the soil, then apply foliar N-P-K fertilizer.

Leaf tips turn brown then curl upwards.

Secondary Nutrient Deficiencies may easily be avoided by mixing one cup of fine dolomite lime per cubic foot of soil before planting. Dolomite supplies soil with Mg and Ca.

Magnesium (Mg) is the most common secondary nutrient to be found deficient. It is most commonly deficient in soilless mixes, but is also found deficient in soil. Lower leaves yellow, veins remain green, the tips and then the entire leaf turns brown. The leaf tips usually turn upward, then die. The entire plant could discolor and die within a few weeks. Cure by watering as usual, adding 1 teaspoon Epsom salts per 2 quarts of water. If the deficiency progresses to the top of the plant, turning the growing shoots lime-colored, you will notice the greening-up effect there first. In a few days, it will move down the plant, turning lower leaves progressively greener. Continue regular watering schedule with Epsom salts added until symptoms totally disappear. In a soilless mix, you may want to use Epsom salts regularly, but it will not be necessary if the fertilizer contains Mg.

Calcium deficiency is uncommon, but when found, it may be too late in life to do anything. If too much Ca is applied early in life, it might stunt growth as well. Deficient signs are a yellowing and dying back of leaf edges. Mixing fine dolomite lime with the soil before planting is the best prevention of this ailment. If you must, use a trace element formula containing Ca to treat the deficiency.

MICRO-NUTRIENT DISORDERS

Sulfur (S) is almost never a problem for soils able to grow marijuana. Many fertilizers contain some form of sulfur. Deficiency shows when leaves turn pale green and general purpose N-P-K fertilizer fails to cure the problem. Very seldom is it a problem, but if it is, remedy with trace element fertilizer.

Iron (Fe) - deficiency is somewhat common indoors. An iron deficient (chlorotic) plant is yellowing between the veins, with the veins of the leaves remaining green. Leaves may start to fall if it is severe. Chlorosis is generally caused by a high pH rather than a lack of iron. To remedy, correct pH. If necessary, foliar feed with fertilizer containing soluble chelated iron. I recommend Compound 111.

Other micro-nutrients, manganese, boron, molybdenum, zinc and copper, are rarely deficient in any soil. By using commercial potting soil, fortified soilless mix, or N-P-K fertilizer with trace elements, you are guaranteed that all necessary trace elements are available. Fertilizers that contain only trace elements are available, but may be very tricky to use. Trace elements are necessary in minute amounts and reach toxic levels easily. I advise NOT to use a special trace element fertilizer more than once or twice a crop (once every 2 months) or unless it is absolutely necessary. If using a trace element mix, Compound 111 is my favorite.

CHAPTER FIVE   HYDROPONIC GARDENING

This system by Humboldt Hydroponics is one of many new units developed for indoor use.

The roots of hydroponics come from two Greek words that were put together: *hydro* meaning "water" and *ponics* meaning "working". Today hydroponics is the science of growing plants without soil, most often in a soilless mix. With hydroponics two very important factors may be totally controlled: (1) nutrient intake (2) oxygen intake via roots.

Hydroponic gardening, like HID gardening, is easy and fun, once the concept and principles are understood. There are a few basic rules that must be followed to make a good system be productive. First let's look at how and why hydroponics works.

In hydroponics, the inert soilless medium contains essentially no nutrients of its own. All the nutrients are supplied by the nutrient solution. This solution passes over the roots or floods around them at regular intervals, later draining off. The oxygen around the roots is able to speed the plants uptake of nutrients. This is why plants grow so fast hydroponically. They are able to take in food as fast as they are able to utilize it. In soil, as in hydroponics, the roots absorb nutrients and water; even the best soil rarely has as much oxygen in it as a soilless hydroponic medium.

Hydroponics works well for horticulturists who are willing to spend 10-20 minutes per day in their garden. The garden requires extra maintenance; plants grow faster, there are more things to check and have the potential to go wrong. In fact, some people do not like hydroponic gardening because it requires too much additional care. I have never seen a hydroponic garden that was less work than a comparable soil or soilless garden.

All too often, people that just started indoor gardening get so excited about it, that they go too far too fast. They buy all these new little gadgets and have many more projects going than they can properly manage. The biggest problem people have in purchasing hydroponic units, is following the directions to assemble the system. This is important to remember when thinking about constructing and/or inventing your own unit. It will take a month or two to work out most of the bugs in a home-made unit. Do not expect the best crop in the world the first or second time.

Hydroponic gardening is very exacting and not forgiving like soil gardening. The soil works as a buffer for nutrients and holds them longer than the inert medium of hydroponics. In fact, some very advanced hydroponic systems do not even use a soilless mix. The roots are suspended in the air and misted with nutrient solution. The misting chamber is kept dark so algae does not compete with roots.

I have found that plants, properly maintained, grown hydroponically under HID lamps tend to grow a little more lush foliage and at a faster rate than plants grown in soil. The garden calendar is usually moved up one or two weeks. The real benefit with hydroponics is realized later in life. When roots are restricted and growth slows in containerized plants, hydroponically grown plants are still getting the maximum amount of nutrients.

The principles involved in hydroponics are simple and direct, but the application of these principles can become very complex. Gravel is the inert medium most commonly used to hold the roots and stabilize the plant while the nutrient solution passes over the roots in one of many ways. The nutrient solution drains away from the roots, so the oxygen will have a chance to work with the roots to draw in the nutrients. These are the basic principles of hydroponics; the nutrient solution, its application, and the growing medium are the main variables in hydroponic gardening.

DIFFERENT KINDS OF SYSTEMS

The way the nutrient solution is applied distinguishes the various systems. It also dictates the soilless medium used.

Hydroponic systems may be classified as active or passive. An active system actively moves the nutrient solution. Examples of active systems are: (1) fill and drain (2) top feed.

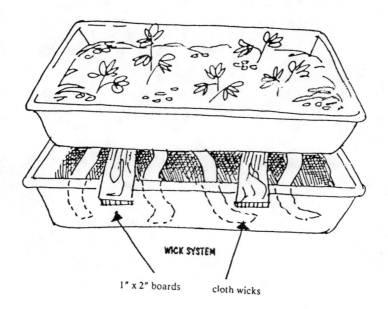

WICK SYSTEM

1″ x 2″ boards   cloth wicks

WICK SYSTEM

Passive systems rely on capillary action of the wick and the growing medium. The nutrient solution is passively absorbed by the wick, medium and roots. The mediums that are normally used in a wick system are vermiculite, sawdust, peat moss, etc. For rapid growth, the average wick system keeps the medium too wet, consequently, not enough air is available to the roots. However, the wick system works very well if engineered properly. The soilless medium used, the number of wicks, their gauge and texture are the main variables involved in a wick system. The wick system has no moving parts. There is nothing mechanical to break, replace, or malfunction. The wick systems also boast a low initial cost and once set up, and functioning properly, they are little work to maintain. One very efficient use of the wick system has been to root clones.

Hydroponic systems may be further classified as recovery and non- recovery. Non-recovery means just what it says. Once the nutrient solution is applied to the inert growing medium, it is not recovered. These systems use sand, sawdust or some other readily available substance as its medium. No nutrient is recovered, less is applied, promoting less waste, complication and labor. The non-recovery systems are used mainly for commercial applications where the soilless medium is in great supply and the soil is not arable.

Two huge Thai plants produced 8 ounces of dried tops in this hydroponic system.

The flood and top feed methods are active recovery systems. They actively work by moving a volume of nutrient solution into contact with the roots. Recovery, because the nutrient solution is recovered after it has drained off and will be used again. These systems tend to use mediums that will drain fairly rapidly and hold lots of air, like pea gravel, light pumice rock or crushed brick. The flood method is used by most commercial hydroponic operations and many home systems. This system has proven to be low maintenance and easy to use.

The top feed method is a little more intricate but used in hydroponic units with excellent results.

In a flood system, the water floods into the bed, usually from the bottom, pushing the CO_2 rich, oxygen poor, air out. When the medium drains, it sucks the new oxygen rich air into the growing medium. Top feed systems apply the nutrient solution to the base of each plant with a small hose. The solution is aerated as it flows through the air.

THE GROWING MEDIUM

The purpose of the growing medium is to harbor oxygen, water, nutrients and support the root system of a plant. Like soil, the texture of the soilless medium is of utmost importance. The texture of the medium should be one that lets the solution drain rapidly enough for the roots to get a good supply of oxygen. A fast draining medium, holding little water for a long time, is ideal for active recovery hydroponic systems.

Fibrous materials, like vermiculite, hold moisture within their cells and water retention is high. This type of medium is desired with a passive, capillary action, wick system.

The size of the medium is important. As with soil, the smaller the particles, the closer they pack, and the slower they drain. The larger the particles, the faster they drain and the more air they hold.

Irregular materials have more surface area and hold more water than round ones which hold less water. Avoid gravel with sharp edges that could cut a plants roots if it fell or was jostled around much. Round pea gravel, smooth, washed gravel, crushed brick or some form of lava are the best kinds of mediums for growing marijuana in an active recovery system. Rock should be of igneous (volcanic) origin. This type of rock tends to have a neutral pH and will not break down under hydroponic growing conditions. Gravel is the most widely used hydroponic growing medium for marijuana. It holds the exact amount of moisture and nutrients and does not stay too wet. The best kind of gravel to use for growing indoors is a pea gravel 1/8 to 3/8-inch in diameter. Ideally, over half of the medium should be about 1/4-inch in diameter. Geolite™, a new ceramic hydroponic medium that could be better than gravel. In any case, wash rock thoroughly to get out all the dust that turns to sediment.

The medium should be clean so as not to react to nutrients. For example, gravel from a limestone quarry is full of calcium carbonate and old concrete is full of lime. When mixed with water, calcium carbonate will raise the pH, the concrete will just kill the garden. Sawdust holds too much water for marijuana growth and is too acidic. Other mixtures made from pebbles or anything near the ocean, very well could be full of ocean salt. If suspicious of this, it may be easier to get another load of medium rather than trying to clean out the salts.

ROCKWOOL

Rockwool is the neatest invention since the sun! It is an inert, sterile, porous, non-degradable growing medium that provides firm root support. Like all soilless mediums, rockwool acts as a temporary reservoir for .nutrients This affords the grower a tremendous amount of control over plant growth through nutrient uptake.

This revolutionary new growing medium consists of thin strand-like fibers made primarily from limestone, granite or almost any kind of rock. With the appearance of lent collected by a cloths dryer, rockwool does not resemble any other growing media.

Rockwool has been used for many years as home and industrial insulation. In fact, the walls in your home may be packed full of rockwool. The rockwool used for insulation is similar to the horticultural grade.

Rockwool is the growing medium of choice in Holland. This entire greenhouse is watered automatically.

Definite advantages are reaped when growing in this soilless substrate. It is economical, consistent and easy to control. Best of all, rockwool's fibrous structure and will hold up to 20 percent air even when it is completely saturated.

Rockwool was introduced into the U.S. in 1985. The word travels slowly and the American horticultural community has been slow to adapt. Most gardeners have not even heard of rockwool.

Rockwool has been used in European greenhouses for over 15 years. It was first discovered in Denmark in 1969. Growers began using rockwool as a way around the ban on soil-grown nursery stock imposed by some of the European community. Today, an estimated 50 percent of all Western European greenhouse vegetables are grown exclusively in rockwool.

Other mediums like peat and soils are becoming more expensive to produce and can easily vary in quality. This fact, coupled with the high cost of sterilization, prompted European growers to explore new alternatives.

Rockwool can be used in both recovery and non-recovery hydroponic systems. As explained earlier, the nutrient solution in a recovery system is constantly changing. Salts soon build up to toxic levels as plants use selected nutrients in the solution. The nutrient solution must be monitored constantly and adjusted to provide the exact concentration of nutrients for optimum growth. However, with a non-recovery system, the excess nutrient solution drains off and is not recovered. The plants get all the nutrients they need and any nutrients that are not used will simply drain off. A fresh nutrient-rich solution is used for the next watering.

Enough nutrient solution is applied to get a 10 to 20 percent drain or leaching effect. Leaching flushes out excess salts from the medium and applies adequate nutrient solution to the medium.

European growers switched to rockwool because it is inexpensive and easy to control. They not only changed, growers continued to use it.

Rockwool is produced from rock alone or a combination of rock, limestone and coke. The rigid components are melted at temperatures exceeding 2,500° F. This molten solution is poured over a spinning cylinder, very similar to the way cotton candy is made with liquefied sugar. As the molten solution flies off the cylinder, it elongates and cools to form fibers. These fibers could be likened to cotton candy fibers. The product of these fibers, rockwool, is then pressed into uniform blocks, sheets, cubes or granulated. The blocks are rigid and easy to handle. They can be cut into just about any size desirable. Granulated rockwool is easily placed into growing containers or used like vermiculite and perlite as a soil amendment.

When used with an open ended drip system, rockwool is easily irrigated with a nutrient solution controlled by a timer. The usual procedure in Europe is to apply a small amount of fertilizer two or three times a day. Enough excess solution is applied to obtain a 10-25 percent leeching effect every day.

A plastic covering prevents the growth of algae n rockwool slabs. The convenient square shape makes the slabs easy to stack and use for individual plants.

Do not let all of this control fool you. Even though rockwool will hold 10-14 times as much water as soil, it does not provide the buffering action available in soil. The pH of rockwool is about 7.8. An acidic fertilizer solution (about 5.5 on the pH scale) is required to maintain the actual solution at a pH of about 6.5 or lower. Errors made in the nutrient solution mix or with pH level, will be magnified. Be careful to monitor both the pH and nutrient level with a watchful eye.

There are some tricks to handling rockwool. Dry rockwool can be abrasive and act as an irritant to the skin. When handling dry rockwool, use gloves and goggles. Once the rockwool is thoroughly wet, it is easy and safe to work with it creates no dust and does not irritate to the skin. Keep out of the reach of children and wash clothes thoroughly after prolonged use around rockwool as a safety precaution.

Rockwool stays so wet that algae rows on surfaces exposed to light. While this green slimy algae s unsightly, it does not compete with plants for nutrition. However, harmless fungus gnats could take up residence. Avoid the unsightly algae y covering the rockwool with plastic.

STERILIZING

The medium must be *sterilized* between each crop. This is much easier than replacing the medium as advised to do with soil. For apartment dwellers, Hydroponics provides an alternative to heavy, messy soil gardening. Instead of toting copious quantities of soil in and out of the building, the soilless medium is sterilized between each crop. Large amounts of soil are not only conspicuous but expensive. It looks very strange when you are packing pickup loads of soil into a small apartment in the middle of winter. The reasons for sterilization are obvious, cleanliness to prevent any bad microorganisms from getting started in the beautiful garden.

Before sterilizing, the roots will have to be removed from the medium. An average marijuana plant (4-5-foot tall or 3-4 months old) will have a root mass about the size of a desk telephone. Roots can create a huge mass in larger bed systems. It really does not matter if a few roots are left in the system, but try to get at least 90-95%. The fewer roots, the less chance the system has of clogging up. A clogged system does not work.

The roots will tend to mat up near the bottom of the bed. It is easy to remove them in one large mat. Some of the medium may be embedded in the roots. It is easier to get more medium than trying to pick it from between the roots.

There are many ways to sterilize the garden. The one used by most systems is very easy. First, remove the nutrient solution from the tank, then make up a solution of ordinary laundry bleach (calcium or sodium hypochlorite) or hydrochloric acid, the kind used in hot tubs and swimming pools.

Apply one cup of bleach per 5 gallons of water, flood the medium with the sterilizing solution for at least one half hour, then flush. Use lots of fresh water to leach and flush the entire system: beds, connecting hoses and drains. Make sure all of the toxic chemicals are gone by flushing entire system for at least one hour (two intervals of 1/2 hour each) before replanting.

HYDROPONIC NUTRIENTS

To gain a more complete background on nutrients, etc., read Chapter 4, "Water and Fertilizer." The same principles that apply to soil, apply to the hydroponic medium.

Always use the best fertilizer you can find. The fertilizers recommended in this book have worked well for hydroponic gardening. Eco-Gro and Dyna Gro lead in popularity because of their complete formulas. All hydroponic fertilizers should have all of the necessary macro- and micro- nutrients.

Whether or not a hydroponic garden is organic or chemical is up to you, Mother Nature. An organic garden will be more work to maintain than the ones using prepared chemical fertilizers.

Organic teas must be prepared in the tea bag to ensure the pipes do not plug up from sludge. Cheap fertilizer (not recommended), like organic fertilizers will contain sludge, which could build-up and require more frequent cleaning of the system.

THE NUTRIENT SOLUTION

The nutrient solution should be changed at least every two (at the most every three) weeks. It can go longer, but growth could slow and deficiencies result. Changing the solution as often as every week would not hurt anything. Plants absorb nutrients at different rates and some of the elements run out before others. The best form of preventative maintenance is to change the solution often. Fertilizer is probably the least expensive necessity a garden needs. By skimping on fertilizer or trying to save it, the garden might be stunted so badly, it would not recover in time to produce a good crop. The pH is also continually changing, due to its reaction to the nutrient uptake, providing another reason to change the nutrient solution frequently. The nutrients being used at different rates could create a salt (unused fertilizer) build-up. This problem is usually averted by using pure nutrients and flushing the soilless medium thoroughly with fresh, tepid water between nutrient solutions.

 RULE OF THUMB - Change the nutrient solution every two weeks.

Hydroponics gives the means to supply the maximum amount of nutrients a plant needs, but it can also starve them to death or over-fertilize them rapidly. Remember this is a hot or fast high performance system. If one thing malfunctions, say the electricity goes off, the pump breaks, the drain gets clogged with roots, or there is a rapid fluctuation in the pH, all of these things could cause severe problems with the garden. A mistake could kill or stunt plants so badly, they never fully recover.

pH

Marijuana grows hydroponically within a pH range of 5.8-6.8, with 6.3 being ideal. The pH in hydroponic gardens requires an extremely vigilant eye by Mother

Nature. All of the nutrients are in solution. The pH of the nutrient solution changes easily. The roots use nutrients at different rates. The changes in the amounts of nutrients in the solution will change the pH. If the pH is not within the acceptable hydroponic range (6-6.5), nutrients may not be absorbed as fast as possible.

RULE OF THUMB - Check the pH every day or two to make sure it is at or near the perfect level.

Do not use sodium hydroxide to raise pH. It is very caustic and difficult to work with. Potassium Hydroxide is much easier to use. Show picture of pH check and perpetual change in it.

THE RESERVOIR

The reservoir should be as large as possible. Be prepared! Forgetting to replenish the water supply and/or nutrient solution, could easily result in crop failure! Plants use much more water than nutrients and water also evaporates from the system. An approximate water loss of about 5-25% per day, depending on climate conditions (mainly humidity and temperature) and the size of plants can be expected. This amounts to many, many gallons of solution per week. Less evaporation occurs when there is a top on the reservoir. When the water is used, the concentration of elements in the solution increases; there is less water in the solution and nearly the same amount of nutrients. More sophisticated systems have a valve (usually a float valve like the kind found in a toilet) that adds more water as it is used from the reservoir. Most systems have a full line on the inside of the reservoir tank to show when the solution is low. Water should be added as soon as the solution level lowers. This could be as often as every day! The reservoir should contain at least 20% more nutrient solution than it takes to fill the beds to compensate for evaporation. The more volume of liquid, the more forgiving it is and the easier it is to control.

RULE OF THUMB - Check the level of the reservoir daily and replenish if necessary.

It is a big job to empty and refill a hydroponic unit with 20-60 gallons of water. In order to do this with ease, the system should be able to pump the solution out of the reservoir. If the water must set for a couple of days to let chlorine dissipate or to alter the pH before putting it into the tank, the system should pump water back into the reservoir. This will greatly ease your task as a hydroponic horticulturist. The used nutrient solution may be pumped into the vegetable garden or down the nearest drain but not into a septic tank. Do not try to use this used nutrient solution on other indoor marijuana plants.

If the system is unable to pump the used nutrient solution out of the bed, place the unit at such an altitude that it may be siphoned or gravity flow into a drain or outdoor garden.

THE IRRIGATION CYCLE

The irrigation or watering cycle depends on the same things as does the soil: plant size, climate conditions and the type of medium used. If the particles are large, round, smooth, and drain rapidly like pea gravel, the cycle will be often: 2-4 times daily. Fibrous mediums like vermiculite with irregular surfaces drain slowly. These mediums are watered less often or utilize a capillary wick system.

Flood systems with pea gravel are generally flooded two or three times daily for 30 minutes. The water comes to within 1/2-inch of the top of the gravel and should completely drain out of the medium at each watering. Top feed systems are usually cycled for about 30 minutes and should be watered three to four times daily.

During and soon after irrigation, the nutrient content of the bed and the reservoir are the same concentration. As the time passes between irrigations, the nutrient concentration and the pH gradually change. If enough time passes between waterings, the nutrient concentration might change so much that the plant is not able to use it.

There are many variations on how often to water. As with soil, experimentation will probably tell you more than anything else. One grower explained to me, "After a while you kind of get the feel for it." It took this hydroponic horticulturist two years to make it work right. Now he harvests two lbs. of dried tops a month from two rooms with three lamps. If possible try experiments on one or two plants at a time, instead of subjecting an en- tire bed or garden to an experiment.

The temperature of the nutrient solution should stay somewhere in the 65-75° F range. The nutrient solution may be heated instead of the room if there is a problem with keeping the room warm in winter. To heat the nutrient solution, submerge grounded heat cables. It might take a few days for the cables to heat a large volume of solution. Never place the heat cable in the soilless medium. The heat from the cable could literally fry the roots.

When air is cooler than water, the water evaporates into the air rapidly. The greater the temperature differential, the more humid the air! Remember to weigh the costs when using this technique: temperature vs. humidity vs. cost.

The nutrient solution should be replaced with water that is at least 60° F. Cold water will shock the plants. It could take a few days to warm up, thus stunting all the plants!

Never let the water temperature get warmer than 85° F. If roots get too hot, they could be damaged. Submersible heaters of any kind must be grounded and constructed of materials that give off no harmful residues; the most common one is lead.

HYDROPONIC NUTRIENT DISORDERS

When the hydroponic garden is on a regular maintenance schedule, nutrient problems are usually averted. Change the nutrient solution if the cause of the nutrient disorder is not known for sure. This method is the easiest and the most secure. If able to determine the exact cause of the disorder, add 10 to 20% more of the deficient ingredient for two weeks or until the disorder has disappeared.

Read "Nutrient Disorders". Hydroponic gardens must be watched than a soil garden. If the pH is off and there is a nutrient deficiency, it could severely affect the garden, and the novice gardener may not notice the problem until it is in its advanced stages. Treatment must be rapid and certain, but it will take a few days for the plant to respond to the remedies. Foliar feed the sick plants for fast results. What if two or more elements are deficient at the same time? This might give plants the appearance of having no specific cause, just symptoms! What do you do when the garden enters the unknown nutrient deficiency syndrome? When this sort of mind bending problem happens, change the nutrient solution immediately! This will supply the missing elements. The plants do not have to be diagnosed, just treated.

 RULE OF THUMB - If the garden has a nutrient disorder, change the nutrient solution and adjust the pH.

The most common hard-to-diagnose disorder is a magnesium deficiency. Most fertilizers do not have enough magnesium to overcome the deficiency. Hard water contains more magnesium and calcium. It might contain enough to solve the problem. Water with Epsom salts to solve this one.

Overfertilization once diagnosed, is easy to deal with. Drain the nutrient solution, then flush with fresh water. The number of times the system is flushed depends on the severity of the problem. Flush at least twice. Replace with properly mixed solution.

Nutrient disorders will occur to all the plants at the same time if they are receiving the same solution. Other climactic disorders, wind burn, lack of light, temperature stress, fungi and insect damage, usually show up on the plants that are most affected. For example, plants that are next to a heat vent might show signs of heat scorch, while the rest of the garden looks healthy. Or a plant on the edge of the garden would be small or leggy since it receives less light.

BUILDING YOUR OWN SYSTEM

One option is to build your own hydroponic unit. This is easy, but there are certain things that must be looked after for the system to work properly. Sealing up all joints and using few or no seams are two basic codes of hydroponic unit construction. Seal seams with waterproof caulk or use fiberglass resin and material for no-leak construction. Nothing can bum a person out like going on vacation for a few days, only to return finding the hydroponic system flooded out the upstairs bedroom and house the afternoon you left Not only were the plants dead when you got home, but the entire home had water damage. All that work to build a unit just to save a few bucks. It ended up costing more than the most expensive hydroponic unit, and it took months away from the harvest countdown. Drain holes or pipe connections must be sure fit, with no leakage. Teflon tape is a good companion for threaded connections.

Many hydroponic systems, using the fill and drain method must have elevated beds so the solution may drain back into the reservoir. Consider this when building and installing hydroponic units in rooms with limited ceiling space. The reservoir can be placed in a hole in the floor if ceiling space is limiting. One grower used a sump pump in a concrete basement hole.

A large, covered reservoir is very important. Remember, the larger the reservoir, the more forgiving. The larger the container, the more solution. The more solution there is, the longer it will take for it to become depleted; the pH will fluctuate less and it will generally be more stable.

The size of the hydroponic container is important. The roots have to grow big enough to support a plant. In large bed systems, the roots glob up at the bottom of the tank. In fact, they get so big they look like a large mat or mattress of roots. In smaller beds, one to three gallons, roots could fill the container and grow out the bottom in two to six weeks. As with soil, the size of hydroponic container dictates its buffing or forgiving effect.

Roots will clog the drain. Place a small mesh (1/4-inch or less) screen made from a non-corrosive material like or plastic over the drain. The screen should be easy to remove and clean.

The frequency of watering depends on the kind of soilless medium used. A fast draining medium like pea gravel requires watering 2-4 times daily, while slow draining vermiculite requires watering only once a day or less. Fill the bed so it is evenly moist; drain it completely and rapidly so oxygen will be available to roots as soon as possible.

The flood system could be as simple as using a 5 gallon plastic bucket medium filled with washed gravel and a drain gravel hole in the bottom. The hole is plugged with a cork, then nutrient solution, kept in another 5 gallon bucket, is poured in. After 20-30 minutes, the cork is removed, and the nutrient solution is drained back into the other bucket for application later that day or the next day. This method is a little sloppy since the liquid is poured through the air (which also aerates it). This system provides an easy, inexpensive way for soil gardeners to get a look at hydroponic gardening. It is not the most efficient nor the most productive system, but it will get your feet wet!

medium gravel

drainage hole covered with screen

hole cut in table

plastic bucket to collect runoff

Bucket is raised twice a day to allow nutrient solution to flow into plant container.

Another manual, gravity flow system attaches a reservoir bucket to a soilless medium or bed bucket with a flexible hose. The reservoir bucket is then raised above the pot so the nutrient solution flows into it. After a couple of hours, the bucket is lowered to let the solution flow back into the reservoir bucket. This

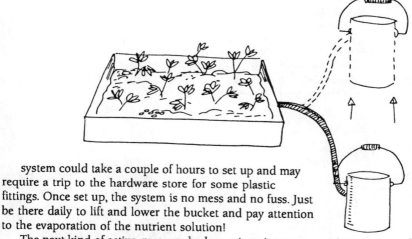

system could take a couple of hours to set up and may require a trip to the hardware store for some plastic fittings. Once set up, the system is no mess and no fuss. Just be there daily to lift and lower the bucket and pay attention to the evaporation of the nutrient solution!

The next kind of active, recovery hydroponic unit uses a aquarium pump and works on the bottom flood method as well. It pumps air into a sealed container full of nutrient solution. The pressure from the pump makes the solution pump up into the hydroponic bed. The pump actually pumps air into the nutrient solution! After the solution is in the bed, the pump continues forcing air through the solution. It aerates the nutrient solution while in contact with the roots. This system is easily automated. An inexpensive timer may be attached to the pump so the unit may operate automatically, keeping the solution in the bed for about 2 hours. This method is good for people that will not be there every day to cycle the nutrients manually. Watch out for running the pump dry when automated.

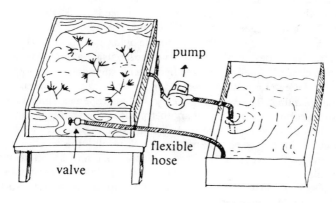

pump

valve

flexible
hose

plastic nutrient
solution tank

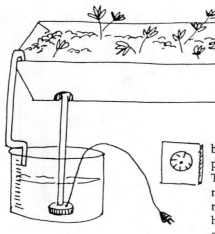

Another kind of active, recovery, bottom flood system uses a submergible pump which is a little more expensive. This type of system is able to recycle the nutrients several times daily at 20 to 30 minute cycles. This is the system many home gardeners and professionals use. It is one of the most successful, because of its ease of operation and the control that may be exercised. The nutrient solution is cycled several times per day; maximum nutrient application and uptake are achieved. A timer is attached to the irrigation cycle which automates the system. Make sure the system is designed to keep the pump submersed to prevent air lock. Also, watch out for unwanted siphoning.

GETTING STARTED

Starting seeds in the medium may not be very easy. Tiny seeds easily wash away, get too deep or dry out. Many people prefer to plant seeds or clones in a peat pot or root cube. The pot or cube are transplanted into the medium after the plant is two or three weeks old. Remember to remove the nylon netting around the peat pots. Clones transplant best into a hydroponic garden using a root cube or peat pot. This way, when clones are placed into the hydroponic medium, the root cube will be able to hold the extra moisture it needs for the dry times in between waterings.

Read "Transplanting". Transplanting is easy with hydroponics, simply remove the plant from the medium, and place it in another place in the medium. The younger the plant the better this works. If the roots are allowed to grow very long, they will break when moved during transplanting. Shock will result if the roots are broken off and not gently returned to the medium. After transplanting, scoop up some of the nutrient solution or mix a B_1 solution and pour it over the newly moved transplant, then cycle the nutrient solution through the system so it gets adequate moisture to let roots settle in.

It is OK to water a bed four to six times per day, as long as the nutrient solution drains completely out each time and there is not water that is still soaking roots, keeping them too wet. The maximum watering cycle should be no longer than 30 minutes.

CHAPTER SIX AIR

Large fan is placed in an open doorway.

Fresh air is at the heart of all successful indoor gardens. Think about your role as Mother Nature. In the great outdoors, air is abundant and almost always fresh. The level of CO_2 in the air over a field of rapidly growing vegetation could be only 1/3 of normal on a very still day. Soon, the wind blows in fresh new air. Rains wash the air and plants of dust and pollutants. All of this happens in the atmosphere, a very huge place. When plants are growing in a small room, Mother Nature really has to be on her toes to replicate the air of the great outdoors. Since there are none of the natural elements to make CO_2 rich, fresh air, you, Mother Nature, must take on the task!

Air is also used by the roots. Oxygen must be present along with water and nutrients for the roots to feed properly. If the soil is compacted or water saturated, the roots have no air.

Air provides essential elements for plant growth. A plant uses carbon dioxide (CO_2 and oxygen (O_2) from the air. Oxygen is used for respiration, burning carbohydrates and other foods, which gives energy. Carbon dioxide must be present during photosynthesis. Without CO_2 a plant will die! CO_2 uses light energy to combine with water, producing sugar. These sugars are used to fuel the growth and metabolism of the plant. With reduced levels of CO_2 growth slows rapidly. Oxygen is given off as a by-product of this process. A plant will release more O_2 than is used and use much more CO_2 than it releases, except during darkness when more oxygen is used.

Plants and animals (remember people are animals too) complement one another. Plants give off oxygen as a by-product, making it available to people. People give off CO_2 as a by-product, making it available to plants. Without plants, animals could not live, and without animals, plants could not live as we know life today. Animals inhale air using O_2 to carry on life processes and exhale CO_2 as a by-product.

AIR MOVEMENT

In order to have a good flow of air through the stomata, adequate air circulation and ventilation are necessary. Indoors, fresh air is one of the most commonly overlooked factors contributing to a bountiful harvest. Fresh air is the least expensive element that can be made available to a plant. Experienced growers really understand the importance of fresh air is and take the time to set up a vent fan. Three factors affect air movement: (1)stomata (2) ventilation and (3) circulation.

Vent Fan

Fresh air is easy to come by and inexpensive to maintain. The main tool used to maintain fresh air is an *exhaust fan placed near the ceiling of the room.*

STOMATA are microscopic pores on the leaf's underside, similar to an animal's nostrils. Animals regulate the amount of O_2 inhaled and CO_2 exhaled through the nostrils via the lungs. In a plant, O_2 and CO_2 flows are regulated by the stomata. The larger the plant, the more stomata it has to take in CO_2 and release O_2. The greater the volume of plants, the more CO_2 rich air they will need to keep them growing fast. Dirty, clogged stomata restrict the air flow. Stomata are easily clogged by dirt, polluted air or sprays that leave a filmy residue. Dirty, clogged stomata are essentially sealed off and unable to function. In nature, stomata are cleaned by rain and wind. Indoors, the horticulturist must make rain with a sprayer and wind with a fan.

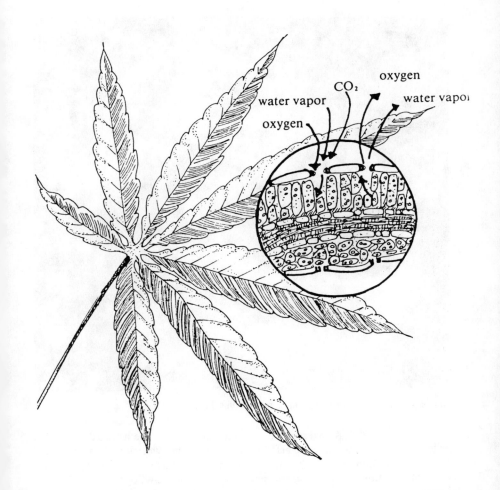

 RULE OF THUMB: Plants should be washed with clean, tepid water on both sides of the leaves at least once a month. See: "About Spraying".

CIRCULATION - If air is totally still, plants tend to use all of the CO_2 next to the leaf. When this air is used and no new CO_2 rich air is forced into its place, a dead air space forms around the leaf, stifling the stomata and slowing growth. Air also tends to stratify. The warm air stays near the

ceiling and cooler air, close to the floor. All of these would-be problems
are avoided by simply opening a door, window and/or installing an
oscillating fan or Heat Siphon. Air circulation is also important for insect
and fungus prevention programs. Mold spores may be present in a room,
but kept from landing and growing when the air is stirred up by a fan.

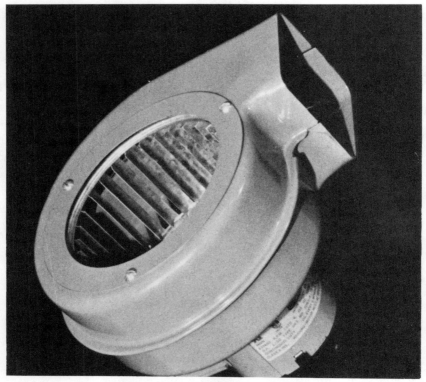

Above fan is easily attached to 4-inch dryer hose

VENTILATION - An average 10 x 10-foot garden will use from 10 to 30
gallons or more of water per week. Where does all that water go? It is transpired
or evaporated into the air. Therefore, gallons of water will be held in the air every
week. If this moisture is left in the small room, the leave will get limp,
transpiration will slow and the stomata will be stifled. This moisture must be
replaced with dry air that lets the stomata function properly. A vent fan that pulls
air out of the grow room will do the trick!

Successful indoor growers know that a vent fan is as important as water, light,
heat and fertilizer. In some cases fresh air is even more important. All
greenhouses have large ventilation fans. Grow rooms are very similar to
greenhouses and their example should be followed. In most grow rooms, there is a

window or some easy-to-use opening in which to mount a fan. If no vent opening is available, one will have to be made.

Squirrel cage vent fan

The main concerns when installing a vent fan are for no light or odors to escape from the exterior vent, while letting out ample air. This can be accomplished in several ways. Baffle or turn the light around a corner so there is little or no chance of it escaping. Use a 4-inch flexible dryer hose for smaller grow rooms and 8-inch galvanized heat duct pipe for large installations. Place one end of the hose outdoors. It should be placed high enough, preferably over 12 feet, so the odor is above most peoples heads. One of the best vents is the chimney. The outlet may be camouflaged by using a dryer hose wall outlet. The other end of the hose is attached to the vent fan. The vent fan is then placed near the ceiling so it vents off hot, humid air. Check for leaks. Set the fan up, then go outdoors after dark to inspect for light leaks. See: "Setting Up the Vent Fan".

Greenhouse fans are equipped with baffles or flaps to prevent backdrafts. During the cold winter or hot summer, backdrafts could change the room temperature and stifle the crop or encourage a menagerie of bad bugs and fungi. Backdrafts are eliminated by installing a vent fan with flaps.

Why use a vent fan? The reason is simple, efficiency. A vent fan is able to pull air out of a room many times more efficiently than a fan is able to push it out. Vent fans are rated by the number of cubic feet per minute (CFM) they can replace or move. Buy a fan that will replace the volume (cubic feet) of the grow room in about 5 minutes. The air pulled out is immediately replaced by fresh air that is sucked in through the numerous tiny cracks or openings in the room. If the grow room is sealed tightly and has few cracks, an open window or air intake vent may be necessary to allow for enough inflow of air.

The fan setup in the middle of a room that pushes the air out of a room is up against a tough physical principle. It is all a matter of pressure. The fan pushes air, increasing the air pressure within the room. This pressure must increase substantially in order for -a rapid exchange of air to take place. The vent fan, on the other hand, is able to change the pressure rapidly. It is much easier to lower the air pressure, causing new fresh air to rush in to fill the vacuum.

TEMPERATURE

All grow rooms should be equipped with an accurate thermometer to measure the temperature. The mercury or liquid type are usually more accurate than the spring or dial type. Thermometers are inexpensive and easy to acquire. They will be necessary to find out all kinds of important stuff, so make sure to get one. The ideal thermometer is a day-night or maximum- minimum type. Using this thermometer, the horticulturist is able to see how low the temperature drops at night and the maximum it reaches during the day. This is very important for many reasons that are explained below.

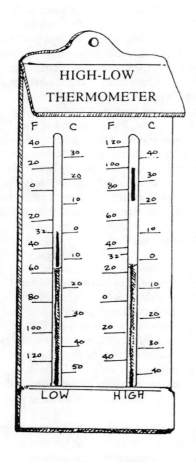

Pins record High-Low

temperatures.

Under normal conditions, the ideal temperature range for indoor marijuana growth is 72-76° F. At night, the temperature can drop 10-15° with no noticeable effect on growth rate. The temperature should not drop more than 20° F, or excessive humidity and mold might become a problem. Daytime temperatures over 100° F and below 60° F seem to slow down growth. Maintaining the proper, constant temperature in the grow room promotes strong, even, healthy growth. Make sure plants are not too close to a heat source, like a ballast or heat vent, or they may dry out, maybe even get heat scorch!

Temperatures above 90° F are not recommended, except with CO_2 enrichment, when the temperature could go as high as 100°. Since the increase in temperature makes the chemical activity faster, everything else must be increased including ventilation. As explained in the following section on humidity, the warmer it is, the more water the air is able to hold. This moist air stifles the stomata and slows rather than speeds growth. All kinds of other problems could result as well from the excess moisture condensation when the temperature drops at night.

Heat build up can really become a problem during the summer months indoors. The ideal grow room is located underground, in a basement, with the insulating qualities of the earth. With the added heat of the HID, and 100° temperatures outdoors, a room can heat up real fast. Several growers have lost their crops to heat stroke during the fourth of July weekend. This is the first big summer holiday and everybody in the city wants to get away to enjoy it.

There are always some gardeners that forget or that are too paranoid to maintain good ventilation in the grow room while on vacation. In a grow room that is improperly set up, with no vent fan and no insulating walls, the summer temperatures may climb to 120° +. There is no way a plant can live in this climate without incredible amounts of water and ventilation. Mother Nature would never let her climate change so much, would you?

The cold of winter is the other extreme. Last winter it was colder than normal in most of the United States. In Portland, the electricity went out, the heat went off and the pipes froze. Residents were driven from their homes until the electricity was restored a few days later. Several growers returned to find their lovely garden wilted, with the deepest, most disgusting green only a freeze can bring. The broken water pipes spewing water everywhere. It is very important to keep the grow room above 30° F. If it goes far below this, the freeze will destroy the cells of the plants, and foliage will die or not be able to grow very fast. Growth slows when the temperature is below 50° F, so try to keep the grow room warm. If you are into stressing the plant by a freeze test, do so at your own risk!

A thermostat regulates the temperature in a room. It measures the temperature, then turns a heat or cooling source, on or off, so the temperature stays within a given range. A thermostat may be attached to an electric or combustion heater. In fact, many homes are already set-up with electric baseboard heat and have a thermostat in each room.

The thermostat is attached to a vent fan in all but the coldest grow rooms. When it gets too hot, the thermostat turns the vent fan on, forcing the hot, stale, air out of the room. The vent fan remains on until the desired temperature is reached, then the thermostat turns off the fan. The vent fan should be all the temperature control necessary. A refrigerated air conditioner can be installed if the heat and humidity are a big problem. If excessive heat is a problem, but humidity is not a concern, a swamp cooler will work well.

There are two types of thermostats: single stage and two stage. The single stage, costs from $20-30 and is able to keep the temperature the same, both day and night. The two stage thermostat is more expensive, about $50, but can maintain different day and nighttime temperatures. This is very convenient, and can save quite a bit of money since the room temperature may drop 10-15° at night with no effect on growth.

Uninsulated grow rooms with a wide change in temperature require special considerations. First, it would probably be easiest to grow somewhere else, but if forced to use an attic or hot spot, get lots of ventilation. Make sure to enclose the room so heating and cooling are easier and less expensive.

When CO_2 is enriched to .12 - .15%, a temperature range from 85 to 100° F promotes more rapid exchange of gases. Photosynthesis and chlorophyll synthesis are able to take place at a more rapid rate and plants grow faster. Remember, this extra 15-25° increases water, nutrient and space consumption, so be prepared!

Seeds germinate faster and clones root quicker when ,the temperature range is from 80-90° F. Two easy ways to increase temperature when cloning are:

(1) use soil heating tape (2) build a (plastic) tent to cover young germinating seeds or clones. This not only increases temperature, but humidity as well. Remove the tent cover as soon as the seeds sprout above the soil to allow for circulation. Clones, however, should remain covered throughout the entire rooting process. Always watch for signs of mold or rot when using a humidity tent with clones. Allowing a bit of air circulation and ventilating clones under the tent helps prevent fungus.

The temperature in the grow room tends to stay the same, top to bottom, when the air is circulated with an oscillating fan. Normally, in an enclosed grow room, the 1000 watt HID lamp and ballast will provide enough heat. A remote ballast, placed on a shelf or a stand near the floor, also helps break up air stratification by radiating heat upwards. Cooler climates have enough heat during the day when the outdoor temperature rises, but not enough when cold temperatures set in at night. The lamp is adjusted to be on during the cool nights. This will warm the room to an acceptable level during both night and day.

Sometimes it is just too cold for the lamp and ballast to maintain adequate room temperatures. Many grow rooms are equipped with a central heating and/or air conditioning vent. This vent is usually controlled by a central thermostat that regulates the entire home's heat. By adjusting the thermostat to 72° F and opening all the internal doors in the home, the grow room can stay a cozy 72°. For most growers, this is too expensive and very wasteful. Usually, keeping the thermostat between 60 and 65°, coupled with the heat from the HID system, is enough to sustain the desired temperature range. Other supplemental heat sources may work better than the above. Incandescent light bulbs and electric heaters are expensive, but provide instant heat. The incandescent bulbs even increase light intensity and add to the spectrum. Propane and natural gas heaters not only heat the air, but burn oxygen from the air, creating CO_2 as a by-product. This dual advantage makes their use even more economical.

There are several new kerosene heaters on the market today that work OK for heating and CO_2 generation. Look for a heater that burns its fuel completely and leaves no tale-tale odor in the room. Watch out for old kerosene heaters or inefficient fuel oil heaters of any type. They could be dangerous!

Diesel oil is a common type of indoor heat. Many furnaces use this dirty and polluting heat source. Wood heat is not the cleanest, but works well as a heat source. A vent fan is extremely important to bring new fresh air into a room heated by a polluting furnace.

Insect populations and fungi are also affected by temperature. In general, the cooler it is, the slower the bugs and fungus reproduce and develop. Temperature control is integrated into many insect and fungus control programs.

HUMIDITY

Relative humidity is the ratio between the amount of moisture in the air and the greatest amount of moisture the air could hold at the same temperature. The hotter it is, the more moisture air can hold; the cooler it is, the less moisture the air can hold. When the temperature in a grow room drops, the humidity climbs and moisture condenses. For example, a 800 cubic foot (10 x 10 x 8 feet) grow room will hold a maximum of about 14 ounces of water when the temperature is 70° and relative humidity is at 100%. When the temperature is increased to 1000 the same room will hold about 56 ounces of moisture at 100% relative humidity. That's four times as much moisture! Where does this water go when the temperature drops?

A 10 x 10 x 8-foot (800 cubic feet) grow room can hold:

> *4 oz. of water at 32°*
>
> *7 oz. of water at 50°*
>
> *14 oz. of water at 70°*
>
> *18 oz. of water at 80°*
>
> *28 oz. of water at 90°*
>
> *56 oz. of water at 100°*

Relative humidity increases when the temperature drops at night. The more temperature variation, the greater the relative humidity variation. Supplemental heat or extra ventilation may be necessary at night if temperatures fluctuate more than 15° F.

 RULE OF THUMB - The moisture holding capacity of air doubles with every 20° F increase in temperature.

Cannabis grows best when the relative humidity range is from 40 to 60%. As with temperature, more or less constant humidity promotes healthy, even growth. Humidity affects the transpiration rate of the stomata. When high humidity exists, water evaporates slowly. The stomata close, transpiration slows, and so does plant growth. Water evaporates quickly into dryer air causing stomata to open, increasing transpiration and growth.

Transpiration in arid conditions will be rapid only if there is enough water available for roots. If water is

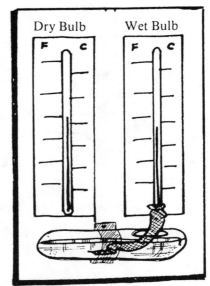

HYGROMETER

inadequate, stomata will close to protect the plant from dehydration, causing growth to slow.

Relative humidity control is an integral part of bug and fungus prevention and control. High humidity (80% plus) promotes fungus and stem rot. Maintaining low (50% or less) humidity, greatly reduces the chances of fungus formation. Some bugs like humid conditions, others do not. Spider mites take much longer to reproduce in a humid room.

Relative humidity is measured with a hygrometer. This extremely important instrument could save you and your plants much frustration and Dry Bulb Wet Bulb fungus. By knowing the exact moisture content in the air, the humidity may be adjusted to a safe 50% level that encourages transpiration and discourages fungus growth.

There are two common types of hygrometers: the spring type, which is curate to 5-10%. This hygrometer is inexpensive (less than $10) and fine for most grow rooms, since the main concern is to keep the humidity near 50%. The other type of hygrometer, actually called a psychrometer, is a little more expensive ($30-50) but is very accurate (see drawing). This hygrometer (psychrometer) uses the wet and dry bulb principle. It is recommended if HYGROMETER using several lamps and/or extreme accuracy is important.

A humidistat is similar to a thermostat, but regulates humidity instead. Humidistats are wonderful! They make playing Mother Nature a snap! Humidistats cost $30-50 and are worth their weight in resin glands. The more expensive models are more accurate. The humidistat and thermostat are wired in line to the vent fan (See diagram below). Each can operate the fan independently. As soon as the humidity (or temperature) gets out of the acceptable range, the fan turns on to vent the humid (or hot) air outdoors.

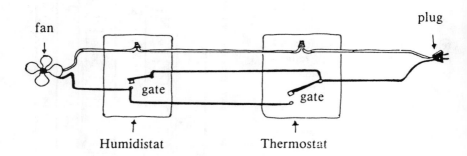

fan

plug

gate

gate

Humidistat   Thermostat

RULE OF THUMB - A vent fan offers the best humidity control possible in most gardens.

The HID lamp and ballast radiate a dry heat, which lowers humidity. Dry heat from the HID system and a vent fan are usually all the humidity control necessary. Other dry heat sources, such as a heat vent from the furnace, wood stove or natural gas, work well to lower humidity. If using forced air from a furnace to lower humidity, make sure warm, dry air does not blow directly on plants. This dry air will dehydrate plants rapidly. One grower swears by silicon packets to absorb excess moisture.

Humidity is easily increased by misting the air with water or setting a bucket of water out to evaporate into the air. A humidifier may be purchased for $100-150. They are essentially a fan over a bucket of water controlled by a humidistat. The fan evaporates water vapor into the air. A humidifier is not necessary unless there is an extreme problem with the grow room drying out. A dehumidifier removes moisture in a room. These units are a bit more complex, since the water must be condensed from the air. A dehumidifier can be used anytime to help guard against fungus. Just set the dial at the desired percent humidity and presto, perfect humidity. They cost from $150-200, but are worth the money to growers with extreme humidity problems that a vent fan has not yet cured. The best price on dehumidifiers has been found at Montgomery Wards and Sears. Dehumidifiers may also be rented if only needed for a month or so.

Young seedlings and rooting clones do better when the humidity is from 70 to 80%. Under arid conditions, the underdeveloped root system is not able to supply water fast enough. High humidity prevents dehydration.

CO_2 ENRICHMENT

CO_2 generator hanging from the ceiling.

Carbon dioxide (CO_2) is a colorless, odorless, non-flammable, non-toxic gas. The air we breathe contains .03-.04% CO_2. Plants use all of the available CO_2 in an enclosed grow room rapidly. Photosynthesis and growth slow to a crawl when the CO_2 level falls below .02%.

CO_2 enrichment has been used in commercial greenhouses for many years. It makes more CO_2 available to plants, thus stimulating growth. Indoor *cannabis* cultivation is similar to conditions in a greenhouse, and the same principles may be applied to the indoor garden. Marijuana is able to use more CO_2 than the .03 to .04% that naturally occurs in the air. By increasing the amount of CO_2 to .12-.15% (1200 to 1500 parts per million (ppm)), the optimum amount widely agreed upon by professional growers, plants may grow two to three times as fast, *providing that light, water, and nutrients are not limiting.* CO_2 enrichment has little or no affect on plants grown under fluorescent lights. The tubes do not supply enough light for the plant to process the extra available CO_2. On the other hand, HID lamps supply ample light to process the enriched CO_2 air. In a grow room using a HID light source, CO_2 enriched air, adequate water and nutrients, mind boggling results may be achieved. In fact, with this basic combination, *cannabis* grows much faster and more efficiently than it grows outdoors. Several growth chambers on the market use this basic combination of growth influencing factors with remarkable results.

CO_2 enrichment does not make plants produce more potent THC. More foliage is produced in a shorter period of time. The larger the volume of THC potent marijuana, the larger the volume of THC produced.

The demands of CO_2 enriched marijuana are much greater than normal and plants must have increased maintenance. They will use nutrients, water and space about twice as fast as normal. A higher temperature range from 85 to 100° F will help stimulate more rapid chemical processes within the super plants. Properly maintained, they will grow so fast and take up so much space, that flowering will have to be induced sooner than normal.

In fact, some people get frustrated using CO_2. It causes plants to grow so fast, unsuspecting growers are unable to keep up with them. With CO_2 enriched air, plants that do not have the support of the other critical elements for life, will not benefit at all and the CO_2 is wasted. The plant can be limited by just one of the critical factors. For example, the plants use water and nutrients a lot faster and if they are not supplied, they will not grow. They might even be stunted. or, if plants need a larger pot but do not get it soon enough, they will not grow and be stunted.

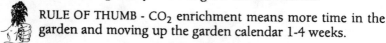

RULE OF THUMB - CO_2 enrichment means more time in the garden and moving up the garden calendar 1-4 weeks.

Increasing light intensity by adding another HID lamp helps speed growth, but may not be necessary. The extra lamp just might make the garden grow so fast, it is impossible to keep up with. More CO_2 does not mean more hours of light per day. The photoperiod must remain the same as under normal conditions for healthy growth and flowering.

To be most effective, the CO_2 level must be kept near .15% everywhere in the room. To accomplish this, the grow room must be completely enclosed. Cracks in and around the walls over 1/8 should be sealed off to prevent CO_2 from escaping. Enclosing the room makes it easier to control the CO_2 content of the air within. The room must also have a vent fan with flaps or a baffle. The vent fan will remove the stale air that will be replaced with CO_2 enriched air. The flaps or baffle will help contain the CO_2 in the enclosed grow room. Venting requirements will change with each type of CO_2 enrichment system. Venting is discussed in detail in the "CO_2 Generator" and the "Compressed CO_2 Gas" sections.

PRODUCING CO$_2$

There are many ways to raise the CO_2 content of an enclosed grow room. CO_2 is one of the byproducts of combustion. Any fuel can be burned to produce CO_2, except for those containing sulfur dioxide and ethylene, which are harmful to plants. See "CO_2 Generators" below. A by-product of fermentation and organic decomposition is CO_2 gas. The CO_2 level near the ground of a rain forest covered with decaying organic matter could be 2-3 times as high as normal. But bringing a compost pile inside to cook down is disgusting! Dry ice is made from frozen CO_2. The CO_2 is released when it comes in contact with the atmosphere. It can get expensive and be a lot of trouble keeping a large room replenished with dry ice.

There are lots of spin-offs to all of these principles and they all work in varying degrees. It is difficult to calculate how much CO_2 is released into the air by fermentation, decomposition or dry ice, without using very expensive equipment to measure it. Dry ice gets very expensive after prolonged use. Two pounds of dry ice will raise the CO_2 level in a 10 x 10-foot grow room to about 2000 ppm. for 24 hours. One chagrined grower remarked: "I can't believe that stuff melts so fast". A filthy, decaying compost pile is simply out of the question indoors! Besides, a new compost pile would need to be moved twice a day to release enough CO_2.

Fermentation is an OK way to produce CO_2, but it is difficult to tell how much is produced. Below is a recipe for brewing CO_2. A one gallon plastic milk jug works best, but any other container will do. Mix one cup of sugar and a packet of brewers yeast with about 31/2 gallons of warm water. The concoction smells horrid, but produces a fairly decent burst of CO_2. This method is one of the least expensive ways of producing CO_2. It works best when used in a small growth chamber. Seedlings that get started with CO_2, seem to get a head start that is maintained throughout life. The CO_2 produced by the fermentation is soon released in the enclosed chamber. The concoction is changed one to four times daily. Half of the solution is poured out, then 1.5 quarts of water and another cup of sugar are added. The yeast will continue to grow during the fermentation process. The first packet of yeast is all that needs to be added. This CO_2 mix is like a sourdough batter starter mix, do not let it die! As long as the yeast does not die, this fermentation mix may be used continually to generate CO_2. In fact, if a person were really into it, there could be several gallons and one would be changed every couple of hours. The smell would soon gag a maggot!

CO_2 GENERATORS

Commercial nurseries produce CO_2 with large generators. These generators produce CO_2 by using propane, butane or natural gas to burn oxygen out of the air in a chamber. The CO_2 rich air is then circulated among the plants. Heat, CO_2 and water are by products of combustion. Each lb. of fuel burned = 3 lbs. CO_2, 1.5 lbs. water and approximately 22,000 BTU's (British Thermal Units) of heat. Small, one lamp grow rooms can burn ethyl or methyl alcohol in a kerosene lamp. In a 10 x 10-foot grow room, 3 ounces of fuel will produce about 2000 ppm of CO_2 in 24 hours.

Heat build-up makes large CO_2 generators impossible to use in the heat of summer. The CO_2 generators used in greenhouses are too large to be practical for the average grow room. Several N.W. companies manufacture small scale CO_2 generators that are similar to the large commercial ones. These smaller CO_2 generators were designed for 200-400 square feet grow rooms.

These CO_2 generators work very well for larger or cool grow rooms. The generators can create quite a bit of heat. Remember for each pound of gas burned, it will create about 22,000 BTU's and 1 1/2 pounds of water. In a small grow room, the heat and moisture produced could make it impractical to use.

The CO_2 generators that I have seen are of two basic designs. The first is hung from the ceiling. CO_2 rich air is produced and cascades over the plants. This model uses a pilot light with a flow meter and burner. This unit essentially looks like a gas stove burner and pilot light in a protective housing. The generator must have a top covering the open flame at all times. The unit is equipped with a safety valve and a pilot light. It may be operated manually or placed on the same timer as the lamp via the solenoid switch. An oscillating fan is placed near the floor to keep the

CO_2 rich air stirred up. This model is designed for a 200-400 square feet room.

The second model is placed on the floor and has a fan located on the side of the burner housing. The fan circulates the warm CO_2 rich air among the plants. The unit has an electronic pilot with a safety timer that is electronically controlled to relight safely. If the flame blows out for any reason, it will relight safely with an electronic spark. This unit easily adapts to a timer and designed for a 100-200 square feet room.

> NOTE: CO_2 is used by humans at low levels. Levels above .4% (4000 ppm) could be hazardous if inhaled for long. The CO_2 level is easy to control with the proper metering system. Besides being hazardous to people at high concentrations, plants can not use CO_2 in levels above .2% (2000 ppm).
>
> A relatively small flame will alter the CO_2 level in an enclosed grow room. With the help of a vent fan, there is little chance of any CO_2 gas buildup. Apply a solution of 50% water and 50% concentrated dish soap to all connections to check for leaks. When the bubbles appear, gas is escaping. Never use a leaky system!!

The LP gas is readily available at gas stations; the tanks are inconspicuous, easy to carry around and light when empty.

Propane tanks are easy to acquire, inconspicuous and easy to fill, unlike the heavy awkward compressed CO_2 tanks discussed below. The LP gas is readily available at gas stations.

Some new propane tanks are filled with an inert gas to protect them from rust. Empty the inert gas out before filling a new tank for the first time. The inert gas does not mix well with propane nor will it burn.

Never over fill the tank! The gas will expand and contract with temperature change.

I think it is easiest and least expensive in the long run to purchase a CO_2 generator from a reputable dealer that stocks a good brand. But there are many people that prefer to manufacture their own. To make a CO_2 generator, find a heater that burns clean and has a knob to control the exact flame produced. A blue flame is produced by propane or natural gas that is burning clean. A yellow flame has unburned gas and needs more oxygen to burn clean. Good examples of home made CO_2 generators are propane heaters, stoves or lamps. Follow the formulas given below for CO_2 generators. Examples are given to find out how much CO_2 to generate in a room. First, the TOTAL VOLUME of the room is found, then the amount of fuel burned to produce the desired amount of CO_2 is calculated.

To find out how much CO_2 it will take to bring the grow room up to the optimum level, find the total volume of the grow room, then divide by the optimum level of CO_2.

Example:

TOTAL VOLUME = L x W x H

TOTAL VOLUME = 10 x 8 x 10-foot

TOTAL VOLUME = 800 cubic feet

OPTIMUM LEVEL = .0015

.0015 x 800 cubic feet 1.2 cubic feet

It will take 1.2 cubic feet of CO_2 to bring the 800 cubic feet grow room up to the optimum level.

Each pound of fuel (kerosene, propane or natural gas) burned produces approximately 3 lbs. of CO_2. One third of a lb. (5.3 oz.), produces about one lb. of CO_2. At 680, one lb. of CO_2 displaces 8.7 cubic feet

Total amount of CO_2 needed / 8.7 x .33 = lbs. of fuel needed

1.2 / 8.7 x .33 = .045 lbs. of fuel needed

.045 x 16 = .72 oz. of fuel

To measure the amount of fuel used, simply weigh the tank before it is turned on, use it for an hour, then weigh it again. The difference in weight is the amount of gas or fuel used.

It is easier to measure the amount of CO_2 produced rather than measuring the amount of CO_2 in the atmosphere of the grow room. Measuring the content of CO_2 is not a very common among indoor growers yet. There are not any inexpensive kits on the market to measure it yet. The least expensive kit costs about $250 and each test requires chemicals within and glass tube and costs about $5. These kits may be purchased from National Dragger, Inc., P.O. Box 120, Pittsburgh, PA, 15275. There are several people working on less expensive kits to measure CO_2, but they are not on the market yet.

Exact venting requirements are difficult with CO_2 generators. Since it is difficult to tell the exact amount of CO_2 present in the room, it is difficult to tell exactly how much to vent the room. One experienced grower says that he is able to sense the level of CO_2 in the air. The best way to figure out how much to vent a grow room is to measure the amount of CO_2 present in the air, then vent the room accordingly. However this is too expensive for most people. To vent a room using a CO_2 generator, wire a vent fan in line to a humidistat and thermostat. Set the humidistat at 50% relative humidity and the thermostat at 90° F. This will maintain the CO_2 level close to the perfect level. If the vent fan is on all the time, something must be wrong! The fan should not come on over once an hour for the CO_2 level to remain near the perfect level.

Compressed CO_2 gas generally works best in grow rooms smaller than 200-300 square feet. The generators are designed for rooms 100-400 square feet or larger where heat buildup is not a problem. The CO_2 is injected into the room from the compressed tank. It creates no heat and is able to meter out the exact amount of CO_2 desired. This means that a room could be virtually any size and the exact amount of CO_2 could be metered in. CO_2 tanks reach a point of diminishing returns. That is, rooms over 200-300 square feet have is more room for the heat produced by the CO_2 generator to dissipate and it creates the proper level of CO_2 for the cubic footage of the room. The CO_2 generator is also more cost effective for larger rooms than the compressed CO_2. Some people just do not want any kind of an unattended flame burning in their home. Only use the CO_2 burner if you feel comfortable.

A. Short range timer B. Solenoid valve C. Regulator D. Flow meter E. Tank of compressed CO_2 gas

COMPRESSED CO_2

Compressed CO_2 gas is very safe, versatile and easy to control. For use with many HID systems, compressed CO_2 is, an excellent choice.

Compressed CO_2 enrichment systems contain a combination regulator/flow meter, solenoid valve, short range timer and tank of compressed CO_2 gas.

Compressed CO_2 gas passes out the tank into the flow meter/regulator. The solenoid valve opens and closes to let the CO_2 into the room. Most flow meter/regulators emit 10 to 50 cubic feet of CO_2 per hour. If the flow meter/regulator were set at 10 cubic feet per hr. and left on for one half hour (0.05 hour), 5 cubic feet of CO_2 would enter the room in one half hour. The total amount of CO_2 needed to bring the level up to 1500 ppm for a 10 x 8 x 10-foot grow room is 1.2 cubic feet By altering the flow rate and time, the exact amount of CO_2 can be injected into the grow room.

For example:

Total amount of CO_2 needed / flow rate = time

1.2 / flow rate = time

1.2 / 10 = .12 hr.

.12 hr. X 60 minutes = 7.2 minutes

If the flow meter is set at 10 cubic feet per hr., the timer will need to be on 7.2 minutes to bring the CO_2 level up to the optimum 1500 ppm.

A short range timer measures short periods of time accurately. The regular 24 hour timer will not measure increments of time less than one hour accurately. If the short range timer were set to be on for 7.2 minutes every few hours, the CO_2 level of the room would go up to the optimum level then taper off until the next burst of CO_2 were injected. It is a good idea to split the 7.2 minutes down into smaller increments so there is a regular supply of CO_2 in the room.

Vent the room using a CO_2 tank about 10 minutes before the CO_2 is injected into the room. Make sure the vent fan is not on during or for at least an hour after the CO_2 is injected into the room.

THE SMELL OF THE SKUNK

A good exhaust fan, vented outdoors, is the best way to keep the house reeking of fresh marijuana. If the odor is strong and venting is a problem, a deionizer or negative ion generator will help. The deionizer generates negative ions, which purifies the air and removes the odor. They produce a negative electrical charge or negative ions. The negative ions pour out into the air. They seek out and attach themselves to particles (pollutants, fungus spores, etc.) in the air and neutralize them.

Negative ion generators are used indoors mainly to get rid of the incredible odor or bouquet produced by poorly vented gardens. The negative ion generators can be used all the time to clean the air of pollutants. Plants grown in such an environment are generally very healthy. The generator uses very little electricity and plugs into a regular 110 volt current. Visually check the filter every few days and make sure to keep it clean.

One grower thought the idea was so good, he put five deionizers in a room with five lights. They worked so well, the marijuana had no odor at all, even after it was harvested! If the bouquet of the harvest is a big concern, vent the air up the chimney or into the attic or a similar collection chamber. Run the deionizers in the collection chamber. This way, the marijuana stays pungent.

Exhaust fans are rated in the amount of square feet of air they can displace, or move in a minute.

> RULE OF THUMB : Use a vent fan that is able to replace all of the air in the grow room within five minutes, or less.

SETTING UP THE VENT FAN

Step One: Figure out the total volume of the grow room. Length x width x height = total volume. A grow room 10 x 10 x 8 feet has a total volume of 800 cubic feet (10 x 10 x 8 feet 800 cubic feet)

Step Two: 2. Find a VENT fan that will remove the total volume of air in 5 minutes or less. Buy a fan that can easily be mounted to the wall (8-inch fans are my favorite for a 2-3 lamp room) or attached to the flexible 4-inch dryer hose. A high speed squirrel cage fan will be necessary to maintain enough air flow through 4-inch flexible duct.

Step Three: Place the fan high on a wall or near the ceiling of the grow room so it vents off hot, humid air.

Step Four: If possible, cut a hole in the wall and secure the fan in place over the hole. Do not worry about the hole, it can be patched, and the garden will love it. However most locations require special installation. See: 5-9 below.

Step Five: To place a fan in a window, cut a 1/2-inch piece of plywood to fit the window sill. Cover window with a light proof black paint or similar covering. Mount the fan in the top of the plywood venting out. Secure the plywood and fan in the window sill and open the window from the bottom.

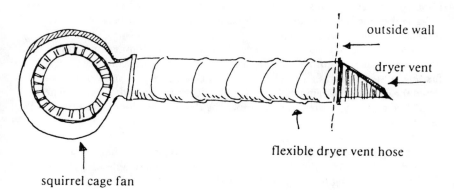

outside wall

dryer vent

flexible dryer vent hose

squirrel cage fan

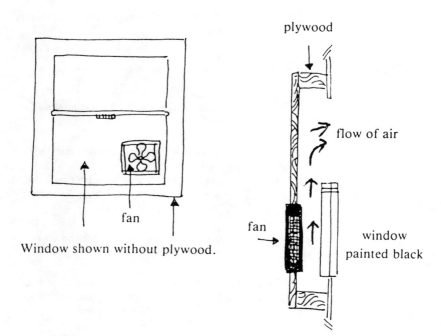

plywood

flow of air

fan

fan

window
painted black

Window shown without plywood.

Step Six: Another option for a light proof vent is to use a 4-inch flex dryer hose. Simply vent the hose outdoors and attach a small squirrel cage fan to the other end of the hose. Make sure there is a tight connection between the fan and the hose by using a large hose clamp.

Step Seven: Another option is to vent the air up the chimney or into the attic where light leakage and odor are not a problem. If using the chimney for a vent, first clean the excess ash and creosote. Tie a chain to a rope. Lower the chain down the chimney, banging and knocking all debris inside to the bottom. There should be a door at the bottom to remove the debris. This door is also used as the vent.

Step Eight: The fan may be attached to a thermostat and humidistat to vent hot, humid air outside when necessary. Instructions are available with the thermostat for wiring to the vent fan. The diagram shows how to wire a thermostat and humidistat to the same fan.

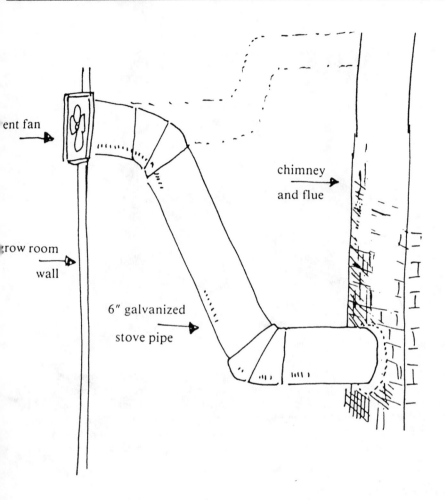

ent fan

chimney
and flue

grow room
wall

6" galvanized
stove pipe

Step Nine: Or attach the vent fan to a timer and run for a specific length of time. This method is generally used with CO_2 enrichment. The fan is set to turn on and vent out used air just before new CO_2 rich air is injected.

CHAPTER SEVEN BUGS & FUNGI

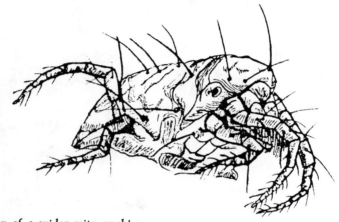

Close up of a spider mite, yuck!

Bugs will creep into your garden, eat, reproduce, and be merry. Bugs live everywhere outdoors. Indoors, bugs will live just about anywhere that you (Mother Nature) let them. Fungus is present in the air at all times. It may be introduced by an infected plant or from air containing fungus spores. Fungus will settle down and grow if climatic conditions are right. Both fungus and bugs can be prevented, but once an infestation has started, severe methods of control may be necessary to eradicate them.

PREVENTION

Cleanliness is the key to bug and fungus prevention. The grow room should be totally enclosed, so the environment may be easily controlled. Keep the floor clean. Keep all debris off soil surface. Do not use mulch. Bugs and fungus like nice hideaway places, dirty corners, old damp leaves and mulch. You, the horticulturist, and your tools could be the transporters of many microscopic bugs and fungi that may be fatal to the garden. This does not mean you and your tools have to be hospital clean every time you enter the grow room, even though that would be nice. It does mean, normal and regular sanitary precautions do need to be taken. Wear clean clothes and use clean tools. Have a separate indoor set of tools to be used only in the grow room. Disinfect tools by dipping them in rubbing alcohol, or wash with soap and water after using them on a diseased plant. Bugs and fungus love to ride from plant to plant on dirty tools.

Personal cleanliness is very important for bug and fungus prevention. Wash your hands before handling plants and after handling diseased plants. Do not walk around your buggy outdoor garden, then visit your indoor garden, do it vice versa. Think before entering the indoor garden and possibly contaminating it. Did you walk across a lawn covered with rust (rust is a rust-colored fungus) or pet the dog that just came in from the garden outside? Did you just fondle your spider mite infested split leaf philodendron in the living room?

Once you have grown a crop in a potting soil or soilless mix, throw it out. Some growers have used the same OLD potting soil over and over with OK results. They place charcoal in the bottom of containers to absorb excess salts and maintain sweet soil. Used soil makes excellent outdoor garden soil. Used soil may harbor harmful bugs and fungi that have developed an immunity to sprays. Starting a new crop in new potting soil will cost more up front, but will eliminate many potential problems.

Most important, once potting soil is used, it loses a good deal of the fluff of its texture. Compaction becomes a problem. Roots have trouble penetrating compacted soil and there is little room for oxygen, so roots do not breathe. Used potting soil is depleted of valuable N-P-K nutrients, as well as secondary and trace elements. A plant with a slow start is a perfect target for disease.

Companion Planting works well to discourage bugs. Bugs, except for thrips, hate garlic. Since garlic cloves are readily available, take up little room, transplant well and discourage bugs, they are by far the best companion plant for indoor marijuana. When sowing seeds or transplanting, just plant a few cloves of garlic about 1/2-inch deep with them. The clones will sprout and grow in a week or two, driving insects away. Garlic will grow straight up, creating very little shade, and has a compact root system attached to the bulb below the soil. When transplanting, just move garlic along with the marijuana. Garlic is very resilient and can take more shock during transplanting than marijuana. *Cannabis* is usually harvested before garlic is mature. These garlic plants may be transplanted to become a companion to another young marijuana plant through life. It is still a good idea to dip the garlic transplant into a insecticide/fungicide solution to prevent disease transferal.

Marigolds also discourage bugs, but not as well as garlic. Marigolds are much prettier than garlic, but they must be blooming to effectively discourage bugs. They take up a lot of space as well.

Plant insect and fungus resistant strains of marijuana. *Most marijuana horticulturists have found various strains of cannabis* indica *to be the most resistant to bug attacks, but some strains have less resistance to fungus. When choosing your mother plants, inspect them regularly and compare them to one another for bug and fungus resistance. It is incredible how some plants attract disease and may be infested, while others growing nearby have little or no problem at all.*

Keep plants healthy and growing fast at all times. *Disease attacks sickly plants first. Strong plants tend to grow faster than bugs can eat or fungus can spread. With strong, healthy, fast growing plants, a few bugs or a little fungus could not do much damage.*

Forced air circulation makes life miserable for bugs and fungus. Bugs hate wind, they can not hold on to the plants or fly very well in wind. Fungus has little time to settle in a breeze and does not grow well on wind- dried soil, stems and leaves.

Fast growing plants rarely have trouble with bugs.

Ventilation will change the humidity of a room quickly. In fact, a vent fan attached to a humidistat is the most fool proof form of humidity control. Mold was a big problem in a grow room that did not have a vent fan . It was terrible! Upon entering the enclosed grow room, with the humidity near 100%, eyeglasses would steam up immediately. If fact, the room was so humid that roots were growing from the stems of plants. The grower installed a vent fan, that sucked the moist, stale air from the grow room, venting it outdoors, and the mold problem disappeared!

Every indoor horticulturist should practice all of these preventative measures. It is much easier to prevent a disease from getting started than it is to wipe out an infestation. If bugs or fungus should multiply and are left unchecked, the entire garden could be devastated in a few weeks.

INSECT & FUNGUS CONTROL

Sometimes, even with all preventative measures taken, bugs and fungus still creep in and set up housekeeping. First they will establish themselves on a weak, susceptible plant, then launch an all-out assault on the rest of the garden. They will move out in all directions from the infested base, taking over more and more space, until they have conquered the entire garden. This can happen in a matter of days. Bugs can lay thousands of eggs that grow into mature adults within a few weeks. For example, say you did not take preventative measures or closely examine plants for disease, and 100 microscopic munchers each laid 1000 eggs, that grew into adults two weeks later. By the end of the month, there would be millions of insects attacking the infested garden.

Sprays essentially kill adults and, all too often, only some of them. Sprays should be applied soon after eggs hatch so young adult bugs are caught in their weakest stage of life. Horticultural oil spray works well alone or as an additive to help kill larva.

The availability of sprays can be seasonal. Garden sections of stores are changed for the winter. The stock is sometimes kept in the storage room, but usually it is sold in a season end sale. All kinds of bargains on sprays are available for the winter growing season at these season end sales. Besides, it looks real suspicious to be buying vegetable insecticides in the middle of winter!

The products recommended have worked before and are readily available. This does not mean they are the best nor the only products to use. There are many local products that are just as good as national or Northwest brands. Always follow the directions on the can!

BUGS

The indoor gardener has many options open for bug and fungi control. As we have seen, prevention and cleanliness are at the top of the list. There is a logical progression to bug and fungi control. It is outlined in the chart below. Notice it starts with cleanliness and progresses through the most basic elements.

RULE OF THUMB - follow the logical progression for bug and fungus control.

LOGICAL PROGRESSION OF BUG CONTROL

1. *Prevention*
   _____*a. cleanliness*
   _____*b. use "new" soil*
   _____*c. one "indoor" set of tools*
   _____*d. disease resistant plants*
   _____*e. healthy plants*
   _____*f. companion planting*
   _____*g.. climate control*
   _____*h. no animals*

2. *Manual Removal*
   _____*a. fingers*
   _____*b. sponges*

3. *Organic Sprays*

4. *Natural Predators*

5. *Chemicals*

Manual removal is just what the name implies: smashing all bugs in sight between the thumb and forefinger or between two sponges. Gloves may be worn so none of the bug juice gets on you, yuck!

If forced to use a spray, always use a natural one. Harsh chemicals are only a last resort. With the development of an environmental conscientiousness and technology, several new natural based sprays have been developed. They offer unique qualities unknown to harsh chemical sprays. As with any spray, it always seems to slow plants down a little, even if it is natural. The plant is covered with the filmy residue of the spray for some time. The stomata are clogged until the spray wears off or is washed off. The stronger the spray, the harder it is on the plant. It is a good idea to spray the plants as little as possible and not spray at all for two weeks before harvest. Please read "About Spraying" at the end of this chapter. Read ALL the labels thoroughly of all sprays before you use them.

Only use contact sprays that can be used for edible plants. Do not use any sprays at all on young seedlings or tender clones. The spray could burn the tender little plant.

Bacillus thuringiensis or Bt

Bacillus thuringiensis commonly referred to as Bt is a disease-causing bacteria. The caterpillar or worm first eats the Bt and within a short time the digestive system becomes paralyzed. Many pests are affected including cabbage loopers, cabbage worms, corn earworms, cutworms, Gypsy moth larvae, hornworms, some nematodes and tent caterpillars. Bt is sold as a dormant spore dust or a liquid under the names of Dipel, Biotrol, or Thuricide.

Bt/H-14 sold under the trade names Vectobac and Gnatrol controls destructive soil nematodes. Destructive nematodes are difficult to see. They cause slow growth and slowly rotting roots.

All of the strains of bacillus thuringiensis are nontoxic to humans, animals and plants.

Diatomaceous Earth

Diatomaceous (DE) earth is formed by the lacy shells of trillions of minute one celled silicate (algae diatoms) that have died and settled to the bottom of oceans or lake beds. These prehistoric lightweight snowflake-like skeletons have been fossilized. They form deposits hundreds of feet thick that are mined, pulverized and sold as a non-toxic wettable powder that is fatal to most soft bodied insects including ,aphids slugs and spider mites. Some beneficial insects are also subject to the piercing DE. The diatomaceous earth (DE) works by puncturing or slicing the pest's body, causing dehydration. If the pest ingests the razor-sharp diatomaceous earth, it disrupts vital body functions. Earthworms, animals, humans and birds however, can digest diatomaceous earth and are not effected by it. DE also contains 14 trace minerals in a chelated (available) form.

Use a protective mask when openly handling this fine powder to guard against irritations.

Spread DE in a quarter-inch deep, two-inch wide border to prevent slugs and snails from crossing over to eat plants. Mix 1 part DE with 3 to 5 parts water and a few drops of biodegradable dish soap to use as a spray. Apply this spray to infestations of pest insects. A dusting of DE is most effective. Use a ketchup bottle or commercial duster to apply DE dust to the undersides of moist foliage. The dust sticks to the moist leaves where it stays until washed off by rain or irrigation. For best results, do not water for 48 hours after application.

Caution! Do not use swimming pool diatomaceous earth. It is chemically treated and heated, This product contains crystalline silica that is hazardous if inhaled. The body is unable to dissolve the crystalline form of silica which causes chronic irritation.

Homemade Sprays

Many homemade spray preparations are outstanding .insecticides A hot taste or smelly odor are the main principles behind most home-brewed potions. The sprays are normally made by mixing repellent plants with a little water in a blender. The resulting slurry concentrate is strained through a nylon stocking or fine cloth before being diluted with water for application.

Cooking or heating preparations generally destroys active ingredients. To draw out ingredients, mince plant and soak in a mineral oil for a couple of days. Add this oil to the water including a little soap to emulsify the oil.

Any nondetergent, biodegradable soap will work as a wetting and sticking agent in these preparations. The soap dissolves best if a teaspoon of alcohol is added to each quart of water.

Chamomile sprays are used to prevent dampening-off and mildew.

Chrysanthemum marigold and nasturtium blossoms, ,garlic chive, onion, hot pepper, bug juice, horseradish, mints, oregano, tomato and tobacco residues repel or kill many insects including ,aphids caterpillars, mites and whiteflies. Be very careful with tobacco sprays. (See "Nicotine & Tobacco Sprays"). These mixes can vary in proportions, but the blended remaining slurry is always filtered before adding with water for the final spray.

One homemade organic spray is made by blending 1 teaspoon of hot pepper or Tabasco sauce, 4 cloves of garlic with a quart of water. Grind this mix up in the blender and strain through a nylon stocking or cheese cloth before using in the sprayer.

A mix of one eighth to one quarter cup of hydrated lime mixed with a quart of water makes an effective insect spray and is especially effective on tiny insects such as spider mites. Mix a nondetergent soap with the lime the soap acts as both a sticking agent and insecticide. Lime can be caustic in large doses. Always try the spray on a test plant and wait a few days to check for adverse effects before applying to other plants.

Another natural spray is made from chopped tomato leaves soaked in water. The water is used as a spray against white cabbage butterflies.

Spray made out of bug guts ground up in a blender, emulsified in water.

Homemade sprays are made from a few drops (a 1% solution: one tablespoon of soap per quart of water) of a biodegradable soap concentrate like Castille or Ivory liquid. It is important to use a soap with no sulfates or harsh agents that will cause leaf spot. The soap is mixed with a quart of water and the juice from a freshly squeezed garlic, chili powder, rubbing alcohol or ground-up bugs. The mix is then shaken up vigorously. Natural, homemade sprays are so effective that some growers will not use anything else. If the homemade mixes does not work after one or two applications, try a stronger spray Safer's or Pyrethrum.

Insecticidal Soaps

Insecticidal soaps are mild contact insecticides made from fatty acids of animals and plants. These soaps are safe for bees, honeybees, animals and humans. The soap controls soft-bodied insects such as ,aphids mealybugs, spider mites, thrips and whiteflies by penetrating and destroying body membranes.

Soft soaps such as Ivory liquid dish soap or Castille's soap are biodegradable and kill insects in the same manor as Safer's, but they are not as potent. Do not use detergent soaps, they may be caustic. Add a few cap-fulls of Ivory or Castille's to a quart of water and spray. These soaps can also be used as a wetting agent when watering down peat moss, dry potting soil or seedlings. The soap reduces the surface tension of the water to give it better penetration. Ivory or Castille's can also be used as a spreader-sticker to mix with sprays. The soaps help the spray stick to the foliage better, which is important when using contact sprays. The soft soaps will only last for about one day before dissipating.

Safer's Insecticidal Soap is the first choice of many horticulturists for an all round organic bug spray. Safer's is made from potassium fatty acid salts and a little alcohol. Exactly how it kills the little pests is not completely known. It is believed to penetrate their bodies, paralyze the nervous system, cause the body fluids to flow away, suffocate by blocking breathing pores, and desiccate the little bodies. Once covered with Safer's, it will take about an hour for death to occur.

Safer has no residual effect. That is, if you spray a plant at 8 am, a bug that lands on the same plant at noon will not be affected by the spray. This is good and bad. It means that the foliage may be ingested soon after spraying, but it could take multiple applications to make sure you get all the bugs.

There is a trick to using Safer's. It is very simple: Apply it heavy. Drench the garden. Since it works by suffocation and penetration upon contact, it is necessary to get a good big dose to completely cover the bugs. However, this does not mean to mix it any heavier than the recommended 1 to 40 ratio. Safer may be applied as often as every two days.

Another neat thing about Safer's is you can use it with no fear of becoming sick. Fatty acids are produced by humans. They are one of our defenses against disease-causing fungi.

Nicotine (sulfate) and Tobacco Sprays

Nicotine is a non-persistent pesticide derived from tobacco. It is toxic to most all insects and humans if a concentrate is swallowed. Many times nicotine is mixed with sulfur. One well known brand on the market is Black Flag's Nicotine Sulfate.

Nicotine sulfate (tobacco juice mixed with sulfur) is an excellent insecticide on all plants except members of the nightshade family (eggplant, tomatoes, peppers and potatoes). You can purchase bottled nicotine sulfate or simply use tobacco diluted in water. Apply the nicotine as a spray to kill aphids and whiteflies.

In small concentrations, nicotine sulfate is not toxic to humans.

Horticultural Oil

Oil spray is a safe, non-poisonous and non-polluting insecticide. Similar to medicinal mineral oil, it kills slow moving and immobile sucking insects by smothering and suffocating them while the thin oily film remains invisible to humans. Oil spray control for ,aphids scale, spider mites and thrips.

Pyrethrum

This extremely powerful insecticide is extracted from the flowers of the pyrethrum chrysanthemum (*Chrysanthemum coccineum* and *C. cinergrii folium*), grown commercially in the tropical mountains of Ecuador and Kenya. A broad-spectrum pesticide pyrethrum is very toxic to most insects, including beneficials and cockroaches. If applied as a spray, pyrethrum is very effective to control flying insects. But if the insect does not receive a killing dose, they may revive. For this reason, pyrethrum is often combined with rotenone or ryana to ensure pest death. Use this non-selective insecticide to spot spray only heavily infested plants.

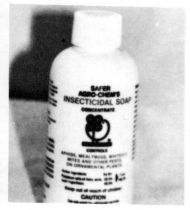
Insecticidal Soap

Pyrethrum

Pyrethrum is not toxic to animals or humans. Purchase in aerosol, dust or liquid. Aerosol spray is very convenient, but can burn foliage if applied closer than one foot. Aerosols also contain piperonyl butoxide which is toxic to people. All forms of pyrethrum dissipates within a few hours in the presence of air and HID light. At least one manufacturer offers an encapsulated pyrethrum in aerosol form. As the spray fogs out of the nozzle, a bubble forms around each droplet of mist.

The outside coating keeps the pyrethrum intact for several days. If an insect should encounter the bubble, pop! The pyrethrum is released.

Pyrethrum in the aerosol can is a relatively new product. This is the best natural product I have seen for killing spider mites and just about any other insect except bees. The natural pyrethrum comes from the pyrethrum flower found in southern Africa. The daisy-like flower is a member of the chrysanthemum family. This natural, contact insecticide is very toxic to insects especially spider mites, but decomposes rapidly when exposed to air and sunlight.

Pyrethrum is easy to spot at the store; it comes in a green can while the rest of the bug sprays come in a red can. Pyrethrum is the fastest selling insecticide on the market! Pyrethrum also comes in pump type applicator bottles. They do not work very well because the method of application does not saturate the air.

It is almost impossible to incorrectly apply the aerosol/fogger, except for standing too close. Even the novice gardener using it the first time has excellent results. The secret is in the fogger method of application. The pyrethrum is shot out in a fog that permeates the grow room. The spray goes everywhere, even bottoms of the leaves, anywhere bugs can hide! Care must be taken to be far enough away from the plants when spraying. When the fog comes out of the nozzle, it is ice cold. If this ice cold spray is applied too close, foliar damage may result. To apply this spray, simply follow the directions on the can.

Wear a respirator or a protective mask with this insecticide. The misty fog permeates the air, making it easy to inhale. Pyrethrums are also toxic to humans.

Do not use synthetic pyrethroids. Synthetic pyrethroids are toxic to honeybees. Always purchase natural pyrethrum.

Sulfur

Sulfur is a common fungicide that has been used for centuries. If you should need to use this strong ,fungicide apply it in very light concentrations. Sulfur easily burns foliage. Be careful.

Traps

Black lights can be used to catch egg-laying moths. Light and fan traps attract many insects including beneficials and their use may do more harm than good.

When using sex lure traps, place them away from sensitive plants so insects will be lured away from them.

Sticky "tanglefoot" resins can be smeared on attractive yellow or red cards to simulate ripe .fruit When the pests land on the ""fruit they are stuck forever!

PREDATORS

A predator may be a small parasite that affixes itself to the host's body, taking many days to consume it, or it may be a huge bug that can devour many victims daily. The rate at which the predators keep the infestation in check is directly proportionate to the amount of predators. The more predators, the sooner they will take care of any infestations. Predators work by out-breeding their victim, producing more predators than the victim is able to keep up with. The predators are the crusading warriors in the never ending battle of pest free horticulture!

Predators are shipped special delivery and may arrive after the daily mail delivery. The inside of a mail box in the hot sun easily reaches 120° +. Check the mail box regularly if ordering predators.

When any predator is introduced into the garden, there must be special precautions taken to ensure the little killer's well-being. Stop spraying all toxic chemicals, malathion, diazinon, etc., at least two weeks before introducing the predators. Pyrethrum and Safer Insecticidal Soap can be applied up to a few days before, providing any residue is washed off. Do not spray for 30 days after releasing predators.

Predators work very well in gardens that are not sterilized between crops. Gardens with perpetual harvests are ideal for predators.

Most of the predators that do well in the HID garden can not fly. Bugs that can fly usually go straight for the lamp. The lady bug is a good example. Say 500 of them are released on Monday, by Friday, only a few die-hards would be left. The rest would have popped off the lamp. If using flying predators, release them when it is dark. They will last longer.

Predators are most often very small and must be introduced to each plant separately. This could take a little time and patience, so budget time for it. The predators also have specific climatic requirements. For best results, pay attention; note the predators needs and maintain them.

Oil sprays are widely used in greenhouses. They are not the same kinds of oils used in the car nor sold at the hardware store. Do not use 3-in-1 oil or anything similar in place of the horticultural petroleum oil. The horticultural oil is refined by removing most of the portion that is toxic to plants. The petroleum oils work well to smother bugs and eggs, as well as generally impair the life cycle of the insect. If using the oils make sure it is a lightweight horticultural oil with a viscosity of 60-70. The lighter weight the oil, the less toxic it is to plants. I prefer to use oil sprays only during vegetative growth. This way, the residue has ample time to dissipate before harvest and will not be tasted when smoked.

Mix two drops of oil spray (no more than a 1% solution) per qt. of water. More than a few drops could burn tender growing shoots and clog stomata. Repeat applications as needed, usually 3 applications, one every 5 to 10 days will do it. The first application will get most of the adults and many eggs. Eggs hatch in about 10 days. The second spraying will kill the newly hatched eggs and the remaining adults. The third application will finish off any survivors.

Bug bombs are very strong insecticides that essentially exterminate everything in the room They were developed to kill fleas and roaches. Bug bombs are used between crops to rid the grow room of all bugs before introducing the next crop. Many manufacturers produce the bug bombs under many brand names containing a menagerie of toxic chemicals. Place the bug bomb in the empty room. Turn it on. Then leave the room. The chemicals are very toxic! Follow directions to the letter!

Spider Mites

Stippling is easy to see

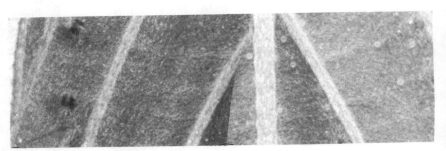

Mites (left) and eggs (right) on leaf underside.

The spider mite is the most common insect found on marijuana indoors. Actually, it is not really an insect, it is a spider. Insects have 6 legs and spiders have 8. These microscopic mites are found on the leaf's undersides, sucking away the plant's life-giving fluids. To the untrained eye, they are hard to spot. Most people notice the tell-tale yellowish-white spots (stippling) on the tops of the leaves first. More careful inspection will reveal tiny spider webs on the stems and under leaves. Webs may easily be seen when misted with water. The spider mites appear as tiny specks on leaf undersides. The naked eye has a hard time distinguishing the pest, none the less they can be seen. A magnifying glass or low power microscope helps to identify the yellow, white, two spotted, brown, or red mites and their light colored eggs.

CONTROL: has a logical progression. First make sure all preventative measures have been taken. NOTE: The spider mite thrives in a dry, 70-80° F climate. It can reproduce in five days if the temperature is above 80° In order to create a hostile environment for mites, lower the temperature to 60° and spray the plants with a jet of water, making sure to spray under leaves. This will literally blast them off the leaves as well as increase humidity. Their reproductive cycle will be slowed and you will have a chance to kill them before they do much damage. If the leaves have been over 50% damaged, remove and throw away, making sure bugs and eggs do not reenter the garden. If mites have attacked only one or two plants, isolate the infected plants and treat them separately. Now that there is a hostile environment and leaves over 50% infected have been removed, the horticulturist may select one or all of the following control methods:

Manual removal: Smash all mites in sight between the thumb and index finger or wash leaves individually with two sponges. Make sure not to infect other plants with filthy hands or sponges. This method is best for just a few mites. It takes forever.

Homemade sprays work very well when there is not yet an infestation of mites. If these sprays have not eradicated the mites after 4-5 applications, switch to another, stronger spray, like Pyrethrum, Safer Insecticidal Soap.

Safer's Insecticidal Soap is a wonderful product and controls mites. Usually two or three heavy applications at 5-10 day intervals will do the trick.

Pyrethrum (aerosol) is the best natural miticide! Apply 2-3 applications at 5-10 day intervals.

Predatory spider mites work very well. There are many things to consider when using the predators. First and foremost, the predators can eat only so many mites a day. The average predator can eat 20 eggs or 5 adults daily. This gives you an idea of how fast they can really control the spider mites, which is their only source of food. As soon as the predators source of food is gone, they die of starvation. A general dosage of 20 predators per plant is a good place to start. You might even want to throw in an few more for good measure. The spider mites have a difficult time traveling from plant to plant, so setting them out on each plant is necessary. In maintaining the predators, the most important factors are temperature and humidity. Both must be at the proper level to give the predators the best possible chance. There are two kinds of predators that are commonly used indoors: amblyseius californicus and phytoseiulus longipes.

When spider mites have infested a garden, the predatory mites can not eat them fast enough to solve the problem. Predatory mites work best when there are only a few spider mites. The predators are introduced as soon as spider mites are seen, and released every month thereafter. This gives predators a chance to keep up with mites. Getting started with predatory mites will cost about $30. Before releasing predators, rinse all plants thoroughly to ensure all toxic spray residues from insecticides and fungicides are gone.

Pyrethrum the best control for spider mite extermination. Spider mites should be gone after 2 or 3 applications, at 5-10 day intervals, providing sanitary, preventative conditions are maintained. The first application will get most of the adults and many eggs. Eggs hatch in 5-10 days. The second spraying will kill the newly hatched eggs and the remaining adults. The third application will finish off any survivors.

Whiteflies

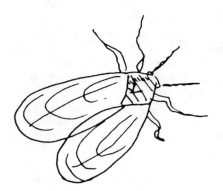

Whiteflies like mites, may cause white speckles (stipples) on the tops of leaves and hide underneath. The easiest way to check for the little buggers is to grab a limb and shake it. If there are any white flies, they will fly from under leaves. Whiteflies look like a small, white moth about one millimeter long. Most whiteflies have wings but some do not. They usually appear near the top of the weakest plant first. They will move downward on the plant or fly off to infest another plant.

CONTROL: Take all preventative measures. Whiteflies are very difficult to remove manually; they fly faster than the hand is able to squish them. Adults are attracted to the color yellow. To build a whitefly trap similar to flypaper, cover a bright yellow object with a sticky substance. Place the traps on the tops of the pots among the marijuana. The traps work very well, but are a mess to clean.

Whiteflies are easily eradicated with natural sprays. Before spraying, remove any leaves that have been over 50% damaged and cure with heat or burn infested foliage.

Homemade sprays applied at 5-10 day intervals work well.

Safer's Insecticidal Soap applied at 5-10 day intervals.

Pyrethrum (aerosol) applied at 5-10 day intervals does it.

The parasitic wasps *encarisa formosa* are the most effective whitefly predator. The small wasps only attack whiteflies, they do not sting people! As with all predators, all toxic sprays must be washed completely off before their introduction. Since the *encarisa formosa* is a parasite, about 1/2-inch long, much smaller than the white fly, it takes them much longer to control or even keep the whitefly population in check. Once the parasite affixes to the whitefly, death is slow. The parasite feeds for some time on the host insect, then hatches its eggs inside its victims body cavity. If you use them, set them out at the rate of 2 or more parasites per plant, as soon as the first whitefly is detected. Repeat every two to four weeks throughout the life of the plants.

Aphid:

Aphids are most common indoors when they are plentiful outdoors. About the size of a pin head, aphids are easily spotted with the naked eye. This insect may be green, yellow, black or even pink, and be with or without wings. Aphids excrete a sticky honeydew and prefer to attack weak plants. The growing tips or buds are attacked first, but aphids love to hide on the leave's undersides.

An infestation of aphids can devastate a garden in a matter of days!

CONTROL: Even though aphids may have wings, manual removal is easy and works well to kill them. They do not fly as well as white flies. Aphids bite into the plant, sucking out life giving juices. When affixed to foliage, aphids are unable to move and easy to squish.

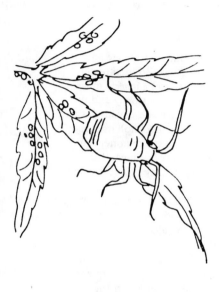

Homemade and Safer's sprays are very effective. Apply 2 or 3 times at 5-10 day intervals, after manually removing as many aphids as possible.

Pyrethrum (aerosol) applied 2-3 times at 5-10 day intervals does it.

Lacewings are the most effective available predators for aphids. Release 1 to 20 lacewings per plant, depending on infestation level, as soon as aphids appear. Repeat every month. If possible, buy adult lacewings rather than larvae, which take some time to hatch and mature into adult aphid exterminators.

Lady bugs also work very well to exterminate aphids. Adults are easily obtained at many retail nurseries during the summer months. The only drawback to lady bugs is their attraction to the HID lamp. Release about 50 lady bugs per plant. About half of them will go directly for the HID, hit the hot bulb and buzz Within 1 or 2 weeks all the lady bugs will fall victim to the lamp, requiring frequent replenishment.

Thrips

Thrips are not common indoors. These tiny, winged, fast moving little critters rasp on the leaves and buds, then suck out the juices for food. They tend to feed inside flower buds or wrap up and distort leaves. Thrips are hard to see but not hard to spot. Upon careful inspection, thrips appear as a herd of specks thundering across foliage.

CONTROL: Preventative maintenance. Manual removal works OK if only a few thrips are present, but they are hard to catch.

Homemade sprays are very effective. Apply 2-4 times at 5-10 day intervals.

Safer's Insecticidal Soap is very effective. Apply at 5-10 day intervals.

Pyrethrum (aerosol) applied at 5-10 day intervals does it.

Thrips have no readily available natural predators.

Mealy Bugs

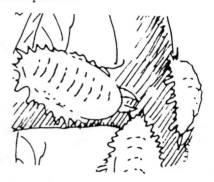

Mealy Bugs are somewhat common. These 2-7 millimeter, oblong, waxy white insects move very little, mature slowly and live in colonies that are usually located at stem joints. Like aphids, mealy bugs excrete a sticky honeydew. Mealy bugs are fairly easy to control, since they reproduce and move slowly.

CONTROL: Preventative maintenance. Manual removal works very well for small populations. Pry them off by getting a fingernail underneath or wet a Q-tip with rubbing alcohol to wash them off.

Homemade sprays work OK especially if they contain a lot of rubbing alcohol. Apply 2-3 times at 5-10 day intervals.

Safer's Insecticidal Soap applied at 5-10 day intervals works well.

The lady beetle and the green lacewing are effective natural predators. Both work very efficiently and have no trouble eating mealy bugs faster than they can reproduce. If using these predators, manually remove all visible mealy bugs; release 5-10 predators per plant, depending on need, as soon as the mealy bugs are noticed. Repeat releases at 2 week intervals. Within a month, there should be a noticeable reduction in mealy bug population.

Scale

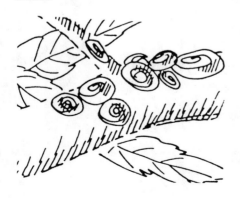

Scale is uncommon on marijuana indoors. Scale looks and acts similar to mealy bugs, but is usually more round than oblong. Scale may be white, yellow, brown, gray or black. Their hard protective shell is 2-4 millimeters across and they rarely or never move. Check for them around stem joints, where they live in colonies. Scale sometimes excretes a sticky honeydew.

CONTROL: Preventative maintenance. Manual removal may be tedious, but is very effective. Wet a Q-tip in rubbing alcohol and wash scale away. A small knife, fingernails or tweezers may also be necessary to scrape and pluck the tightly affixed scale from the plants.

Homemade sprays work well if they contain a lot of rubbing alcohol.

Safer's Insecticidal Soap works well for scale control. Apply at 10 day intervals.

Pyrethrum (aerosol) applied 2-3 times at 5-10 day intervals does it.

Nature holds many natural scale predators, but to date there are no readily available commercial predators.

Bees & Wasps

Bees and wasps - may become a nuisance. They are not harmful to *cannabis*, but hurt like hell when they sting. They sneak into the grow room through vents or cracks, in search of flowering plants, a valuable commodity to bees and wasps in the middle of winter! If they become a problem, manual removal is out of the question! A circulation fan in the room is the best form of preventative maintenance. The artificial wind will impair their flight, causing them to seek a more hospitable garden. There are many aerosol sprays that work well to kill bees and wasps. Sevin, found at the nursery, in either liquid or wettable powder, works as well as aerosol sprays and costs less. Wasp traps are also available and work well. No pest strips do a fair job of eradication. Sweet fly paper is also a viable alternative. Bees and wasps are attracted to the HID lamp. Many will fall victim to its outer envelope....Buzz.. .POP!

Fruit flies and gnats can become a problem. They do no harm to the indoor crop, but are a nuisance to be around. In a few days, they will fall victim to the lamp. If you are not the patient type and the chore of cleaning up bug bodies is not appealing, just about any indoor bug spray in the aerosol form will get rid of them. One friend used 1 cup of Wisk per gallon of water to kill all the larvae in the soil.

The worst case of gnats that I've seen was a bunch that hatched just before the harvest was taken. The gnats flew around the room, landing on the resinous buds. They would stick to the resin coated buds just like flypaper! It was virtually impossible to remove the little gnats. They tasted badly and went snap-crackle-pouf when smoked!

FUNGUS

Fungus is a very primitive plant In fact it is so primitive that it does not produce chlorophyll, the substance giving higher plants their green color. Fungus reproduces by spreading tiny microscopic spores rather than seeds. Many fungi spores are present in the air at all times. With proper conditions, these spores will settle, take hold and start rowing. I know of several cases where entire crops have been wiped out in a matter of days! One of these grow rooms was close to a swamp that is filled with fungus spores. The grower decided to move after four consecutive crops were wiped out by fungus from the swamp. Unsterile, soggy soil, coupled with humid, stagnant air provides the environment most fungi need to thrive. Although there are many different types of fungi, they are usually treated by the same methods.

PREVENTION

Prevention is the first step and the true key to fungus control. In "Setting up the Grow Room", I recommended you remove anything that might attract fungus or harbor mold, such as cloth curtains or clothes. Make sure the advice is followed as part of a preventative program. If the room is carpeted, make sure to cover it with a white plastic (visqueen). If mold should surface on the walls, spray it heavily with the fungicide used in the garden, wash down the wall with Pinesol (made from natural pine oil) or paint damp, fungus covered walls with whitewash. Get all of the mold off when it is washed down. Repeat applications if the mold persists.

The basic ingredients to mold and fungi control are cleanliness and climate control. All the clean, well ventilated grow rooms I have visited had little or no problem with fungi. All of the dingy, ill kept gardens had fungi problems and yield a sickly, below average harvest. If the garden is in a basement, the use of a flat white paint with a fungus inhibiting agent is essential. One garden was literally carpeted with fungi. The walls were whitewashed and lime was spread on the earth floor. The vent fan was cranked up and the room kept clean. There has been no trouble with mold in over a year!

Leafspot is easily prevented.

There are many ways to lower humidity. Ventilation is the least expensive, the easiest and most often used. Remember, one of the by-products of combustion CO_2 generators is water vapor. Dehumidifiers work exceptionally well, offering exacting humidity control. They are not very practical for the average grower to buy, but many rental stores rent them by the month for about $30. Wood, coal, gas, and electric heat all work well to dehumidify the air. Many times, the grow room will have a central heating vent. This vent may be opened to provide additional heat and lower humidity.

CONTROL

Fungus is prevented by controlling all the factors contributing to its growth. If prevention fails and fungus appears, the horticulturist may elect to take preventive measures, remove dead leaves and leaf parts and alter soil, moisture and air conditions, to prevent fungus from spreading. These methods work well in gardens that have only a few signs of fungus. Another method of treating fungus, is to isolate the infected plant and treat it separately. Fungus can spread like wildfire. If it gets a good start, take all preventative measures, as well as spraying the entire garden with a fungicide. Spraying will be necessary if the fungus gets a good start and appears to be spreading, even though preventative measures have been taken.

LOGICAL PROGRESSION OF FUNGUS CONTROL

1. *Prevention*
   a. *cleanliness*

   b. *low humidity*

   c. *ventilation*

2. *Removal*

3. *Copper, lime sulfur sprays*

Damping-off

Damping-off is a fungus condition in the soil that rots the newly sprouted seedlings and occasionally attacks rooting clones at the soil line. The stem will weaken, then grow dark at the soil line and finally fluid circulation will be cut, killing the seedling or clone. Damping-off is normally caused by: (1) fungus already present in an unsterile rooting medium, (2) overwatering, maintaining soggy soil, or (3) excessive humidity.

Prevent all three conditions. Use fresh, sterile soil or soilless mix and clean pots. This will guard against harmful fungus in the soil. Careful daily scrutiny of soil will insure the proper amount of moisture is available to seeds or clones. Many growers prefer to start seeds and root cuttings in fast draining, sterile, coarse sand, fine vermiculite or my favorite, root cubes.

Damping-off

Using these mediums makes it almost impossible to overwater. Do not place a humidity tent over sprouted seedlings. A tent can lead to excessive humidity and damping-off. Clones are much less susceptible to damping-off and love a humidity tent to promote rooting. (See: Chapter 4, for seed and clone water requirements).

Control damping-off in its early stages by watering with a fungicide like Captan or a mild bleach solution (2-5 drops per gallon). Damping-off usually progresses rapidly and kills the young seedling in a matter of days. Over- watering is the biggest cause of damping-off and the key to prevention.

Soil Borne Fungus

Mushrooms grow in soil that harbors soil born fungus.

Soil born fungus attacks the root system. It is usually seen on the soil surface first, then growing around the roots in the soil. Soil born fungus normally starts from using an unsterile planting medium and/or improper drainage. Bad drainage keeps roots too wet, making them susceptible to fungus and rot.

To prevent this type of fungus, a sterile planting medium and good drainage are essential. As explained in Chapter 3, good drainage is easily attained by having adequate drain holes and the proper soil texture.

Control soil born fungus by applying Captan or a biodegradable soap solution to the soil. Three or four applications are usually necessary. Mix the fungicides as per directions and apply in a water solution. Make sure the soil is not overwatered and there is adequate drainage.

Foliar Fungus

Leaf and stem fungus including leaf spot attack foliage. They appear as dark spots or splotches just about anywhere on the foliage. These types of fungus are usually caused by: (1) using cold water when misting plants and fungus like spots are formed as a result of temperature stress (See: "About Spraying". The spots could develop into a fungus. (2) excessive humidity (over 60%).

Leaf at right has leaf spot that turned into leaf fungus.

Prevention of these types of fungi attacks is easy. Spray with tepid water, have a hygrometer to measure humidity, and most important, employ a vent fan to dissipate the excess moisture. Vast quantities of water are applied to actively growing plants. They transpire the water back into the air. If this moist air is allowed to remain in the tiny grow room, it will stifle growth. A vent fan will remove it rapidly. A hygrometer may be purchased for less than $10 at some nurseries and most HID stores. When humidity goes over 60%, many fungi have a chance of getting started. The HID lamp and ballast emit a dry heat. This heat usually along with a vent fan provide enough humidity control to prevent fungus in an enclosed grow room. During the winter or cooler months, dry heat from the HID system may maintain low humidity and 72° temperatures while turned on. At night, when the HID is off, the temperature will drop, causing moisture condensation and raising humidity. Check the humidity, both day and night, to see if there is a substantial variation in day and night humidity. If the humidity registers above 60%, and fungus is a problem, use turn the vent fan on at night. This will vent off all the moist air. If the temperature is a problem, use dry heat to raise the night time temperature to 5-10° below the daytime temperature. This will keep humidity more constant.

Control foliar fungus by removing all seriously damaged foliage, take all preventative measures, then spray with one of the recommended fungicides 3-4 times at 3-5 day intervals.

Blight

The term blight describes many plant diseases. Signs of blight include dark blotches on foliage, slow growth sudden wilting and plant death. Most blights spread quickly through large areas of plants. Avoid blights by maintaining the proper nutrient balance in the soil and supply good .drainage

Mold

Gray mold (botrytis) is a form of fungus that is familiar to all of us. It is grayish, whitish to bluish green in color, with a hair-like appearance. The mold can appear on just about anything in the garden from the walls to the soil surface.

Gray mold spores are always in the air. They can be present even in the cleanest of rooms. But, as long as the proper environment is maintained, they will not grow and reproduce. Gray mold occurs in two stages: non-germinated spores that live on foliage, and germinated spores that grow and penetrate foliage tissue where the spores remain in a latent, inactive form until conditions promote disease outbreak. Gray mold loves to enter plant wounds and attack the weak plants. Spores seldom invade healthy growing tissue.

Plants can have botrytis and have no outward sign at all. It is difficult to tell where the disease came from if there are new plants continually being introduced into the garden. Yellowing of foliage defoliation brown, soft areas on dark-colored leaves. Spots will soon develop into the characteristic fuzzy gray mold during the reproductive stage when spores are released into the air.

Prevent mold by lowering humidity, increasing ventilation and keeping the grow room clean!!

Bud mold is a crippling fungus that attacks ripe buds. It looks like a fast growing mold or rapidly rotting portion of the bud. This condition could spread through the entire garden in a matter of days.

Prevent (bud) mold with low humidity, (50% or less) ample air circulation and especially ventilation. Humid geographic areas with an outside humidity over 70% present the biggest problem to fungus abatement. Bud mold may be triggered when dead foliage rots. When removing yellow leaves between dense buds, pluck the entire leaf so no foliage is left to rot. See box in photo below.

Control mold on the soil or walls by removing it manually. Just use Pinesol in a heavy concentration and . ,-, wash mold from walls or wherever it is growing. Do not use harsh Pinesol on plants. You must use a vegetable fungicide on plants. This kind of, fungus - mold - does best when the grow room is kept dirty and old leaves are allowed to pile up. Keep the garden clean and wash it down with Pinesol between crops if mold is a problem.

If buds show signs of mold, remove the infected bud immediately. Get all of the bud mold by removing 2-4 inches below the mold. Keep the bud from contaminating the other buds and wash your tools after removing it to keep the bud from contaminating the other tops. There is no chemical or spray that is effective against bud Remove leaf stem (petiole) blight, only climate control, to prevent bud mold. cleanliness and harvest.

Remove leaf stem (petiole) to prevent bud mold.

Viruses

Viruses are still a mystery. They act like living organisms in some instances and nonliving chemicals in other cases. We do know that viruses are spread by insect, minute plant, animal, and human vectors. Infected tools often carry viruses from one plant to another.

Typical symptoms of viral infection are sickly growth and low yields of flowers and fruits. In some cases, viral diseases can cause sudden wilt and death.

ABOUT SPRAYING

Phytotoxicity is the injury to plants. It can be caused by sprays. Symptoms include burned leaves, slow growth or sudden wilt. If you are worried about a spray damaging foliage, spray a small portion of the garden and wait a few days to see if the plants wilt or look sick.

Use chemical sprays with extreme care if at all in enclosed areas they are more concentrated indoors than outdoors in the open air. Always wear a mask.

Sprays are beneficial if not overdone. Every time a plant is sprayed with a fungicide or insecticide, the stomata are clogged and growth slows. Rinsing off spray helps, but if sprays are used over and over, the garden will be slow-growing.

Use a respirator or face mask when spraying, especially if using an aerosol/fogger. Spray residues remain very concentrated in the enclosed grow room. This makes it easy for even the safest spray to be irritating if inhaled for long.

A large 1-2 gallon sprayer costs from $15-30 and works well for small and large gardens. All nurseries and many department stores carry these sprayers. Watch for spring and fall sales to get the best deal. The sprayers have an application wand and nozzle attached to a flexible hose, which makes it very easy to spray under leaves, the most important part! Garden sprayers are also made of heavy duty materials and can take frequent use. I like plastic rather than galvanized steel because it does not corrode or rust. Brass nozzle parts with rubber gaskets are easily be cleaned with a paper clip. Just pump the sprayer up, and application is easy.

Electric foggers work well for large jobs. The foggers have an electric blower. The spray is metered out the nozzle with a good deal of pressure. The result is a fine, penetrating fog of spray. The fogger works best with Safer's Insecticidal Soap and various fungicides. Electric foggers are used to mist orchids and are usually available through orchid suppliers.

One serious horticulturist uses a jackrabbit pump as a sprayer. The suction hose is placed in the nutrient solution, insecticide, etc. and the spray is applied with a pumping motion. The jackrabbit pump is used mainly for foliar feeding. This horticulturist notes that with daily, early morning foliar feeding, little or no problem with fungus is realized. The pump works exceptionally well for heavy organic fertilizers.

Another favorite is a small, one or two quart spray bottle. A Windex bottle is OK, but will probably clog up or break in a couple of weeks. The best bottle is found at a nursery. It will have a removable nozzle that may easily be taken apart and thoroughly cleaned if it clogs up. Homemade organic teas clog the most. A straight pin should be handy to punch out the nozzle hole. Get a heavy duty spray bottle that can take a lot of use. It takes about 3A qt. of spray to cover a 10 x 10-foot garden. That is a lot of pumping on a very small plastic spray bottle!

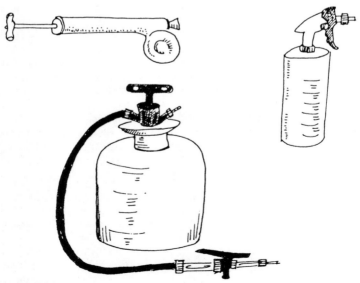

Various sprayers.

Always wash bottle and pump thoroughly before and after each use. Using the same bottle for fertilizers and insecticides is OK. However, for best results: do not mix fertilizers and insecticides or fungicides together when applying. Mixing chemicals will lessen their effectiveness. There could also be a chance the two chemicals are incompatible and one inhibits the others effects.

Mix pesticides and fungicides just before using. Fertilizer solutions may be mixed and used for several months afterward. When finished spraying, empty the excess spray into the toilet. Do not use the same mixed spray another day. It will be diluted and imbalanced. Spray residues have a tendency to build up in a partially clean bottle. Fresh water is the only liquid to leave in the spray bottle overnight.

Always spray early in the day. The moist spray needs a chance to be absorbed and dry out. If sprayed just a few hours before nightfall, moisture left overnight on the leaves could cause fungus or water spots.

Always use tepid or room temperature water. Water too hot or cold shocks the plants and will cause water spots on leaves. Plants are able to absorb and process tepid water more rapidly.

Before spraying fungicides and pesticides, make sure the plants are well watered. With more water in the system, a plant suffers less shock from the killing spray. When foliar feeding the garden with a soluble fertilizer, just the opposite is true. Plants will absorb the soluble nutrients more rapidly when there is less moisture in the plant and soil. This is not a reason to dry plants out!

When mixing, follow directions to the letter, and read entire label before using. Mix wettable powders and soluble crystals in a little hot water to make sure they get dissolved before adding the balance of the tepid water.

Novice gardeners, that have never sprayed before, may want to talk it over with their nurseryperson before starting. Tell him you have spider mites on the dieffenbachia.

Always spray the entire plant, both sides of the leaves, stems, soil and pot. When spraying heavily, be careful with new tender growing shoots, they are easily burned by harsh sprays.

Have an accurate measuring cup and spoon that are only used for the garden. Keep them clean. If the spray is mixed too heavy (easy to do when mixing small amounts) it will not kill any more bugs any deader; it will burn plants. Extreme precision should be exercised when mixing small quantities. A few drops could make the spray too potent and burn tender plants.

It is best to spray only in the vegetative growth stage so sprays totally break-down before harvest. Do not spray with toxic chemicals during the last two weeks prior to harvest. This will ensure there are no insecticides on the plants. Spraying could promote mold once buds form and growth becomes dense. The moisture is trapped in the dense foliage of the flower cluster. If this water is allowed to remain in the flower top a day or longer, mold will find a new home.

Always rinse plants with tepid water one or two days after spraying. The water needs to actually drip from the leaves to have a cleansing effect. Misting plants heavily, washes away all the stomata clogging film and residue left from sprays. Fertilizer left on leaves is dissolved and absorbed by the rinse. Make sure both sides of the leaves are thoroughly rinsed. Many fungicides leave a heavy, powdery film and could require 2 or 3 rinsing.

Always give plants several days of rinsing with a fresh water spray a week before harvesting.

Every time a plant is sprayed with a fungicide, insecticide, or soap, it clogs the stomata and growth slows. Rinsing off spray helps, but if sprays are used over and over, the garden will be slow growing.

In choosing an insecticide or fungicide, use only contact sprays that may be used on edible fruits and vegetables. Read the entire label to find the toxic or active life of the chemical. Wait a few more days than the label recommends and thoroughly wash any foliage before ingesting it. Toxic life is many times longer indoors because sunlight breaks down many chemicals.

Consider using a respirator when spraying, especially if using an aerosol/fogger. In the enclosed grow room, the fumes and contents of a spray remain very concentrated. This makes it easy for even the safest spray to be irritating if inhaled for long.

CAUTION: Raise HID lamp out of the way, so mist from spray will not touch the bulb. Temperature stress, resulting from the relatively cold water hitting the hot bulb, may cause it to shatter. This could not only scare the hell out of you, it could burn eyes and skin. If the bulb breaks, TURN OFF SYSTEM IMMEDIATELY - UNPLUG!

Section II

Stages of Growth

Typically, a marijuana plant goes through three separate stages of growth. The seedling stage lasts about a month. During this stage, the seed germinates or sprouts, establishes a root system, and grows a stem and a few leaves. During vegetative growth, the plant produces much bushy green growth as well as a supporting root system. This stage may last from two months to over a year. The last stage of the life cycle comes when flowers form. If the flowers are pollinated, seeds will form.

Indoors, with artificial light, the photoperiod (the daylight to dark ratio) may be controlled at will. The vegetative stage may be maintained with 18 hour days and flowering induced with the 12 hour days and 12 hours of uninterrupted dark nights.

CHAPTER Eight THE SEED & SEEDLING

Cannabis Sativa Cannabis Indica

Cannabis indica produces flower tops that are twice as heavy as the cannabis sativa.

Indica leaf   Sativa leaf

The seed contains all the genetic characteristics of a plant. A seed is the result of sexual propagation, having genes from both male and female parents. An exception to this rule is found in hermaphrodite plants that bear both male and female flowers. The genes within a seed dictate the plant's size, disease and pest resistance, root, stem, leaf and flower production, yield, cannabanoid levels and many other variable growth traits. *The genetic make up of a seed is the single most important factor dictating how well the plan t will grow under HID lamps and levels of THC it will produce.*

Since genetic make up largely determines THC levels, it makes sense to choose seeds from the most potent marijuana you can find. Most growers believe the seed, strain or variety, containing the most favorable genes for indoor HID cultivation is from various strains of *cannabis indica*. *Cannabis indica* grows squat and bushy with a condensed root system, stout stems, broad leaves and dense flowers. *Indica* is usually very resistant to bugs and somewhat resistant to fungus. It matures rapidly and produces high levels of THC under HID lamps. In fact, many people prefer indoor smoke to outdoor! The ideal *cannabis indica* seed comes from plants that have been grown under HID systems and selectively bred for many generations. When grown indoors for generations, plants have time to acclimate and grow even stronger in the indoor climate they have grown accustomed to. The famous Skunk Weed, Kush and Afghani are examples of *cannabis indica*. The *cannabis sativa* family includes marijuana originating in Thailand, Hawaii, Columbia, Mexico, etc. Some growers prefer to cultivate these varieties, with Thai and Hawaiian at the top of the list. The *sativa* family generally grows tall and leggy, producing sprawling roots, long stems, narrow leaves, sparse flowers, and an overall lower yield per square foot of space and grow time than indoor *indica*. The THC production is generally high, but weight of flower tops is lower. *Sativa* grows much better outdoors than it does indoors.

A simple picture of a seed reveals an embryo, containing the genes and a supply of food, wrapped in a protective outer coating. Mature seeds are hard, dark brown or spotted in color and will have the highest rate of germination. Soft, pale or green seeds are usually immature. These seeds should be avoided. They do not germinate as well and could produce a sickly plant. Fresh, dry, mature seeds sprout quickly, while older (one year or more) seeds may take longer to sprout.

Cannabis seeds need only water, heat and air to germinate. They sprout without light in a wide range of temperatures. Seeds, properly watered, will germinate in 2-7 days, in temperatures from 70-90° F. The warmer it is, the faster germination takes place. Germination temperatures above 90° F are not advised. When the seed germinates, the outside protective shell splits, and a tiny, white sprout pops out. This sprout is the tap root. The seed leaves emerge from within the shell as they push upward in search of light.

There are two popular ways to germinate seeds. (1) In a warm room (70-90° F) place seeds in a moist paper towel or cheesecloth, making sure they are in darkness. Water the cloth daily, keeping it moist, letting excess water drain away freely. The cloth will retain enough moisture to germinate the seed in a few days. The seed contains an adequate food supply for germination, but watering with a mild mix of liquid fertilizer or Up-Start will hasten growth. If living in a humid climate, water with a mild bleach or fungicide solution (2-5 drops per gallon) to prevent fungus. Once the seeds have sprouted, and the white sprout is visible, plant them. Take care not to expose the tender rootlet to prolonged, intense light or wind. Plant the germinated seed in fine planting medium with the white sprout tip (the root) pointing down.

The second popular planting and germination method is to sow the seed in a shallow planter, one to five gallon pot, peat pellet or rooting cube. The planting medium is then maintained evenly moist. If the seedling is to be transplanted from the shallow planter, use a spoon to contain the root ball. Peat pellets or root cubes may be transplanted in 2-3 weeks or when the roots show through the sides. Do not forget to fertilize them if they begin to yellow.

Some friends place the seeds in a couple of nursery flats and place them in the drawer of their heated water bed. As soon as the seeds sprout, they are placed on top of the waterbed for a few more days to take advantage of the bottom heat. Then they are placed into the grow room.

A moisture tent may be constructed over the seedling container. Just put a baggie or cellophane over the seeded soil. This will maintain high humidity and temperature. Usually, the seeds only need one initial watering when this method is used. Remove the bag as soon as the first sprout appears. Leaving it on will lead to damping-off or other fungi.

It is not necessary, but the planted seeds may be placed under the HID lamp while germinating. The lamp will add dry heat, but the soil will require more watering. Placing heat tape under or in soil will expedite germination, without drying the soil out as fast.

The biggest problem most people have with germinating seeds is over- watering. The soil is to be uniformly moist. A shallow flat or planter with a heat pad underneath may require daily watering, while a deep, one gallon pot will need watering every 2 or 3 days. When the surface is dry (1/2-inch deep) it is time to water. Remember there are few roots to absorb the water early in life and they are very delicate.

It is a good idea to plant many times the number of seeds that are expected to mature to harvest. This is the best way to ensure success and a full grow room. When plants are small, they take up very little room. The HID lamp-uses the same amount of electricity to grow 10 small plants as it does to grow 100. As the plants mature, the small and sick may easily be weeded out. The strong and healthy plants may be transplanted to larger containers, traded or given to friends! A female clone of premium smoke takes on a new value to indoor growers. Just one of these females will start an entire grow room!

When the seed sprouts, the first leaves that appear are called seed or seedling leaves. The seed leaves will then spread out as the stem elongates. Within a few days, the first true leaves will appear. The plant is now in the seedling stage, that will last about three more weeks. During this time, a root system grows rapidly and green growth is slow. Water is critical at this point of development. The new root system is very small and requires small but constant supply of water. Too much water will drown the roots and may cause root rot or damping-off. Lack of water will cause the infant root system to dry up. As the seedlings mature, some will grow faster, stronger and appear generally more healthy. Others will sprout slowly, be weak and leggy. If many seeds were planted, the sick and weak can be thinned out and the strong kept. This thinning process should take place around the third to fifth week of growth. Seedlings may also be transplanted easily without any damage.

CHAPTER NINE VEGETATIVE GROWTH

After the seedling is established, it enters the vegetative growth stage. When chlorophyll production is in full swing, the plant will produce as much vegetative or green, leafy growth as light CO_2, nutrients and water will permit. Properly maintained, marijuana will grow from 1/2-2 inches per day. If the plant is stunted now, it could take weeks to resume normal growth. A strong, unrestricted root system is essential to supply much needed water and nutrients. UNRESTRICTED VEGETATIVE GROWTH IS THE KEY TO A HEALTHY HARVEST. During vegetative growth, the plant's nutrient and water intake changes. Transpiration is carried on at a more rapid rate, requiring more water. High levels of N are needed; P and K are used at much faster rates. The larger a plant gets, the faster the soil will dry out. A larger root system is able to take in more water and nutrients. Strong lateral branches are produced. They will soon be filled with flower buds. The more vegetative growth, the more flowers and weight at harvest.

Eighteen hours of halide light is conducive to vegetative growth, after that a point of diminishing returns is reached and the light losses effectiveness. Since most seed is of uncertain origin, the best way to promote maximum vegetative growth is to have the maximum amount of daylight! Marijuana will remain in the vegetative growth stage more than a year (theoretically forever) as long as the 18 hour photoperiod is maintained.

This offers the indoor horticulturist incredible opportunities; once a plant's sex is determined, it may become a Mother plant for a multitude of clones. Or harvested plants may be forced back into rejuvenation. (See: "Second Crops".)

During the vegetative stage, transplanting, pruning, bending, and cloning are normally practiced and are explained next.

CLONING & the MOTHER PLANT

Cloning is the most efficient and productive means of *cannabis* propagation known today. Technically, cloning is taking one cell of a plant and promoting its growth into a plant. For the purpose of discussion in this book cloning is any type of asexual propagation. Marijuana may be reproduced or propagated sexually or asexually. Seeds are the product of sexual propagation; clones are the result of asexual or vegetative propagation. Cloning is: simply cutting some growing branch tips and rooting them. Many people have taken cuttings or slips from a houseplant such a philodendron, ivy or coleus, and rooted them in water or sand. The rooted cutting is then placed in rich potting soil.

This young parent became the mother of many a fine female.

Once the sex of a plant is known (See: "Cloning for Sex") and it is a female at least two months old, you are ready to practice the simple, yet incredibly productive art of cloning. Any female may be used for sinsemilla cloning stock, no matter how old she is or if she is a clone of a clone. One grower has taken clones of clones over 20 times! That is, clones (C-1) were taken from the original female grown from seed. These clones were grown in the vegetative stage, then clones (C-2) were taken from the first clones (C-1). Blooming was induced in (C-1) two weeks later and (C-2) were grown in the vegetative stage. Then, clones (C-3) were taken from the second clones (C-2). This same growing technique is still going on with clones of clones well past (C-20) and there has been no apparent breakdown in the potency or the vigor of the clones!

Identical clones will vary if they are grown in different climates. If the climate is poor for growth, the plant will develop poorly and be stunted. If the grow room is well cared for and has a perfect climate, strong healthy plants will be harvested.

Clones are so popular among indoor growers that good indoor seeds are sometimes difficult to acquire. But, with clones, who needs seeds? Growers are trading clones instead of seeds!

Vegetative propagation yields an exact genetic replica of the Mother Plant. A female plant will reproduce 100% females all exactly like the Mother. Occasionally, a male flower will appear on a clone of a known female. Or, a plant will have mutated or different growth than other clones from the same plant.

These clones will all have the characteristics of the favorite Mother. Fast, squat, bushy growth is at the same rate and lends itself to easy maintenance. Under HID's, clones grow thick, heavy buds, high in THC.

Clones from the same plant grow into identical adults if grown in the exact same environment. The same clones grown in different grow rooms will look like different plants. A broad leafed *indica* clone that was stressed, might grow very narrow leaves.

A one month old clone from a six month old Mother is not really one month old, but six months old, just like the Mother. A six month old plant produces more THC than a one month old plant. By cloning, the horticulturist is planting a THC potent plant that will continue to grow in potency at a rapid rate. The month old, rooted clone thinks it is six months old and can be induced into flowering easily or as soon as desired. The rooted clones are grown two weeks to three months, or until they are 1-4 feet tall, before flowering is induced.

One of the differences that is very apparent between clones and plants grown from seed is their leaf size. The young seedlings have thick, broad leaves, while the mature clones have the leaves of a 4-8 month old plant.

HID lamps are expensive to operate. Cloning reduces the time it takes for a crop to mature from 5-10 months (as when seeds are planted) to 2-5 months, thus saving money on electricity. One grower, using a Living Systems Hydroponic set-up, takes one clone a day and harvests one plant daily. He has 120 plants and they are on a 90 day schedule. That is, 90 days elapse from the time the clone is cut from the Mother plant until the day it is harvested.

Productive growers use two rooms. A vegetative room with a 1000 watt halide hanging over clones, Mothers and seedlings, and a larger flowering room with a 100 watt halide and 1000 watt HP sodium lamps. The flowering plants are able to spread out and bud to amazing highs!

Light intensity is much greater, since the clones do not have a chance to get too tall. Remember, the closer the light is to the entire plant and garden, the faster they grow. Lower branches, heavily shaded by upper branches and leaves, will grow slow and spindly.

Because a clone of any age is larger than a plant grown from seed, the root system is small and compact, making clones well suited for containers. By the time the root system is inhibited by the container, it is time for harvest. A 5 or 6 month old plant, grown from seed, is easily pot bound and stunted. This compounds any bug or nutrient disorder and generally makes for unhealthy growth.

The stronger a plant and the faster it grows, the less chance it has of being affected by disease. A spider mite infestation, developed in the 5th or 6th month of a sexually propagated (seed) crop, may have to suffer through many sprayings until the infestation is arrested. The grow room can not be totally cleaned out and fumigated until the plants have completed flowering and been harvested. This could take several months.

All plants may be removed for a couple of days in order to fumigate the room or paint it with antiseptic whitewash. Moving a room full of 6 month old plants in 50 pound containers of soil is hard work. The plants are sick to begin with and moving beats them up. When returned to the grow room, they will take forever to resume normal growth. On the other hand, clones are not in the grow room as long; the infestations have less time to launch an all-out attack or build an immunity to sprays.

Healthy clones, taken from a proven, disease resistant Mothers are the route to a bountiful harvest. A bug infestation, that gets out of hand among small clones, is easily dealt with. The small clones are easily removed with little or no damage and fumigate the grow room.

Experiments are more easily controlled with clones. Since clones are all the same, different stimuli (fertilizer, light, bending, etc.) may be introduced on selected groups of clones and a true comparative analysis may be made.

Cloning also has some negative points. The Mother plant will produce clones just like her, if she is not disease resistant, clones also share this weakness. A bug or fungus infestation left unchecked, could wipe out an entire clone crop.

A single branch of a Mother plant can be cut into several pieces. Each one of them can be rooted acid will turn into a plant just like the female.

In general, *cannabis indica* has consistently demonstrated disease resistance. This is one of the reasons *indica* is so popular among indoor growers. Taking clones from 3-4 different Mothers will help ensure a crop. The wipe out effect is very uncommon in clean grow rooms. It is most common in gardens that have grown several crops and have not been completely cleaned out after each crop. Infestations are also promoted by continued use of an ineffective spray used to kill bugs or fungus.

The only other bad part I have found in cloning is: the more potent growing tips must be cut from the beautiful Mother and rooted rather than smoked.

Cloning is simple and easy. A consistent 100% survival rate may be achieved by following the simple procedures outlined in this book. The Mother plant can be grown from seed or cloned. She should be at least two months old and possess all the desirable characteristics.

Just about any plant can be cloned, regardless of age or growth stage. Clones taken in the vegetative stage root quickly and grow fast. Clones taken from flowering plants root quickly but take about a month to revert back to vegetative growth and they might flower prematurely. Buds are also very susceptible to fungus attack.

Several Mother plants that are always kept in the vegetative stage are a very good source of cloning stock. The Mother always produces strong, healthy clones. Start new Mothers from seed every year. Clones have a better chance of being strong and healthy when Mothers are not stressed. Taking clones of clones works very well. Clones (C-2) are taken from clones (C-1) just before they (C-1) flower. Both methods work well combined with one another.

Cloning is the most traumatic experience marijuana plants ever go through. Clones go through an incredible change when growing branch tips are cut from the Mother plant. Their entire chemistry changes. The stem that once grew leaves, must now grow roots in order to survive. Sprays should be avoided now as they compound cloning stress.

Research has found that plants tend to root much better when the stems have a high carbohydrate and low nitrogen concentration. By leaching the soil with copious quantities of water, nutrients including N, are washed out. Heavy leaching could keep soil too soggy. An alternative to soil leaching would be to leach the leaves themselves by reverse foliar feeding. Just fill the sprayer with clean, tepid water, and mist heavily every morning for a week. This gets the N out of foliage rapidly. The Mother plant's growth slows as the N is used up, and carbohydrates have a chance to accumulate. Carbohydrate content is usually highest in lower, older more mature branches. A rigid branch that will fold over quickly when bent, rather than bend, is a good sign of high carbohydrate content. Older branches low on the plant give the best results. While rooting, clones require a minimum of N and increased levels of P to promote root growth.

There are several products available that stimulate root growth. They are available in a liquid or powder form. Professionals prefer the liquid type (root inducing hormones) for penetration and consistency. The powder types are avoided because they adhere inconsistently to the stem and yield a lower survival rate.

In order for a cutting to grow roots from the stem, it must change from producing stem cells to producing undifferentiated cells to producing root cells.

The rooting hormone promotes the rooting process by stimulating undifferentiated growth. Substances that are known to stimulate this type of growth are: napthalenaecetic acid (NAA), indolebutyric acid (IBA) and 2,4-dichlorophenoxyacetic acid (2,3 DPA). The following products have been used as rooting hormones with successful results. Many of these commercial rooting hormones have one or all of the above synthetic ingredients and a fungicide to help prevent damping off and mold.

1) Dip-N-Grow   5) Rootone - F
2) Woods Rooting Compound   6) Up-Start
3) Hormodin   7) Willow water
4) Hormex   8) Superthrive

NOTE: Some of these products are not recommended for use with edible plants, so read the label carefully before deciding to use a product.

An all natural root inducing substance is willow (tree) water. The substance in all willow trees that promotes rooting is unknown, but repeated experiments have proven that willow water promotes about 20% more roots than plain water. This willow water may be mixed with commercial rooting hormones for phenomenal results.

To make the willow water rooting compound, find any willow tree and remove some of this years branches about 1/8-1/4 inch in diameter. Remove the leaves and cut the branches in lengths of 1 inch each. Place 1 inch willow sticks on end, so a lot of them fit, in a water glass or quart jar. Add one half inch of water to the container and let it soak 24 hours. After soaking, pour off the willow water and use for rooting hormone. Soak the marijuana clones in the willow water for 24 hours, then plant in rooting medium. If using commercial liquid rooting hormone, just substitute the willow water in place of regular water in the mix, and watch the amazing results.

Clones root faster if the soil is a few degrees warmer than normal. The soil heat promotes faster chemical activity, spurring growth. For best results, the rooting clones' soil should be kept at 70-80° F. The clones will transpire less if the air is about 50 cooler than the soil. Misting clones with water is a good way to cool foliage and lower transpiration. This helps the traumatized clones retain moisture that the roots do not yet supply.

 RULE OF THUMB - Clone 5-10 practice clones before making a serious cloning.

CLONING for SEX

With cloning, sex may be determined 100% of the time and the parent plants growth cycle is not altered.

Cloning for sex is easy and fun. Simply take two cuttings from each parent plant in question. Two are taken in the event that one dies. Make sure to label each clone and corresponding parent plant when sexing more than one parent, and use waterproof labels.

When rooting, give clones only 12 hours of HID light. Set clones in a dark closet or place a box over them. The 12 hour photoperiod will induce flowering. Fluorescent Lamps work when necessary, but are not bright enough. Some growers prefer to start clones under a fluorescent for a week or so, then change to the HID to induce flowering. The clone will show its sex within a week or two. Harvest all males or fathers, except those used for breeding and keep females or Mothers. Males may also be cloned and induced to flower when pollen is needed for breeding.

This method works well because the parent plant is allowed to grow continually under the 18 hour daylength. It does not have to flower, then revert back to vegetative growth. This takes time, diminishes harvest and stresses the heck out of the confused parent.

Leave the parent plant under 18 hours of halide light to maintain vegetative growth. Give the clones only 12 hours of HID light. This may be accomplished by placing the clones in a nursery flat or all in the same place after 12 hours has passed, cover them with a cardboard box or place them somewhere in total darkness. Take the cardboard box off after the lamp turns off. Make sure the clones get 12 hours of light and 12 hours of uninterrupted, total darkness every 24 hours.

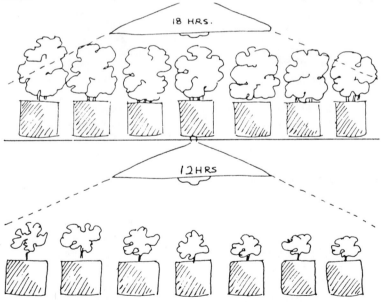

Cloning: Step-by-Step

Step One: Choose a mother plant that is at least two months old and 24 inches tall. Leach the soil daily, with at least one gallon of water per 5 gallons of soil (make sure drainage is good) or wash down leaves (reverse foliar feeding) heavily every morning. Start one week before taking cuttings and leach every morning. This will wash out the nitrogen.

Leaves are trimmed from the stem before the cutting is taken

Step Two: Choose some of the older lower branch tips. With a sharp blade, make a 45 degree cut across firm, healthy 1/8- to 1/4-inch-wide branches and 2 to 8 inches in length. It is very important to keep from smashing the end of the stem when making the cut. Trim off two or three sets of leaves and buds so the stem can fit in the soil. There should be at least two sets of leaves above the soil line and one or two sets of trimmed nodes below the ground. When cutting, make the slice halfway between the sets of nodes. Getting too close to nodes could cause one of the remaining nodes to have mutated growth. Immediately place the cut end in fresh, tepid water. This is a must to keep an air bubble from lodging in the tiny hole in the center of the stem, blocking the transpiration stream. If this hole is blocked, the new cutting will die within 24 hour. Leave the cuttings in the water overnight or no light.

Step Three: If possible, use peat pots or root cubes, because they make maintenance easier and facilitate transplanting. Fill small containers or nursery flats with coarse, washed sand, fine vermiculite, soilless mix or if nothing else is available, use potting soil. Saturate them with tepid water. Use a pencil or chop stick to make a hole in the rooting medium a little larger than the stem. The hole should bottom out at least one half inch from the bottom of the container to allow for root growth.

Step Four: Use a root hormone, Professional nurserypeople prefer a liquid root hormone. Mix it just before using, There will be dilutions for hardwood and softwood cuttings in the mixing instructions. Use the formula for the softwood cuttings. Swirl each cutting in the hormone solution for 10-20 seconds. Place the cuttings in the hole. Pack rooting medium gently around the stem. Powder root hormones require no mixing. Just roll the stem in the powder. When planting, take special care to keep a solid layer of hormone powder around the stem when gently packing soil into place.

Step Five: Lightly water with a mild solution of B_1 or product containing B_1, until the surface is evenly moist. Water as needed.

Step Six: Clones root best with 18 hours (some growers swear that 24 hours is better) of fluorescent light. Use 12 hours of light if cloning to determine sex. If no florescent lamp is available, place the traumatized cuttings 3 to four feet under the halide and shade them with a cloth or screen. The shade will diminish light intensity and prevent excessive shock.

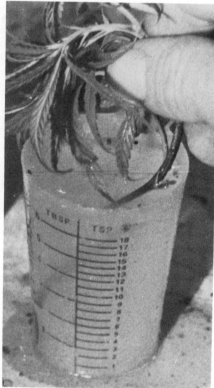

Rooted Clone   *Dipping clone in liquid rooting hormone*

These clones were taken three weeks ago.

Step Seven: Place a tent over rooting clones to keep humidity near 80%. Construct the tent out of baggies, plastic film or glass. Remember to leave a breezeway so the little clones can breathe. An alternative to the humidity tent is to mist the rooting clones with tepid water several times daily. Either method helps retain moisture, since there are no roots to supply the leaves with water.

Step Eight: The humidity tent will maintain the temperature at about 70-80° F. If more heat is needed, just moving the flat up off the cold floor will raise the temperature a few degrees. If this does not raise it enough, place a heat pad, heat tape or incandescent light bulb below rooting cuttings.

Step Nine: Some cuttings may wilt for a few days or the leaves may rot if touching moist soil. Remove rotten leaves. Clones should look normal by the end of the week. If cuttings are badly wilted at the end of a week, they probably won't make it or will be so stunted, they never catch up to the others.

Step Ten: In one to four weeks, the cuttings should be rooted. The tips of leaves will turn yellow, and roots may be seen growing out drain holes, and clones will start vertical growth. To check for root growth in flats or pots, carefully remove a clone to see if it has good root development. Roots will show through the bottom and sides of peat pots and root cubes.

TRANSPLANTING

When plants have outgrown their container, they will need to be transplanted into a larger pot to ensure that the roots have room for continued outward, rapid growth. Inhibiting the root system will stunt plants. Some of the signs are, slow, sickly growth and leggyness. Branches develop with more distance between them on the main stem. In fact, the closest thing I have ever seen to bolting is triggered by root bound plants. The plant will grow straight up. A female maturing in a 4-inch pot could be 4 feet tall and only 6 inches across. It will take forever for them to resume normal growth. This costs the horticulturist money and can really bum out a person! Transplant into the same type of soil, so there is no new soil for the roots to get used to. For clones rooted in vermiculite or sand, just shake away as much of the medium as possible (without damaging roots) before setting the root ball into the new soil. Novice and lazy gardeners, myself included, may want to start seeds or clones in root cubes or peat pots. They are very easy to transplant. Just set the cube or peat pot in the soil.

Next to cloning, transplanting is the most traumatic experience a plant can live through. It requires special attention and manual dexterity. Tiny root hairs are very delicate and may easily be destroyed by light, air or clumsy hands. Roots grow in darkness, where their environment is rigid and secure. When roots are taken out of contact with the soil for long, they dry up and die.

Transplanting should disturb the root system as little as possible. Ortho Up-Start or Vitamin B_1 are recommended to help ease transplant shock. Plants need time to get settled-in and re-establish a solid flow of fluids from the roots through the plant. They will require low levels of N and K, but use large quantities of P. When Up-Start is applied properly and roots are disturbed little, there will be no signs of transplant shock or wilt.

After transplanting, give new transplants filtered or less intense light for a couple of days. If there is a fluorescent lamp handy, place transplants under it for a couple of days before moving them under the HID.

Transplant late in the day so transplants will have all night to recover. The secret to successful transplanting is: manual dexterity, Up-Start and lots of water. Water helps the soil pack around roots and keeps them from drying out. Roots need to be in constant contact with the soil so they can supply water and food to the plant. Transplants will be a little shocked no matter what is done. Think about the plant; it has changed soil and will need to settle-in. During this time of settling-in, photosynthesis and chlorophyll production are at a low, as is water and nutrient absorption through the roots. It needs subdued light to keep foliage growing at the same rate as roots are able to supply water and nutrients. BE GENTLE!

Plants should be as healthy as possible before being traumatized by transplanting. None the less, transplanting a sick, root bound plant to a large container has cured more than one ailing plant.

TRANSPLANTING STEP-BY-STEP

In this example, we will use a one month old clone started in a 4-inch container of coarse sand and transplant it to a 6 gallon pot.

Step One: Water 4-inch clone with 1/2 strength Up-Start or Vitamin B_1, one or two days before transplanting.

Step Two: Fill the 6 gallon container with rich potting soil or soilless mix to within 2 inches of the top.

Step Three: Water soil until saturated.

Step Four: Roll the 4-inch pot between hands to break sand away from the sides of pot. Place hand over top of container with stem between fingers; turn it upside down and let root ball slip out of pot into hand. Take special care at this point to keep the root ball in one integral piece.

Step Five: Carefully place root ball in a prepared hole in the 6 gallon container. Make sure all roots are growing down.

Step Six: . Backfill around the root ball. Gently, but firmly place soil into contact with root ball.

Step Seven: Water with 1/2 strength Up-Start or Vitamin B$_1$, making sure soil is completely saturated, but not soggy.

Step Eight: Place new transplants on the perimeter of the garden or under a screen, so light remains subdued for a couple of days. The transplants should be able to take full light within a day or two.

Step Nine: The new, rich potting soil will supply enough nutrients for about a month. Then, supplemental fertilization will probably be necessary. Soilless mixes require balanced N-P-K fertilization a week or less after transplanting.

Step Ten: See: Chart On "Minimum Container Size" in Chapter 3.

PRUNING & BENDING

Bending and pruning alter the basic growth pattern of a plant. The alteration affects physical shape, liquid flow and growth hormones. Pruning strongly affects the plant, while bending has more subdued affects. When a branch is pruned off, two branches will grow from the nodes just below the cut. This does not mean the plant will grow twice as much. A plant can only grow but so fast. A quick branch amputation is not going to make it grow faster or add any more foliage. In fact, an indoor crop is already being pushed to the limit and trimming or cutting it will slow growth for a few days. Think about it! The crop is only being grown for 2-5 months. Any time it is pruned, valuable foliage is being removed that could be covered with flowers in less than two months!

BENDING is very similar to pruning. Bending alters the flow of hormones, but unlike pruning, it does not remove them. Bending effectively neutralizes the effect of the growth inhibiting hormone. It works well and is much easier on plants than pruning. Bending is simple. Just lean a branch in the desired direction and tie it in place. Branches can take a lot of bending before they pinch over or break. Even if a branch folds, tie it in place, it will heal itself. Young branches take bending much better than old, stiff ones. Bending branches horizontally will encourage the buds to grow vertically towards the light. Each bud will turn into an impressive top, because they all receive more light. It is easy to get a bumper crop practicing bending. A wooden planter box is very handy when practicing bending. A lattice trellis may be nailed to the sides. The bent branches are secured to the trellis. See photo above to see how bending can take the place of pruning.

Tops grow towards the lamp when branches are bent.

Wire ties, like the kind used to open and close bread sacks, can be purchased at the nursery. Wire ties may either be pre-cut or cut by the grower to length. Plastic coated electronic and telephone cable wire work as well as wire ties and essentially cost nothing. They are fastened with a simple twist and stay rigid, leaving the stem breathing room. If a stem is too tight, the liquids can not flow... death by strangulation!

When bending, be gentle, even though *cannabis* can take much abuse. Sometimes a crotch will separate or a branch will fold over, cutting off fluid flow. These mishaps are easily fixed with a small wooden splint, snugly secured with wire ties or duct tape to support the split and broken stem.

Many times a combination of bending and pruning is practiced. It is easy to prune too much, but it is hard to over bend.

PRUNING will make a plant grow bushier. The lower branches will develop more rapidly when the terminal bud is removed. Removing the terminal bud alters the concentration of growth inhibiting hormones. These hormones (auxins) prevent the lateral buds from growing very fast. The further a branch is from hormones at the plant tip, the less effect the auxins have. This is why, when left unpruned, *cannabis* will grow into the classic Christmas tree shape.

Most indoor horticulturists do not prune at all. They usually grow a short clone crop that is only 2-4 feet tall. Short clone crops require no pruning to increase light to bottom leaves or to alter the profile of the garden. This method is the easiest and probably the most productive.

Always use clean instruments when pruning. A single edged razor blade, a sharp pair of pruners, or a pair of scissors all work well. Do not use indoor pruners on anything but the indoor garden. If using pruners outdoors, they will have everything from aphids to dog dung on them. If outdoor clippers must be used, use rubbing alcohol to sterilize them before use.

There are three basic methods or techniques of pruning indoor marijuana. In the first method, the bottom branches are pruned off plants that are over 24-36 inches tall. In fact, many plants are not pruned at all! This concentrates floral hormones so tops are stronger and thicker. This is just the opposite principle from the first. It crams as many plants into as small of an area as possible. The theory is since plants are crowded, they will not get very bushy. The plants (rooted clones) are grown four weeks or less before flowering is induced. The plants never get over 2-3 feet tall. Light is much more intense and the entire plant grows into a flower top with little or no leaves. All the little clones are packed tightly together in one gallon pots, each one of the plants is taking up the minimum amount of space, for the minimum amount of time, to produce the maximum amount of marijuana. Whether this method is more productive than another is debatable. So far, there are no controlled studies, only happy horticulturists.

The second method pinches back tops. This diffuses floral hormones, making the plant bushier. Pruning the plant when it is one or two months old and, again at 2 or 3 months of age, will make it bushier. Continual pruning will keep it in a solid hedge-like shape. Some growers even prune plants into an ornamental shape! With this method, just a few plants are grown for six months or more and require large (10-20 gallon) containers or hydroponic units. The yield of prime, dense tops will probably be less than if not pruned, but the overall harvest is high. Growers that prune say it increases the yield, and who knows, it just might. Growers that prune often, use the pruned cuttings for clones.

The third method uses parts of the other two. This pruning technique removes all but four main branches. The meristem is removed but the four branches are left y intact. This concentrates the floral hormones in the four main branches. Note: Only complete branches are pruned, leaves are left alone! The idea behind this principle is if there are fewer branches, they will be stronger, bearing more and heavier flowers. The seedling or clone is generally one month old when the four main branches are selected. The branches selected are usually the first four that grew or the strongest. The plant is then kept in the vegetative stage until it is 2-3 feet tall before flowering is induced.

Pruning all the branches is not advised. It shocks the plant too much. Just pruning the tall branches that get in the way and rob light from the rest of the garden works well. However, if taking clones from a Mother, you may want to sacrifice her well-being for more clones. Remember, if she is pruned down to stubby branches, it could take her a month to resume much growth.

Pruning too much over a period of time may alter the hormonal balance so much that the plant produces spindly growth. If a plant must be pruned heavily for clones, it is usually best to prune it right down to a few leafy growing tips on the trunk or main stem and let it grow back from there.

For best results, stop pruning one month before inducing flowering. Pruning diffuses the concentration of floral hormones and retards the flowering process somewhat. If heavily pruned, then induced to flower, plants could take an extra week or so to complete flowering. It takes about a month for the hormones to be built up to normal concentrations after pruning.

ALL LEAVES ARE TO BE LEFT ALONE! Somehow a rumor started about how removing large shade leaves would supply more light to smaller growing tips, making them grow faster. This is bad gardening! A plant needs all the leaves it can get to produce the maximum amount of chlorophyll. Removing the leaves slows chlorophyll production and stunts growth. Removing the leaves stresses the plant. Stress is a growth inhibitor, especially during vegetative growth. Only leaves that are clearly dead, bug or fungus infected, should be removed. Leaf removal is not pruning, it is hacking up a normally healthy plant.

Pruning or trimming off lower branches that have spindly, sickly growth, is acceptable. When pruning, cut off the entire branch. Pruning the lower branches has a minimal effect on floral hormone concentration. The only real reasons to cut off lower branches is if they are diseased or you are having a party!

CHAPTER TEN   FLOWERING

A $50 bill easily stuck to this resinous top.

In order for *cannabis* to complete its annual life cycle successfully, it must first flower. Marijuana is a dioecious plant, being either male (pollen producing) or female (ovule producing). Occasionally a hermaphrodite (bisexual) plant, with both male and female flowers on the same plant, will occur.

One of the many, tiny grains of pollen from the male (staminate) flower pod, lands on a pistil of the female (pistilate) flower. Female flower tops are a mass of calyxes with each calyx harboring an ovule and a protruding set of pistils. Actual fertilization takes place when the grain of male pollen slides down the pistil and unites with the female ovule deep within the calyx. Once fertilization takes place, pistils turn brown and a seed will form within the calyx or seed bract. Seeds are the result of this sexual propagation and contain genetic characteristics of both parents. Generally there is a 50/50 chance a seed produces a male or female plant. After fertilization, the female will put all of her energy into producing strong seeds. When the flower tops are full of dark mature seeds, the female will die, having successfully completed her life cycle. The male completes his life cycle and dies after he has produced and dispersed all of his pollen into the wind, in search of a receptive female pistil.

In nature, *cannabis* flowers in the fall, after the long, hot, days of summer. The long nights and short days of autumn signal marijuana to start the flowering stage. Growth patterns and chemistry change: stems elongate, leaves grow progressively fewer blades, cannabanoid production slows at first then accelerates; flower formation is rapid at first then slows. All this causes new nutrient needs. Attention is now focused on flower production, rather than vegetative growth. Green chlorophyll, production, requiring much nitrogen, slows. Phosphorus uptake increases to promote floral formation. Light needs change as well. During autumn, in most climates, the sun takes on a slightly reddish appearance, emitting a more red than a balanced white light. The sun produces this reddish glow by shining at a greater angle through more particles in the atmosphere. Growth and floral hormones are stimulated by this red or harvest sun.

The harvest sun phenomena is not fully understood. However, experiments have proven that by increasing the amount of red light during flowering, floral hormones are stimulated and flower tops get much larger.

Indoors, flowering may be induced just as it is in nature, by shortening the photoperiod from 18 to 12 hours. Once the days are changed to 12 hours, flowers should be clearly visible within one to three weeks. In fact, many growers have two grow rooms: a vegetative grow room with one 1000 watt super metal halide on for 18 hours, the other room for flowering having both a 1000 watt super halide and a HP sodium on 12 hours per day. Using this combination of rooms and lamps, the electricity bill remains relatively low and the horticulturist has the luxury of having both summer and fall every day of the year!

The additional stimulation of a red or harvest sun may be simulated by a 1000 watt H.P. sodium lamp (the phosphor coated halide also emits a little more red than the clear halide). The H.P. sodium may increase flower production 20-30%.

The harvest sun is simulated one of three ways: (1) adding a 1000 watt H.P. sodium lamp to a grow room already containing a 1000 watt metal halide. This more than doubles the available light, especially the red end of the spectrum. The halide maintains blues in the spectrum necessary for continued green chlorophyll production. (2) Replacing the 1000 watt halide with a 1000 watt H.P. sodium. This increases the reds, but cuts the blues. A result of this practice has been more yellowing of vegetative leaves, due to lack of chlorophyll production and more elongation (2-6 inches) than if the halide were present. Growers practicing this technique tend to loose a little on harvest yield, but their halide lamp is available to start another crop of clones at 18 hour days in another room. This subsequent crop will be placed under the H.P. sodium as soon as the first crop is harvested. (3) Adding or changing to a phosphor coated halide. These halides are not only easier on the eyes, their coating makes them produce a little bit more red in their spectrum, thus promoting flowering.

Water needs of a flowering plant are somewhat less than in the vegetative stage. Adequate water during flowering is important to carry on the plant's chemistry and resin production. Withholding water to stress a plant will actually stunt growth and the yield will be less.

Removing large fan leaves to create more intense light to small buds or to stress plants is unacceptable! Large leaves are necessary to keep the plant healthy. Remove only dead or near dead leaves.

MALE

Male *cannabis* reaches maturity and flowers 1-2 weeks before the female. He continues flowering and shedding yellowish, dust-like pollen from his bell shaped pollen sacks (flowers), well into the females flowering stage, insuring her pollination. Male flowers are about 1/2 long, pastel green or sometimes yellowish. Flowers first develop near the top of the plant and hang in clusters, at the base of branches. Gradually, flowers develop further towards the bottom of the male. When they are fully formed, the floral sacks split open, shedding pollen, after about 3-6 weeks of the 12 hour photoperiod.

Males are often, but not always, tall with stout stems, sporadic branching, and few leaves. Since males are tall, wind and gravity can carry pollen to normally shorter females.

Male *cannabis* produces a low volume of flowers that usually contain less THC. They also fertilize females, causing them to stop calyx and high THC production and start seed formation.

Males are usually harvested, except those used for breeding after their sex has been determined, but before the pollen is shed (See: "Cloning for Sex,". There are many ways to discern a male during the seedling or vegetative stage, including chemical additives, genetic background and growth characteristics. One of the, easiest and most successful ways to tell for sure its a boy is to induce flowering via the 12 hour photoperiod, and wait until male flowers are clearly visible.

Male plant

FEMALE

The female plant usually grows squat and bushy, with branches close together on the stem, and leaves growing densely on branches. Within 1-3 weeks of inducing flowering, the first female flowers will appear. The female is prized for her heavy, potent, resin production and weighty flower yield. As with males, female flowers will first appear near the top of the terminal bud, and gradually develop towards the bottom of the plant. Her flower has two small (1/4-1/2-inch) fuzzy, white hairs, called pistils, that form a "V". The set of pistils is attached at the base to an ovule, which is contained in a light green pod, called a calyx. Calyxes form dense clusters, or buds along the stem. A cluster of buds is called a top or *cola*.

The calyxes usually grow rapidly for the first 4 or 5 weeks, then grow at a slower rate for up to 6 months. When the ovule has been fertilized by male pollen, rapid calyx formation and resin production slow and seed growth starts.

Blow up
of a calyx.

Calyxes on this indica female are starting to swell.

SINSEMILLA

Sinsemilla (pronounced sin-semiya) is actually two Spanish words: *sin* without and *semilla* seed. Sinsemilla is used to describe flowering, female *cannabis* tops that have not been fertilized by male pollen.

Highly prized sinsemilla is usually very potent, with a large volume of THC per flower bud, and best of all, it is all smoke, no seeds. The unpollinated female remains in the flowering stage and calyx formation and resin production peak out.

More and larger calyxes develop thicker along the stem, yielding more high quality buds than the fertilized, seeded flower.

Sinsemilla flower top

Any female marijuana plant may become sinsemilla, regardless of origin, by removing the male plants after they are identified. Removal of males essentially guarantees that no male pollen will touch the tender pistils of the female. Sometimes, a few early grains of pollen are shed by premature flowers and find their way to receptive females. I call this *casi* (Spanish for almost) sinsemilla. The few seeds that form are viable, but might not be of great quality.

Unfertilized sinsemilla calyxes waiting to be pollinated.

Sex reversal sometimes becomes a problem when growing only female plants. Mother Nature sets forth both male and female plants. Harvesting all the male plants confuses the females. They have no male counterpart to perpetuate their species. This imbalance is sensed, and a female may produce male flowers, in a valiant attempt to supply pollen for fertilization and successful completion of the life cycle. This phenomena is a natural survival mechanism and nothing to worry about. When it does happen, just pick off the male flowers, as soon as they appear to ensure a sinsemilla crop. A few male flowers on a predominately female plant is technically a hermaphrodite but, when the males flowers are removed, it is all female!

Some growers let the pollen fertilize females, saying that the seeds produced from this sex reversal will be mostly females. This is usually true, but they will also have hermaphrodite tendencies. These seeds may also reproduce weird, deformed plants, with sporadic growth patterns. THC content may decline after two or three generations as well.

HERMAPHRODITES

A hermaphrodite is marijuana that has both male and female flowers on the same plant. There has been much discussion and experimentation concerning hermaphrodites. Some horticulturists claim their seeds will produce a higher percent of female plants. This may or may not be true. My findings have been that hermaphrodites should be avoided, since they are hard to predict and control. Some hermaphrodites are 10% male and 90% female, while others are 90% male and 10% female. Hermaphrodites are freaks of nature, and all too often the product of a stressful and inconsistent indoor environment.

Indoors, the outdoor environment is manufactured and the normal life cycle of *cannabis* is altered. Creating summer in December, cloning, prolonging the life cycle and leaching the soil: all the wonderful things we are able to do indoors mixes up even the strongest plant somewhat. When this necessary stress is coupled with freaky seeds, the outcome is uncertain. High humidity, over pruning and old age seem to promote hermaphrodites more than other environmental factors. I have found that if a plant is stressed or hermaphrodite, it seems to go for the male role every time!

A male flower is blooming at the tip of this hermaphrodite.

Chapter 11 HARVEST

The payoff for all the research, work, risk taking, money spent, and most of all, the long patient wait, is a bountiful harvest. There are many things that contribute to a productive harvest. The plant must be strong and healthy throughout life, wearing all its leaves! Harvesting the large, green, shade leaves to stress the plant or give more light to smaller tops, will stunt the plant and severely reduce the harvest volume. If smoke must be had during the growing season, do not steal it from an immature plant in the name of stress. It is best to remove an entire lower branch, or harvest an entire plant (See: "Survival of the Fittest".

Once the large leaves are fully formed, THC potency has generally peaked out. As long as leaves are healthy and green, the peak potency is retained. Nothing is lost by leaving them on the plant.

Harvest leaves if they show signs of disease or rapid yellowing that fertilizer has failed to cure. Once they start to yellow and die, potency decreases somewhat. This is true especially with fan leaves that grow before the buds. These leaves often yellow just before tops are ripe.

Marijuana needs water throughout life. Withholding water to stress plants before harvest should only be done during the last few days, if done at all.

A grow room that has one pound of dry tops will take about 18 hours to harvest! If this seems too long, think about how much time it will take to cut each and every branch from the plant, then manicure the top, bud by bud before hanging them to dry.

Sure, the plants could be yanked and hung upside down, then thrown in a big bag when dry. The entire process could take less than an hour. Amazingly enough, the smoke would be pretty good. But, if you would like to preserve it as well as promote natural esthetic qualities of the harvest, take some time before harvesting to get the most out of the crop.

Growers that have no clones and do not want to start from seed, because they want specific female plants, go for a "Second Crop". The harvested plants are reverted back to vegetative growth with 18 hours of light and a good big shot of high nitrogen, general purpose fertilizer. Clones may be taken about a month or two later. When there is enough vegetative growth, a mass cloning is made. The tired females are given 12 hours of light to produce another flower harvest a week or two after the clones have been taken. When they are done flowering, the clones may be moved in to take their place. Cloning can really turn even the most passive grower into a year round horticulturist. This practice is a little touchy.

MALE HARVEST

Male flowers take from 2-4 weeks to produce pollen bearing pods from the time they are first seen. watch out for early openers. They continue producing flowers for several weeks after the first pods have begun to shed pollen. Once male flowers are clearly visible, but before they have opened, is the time of peak

THC production. This is the best time to harvest. Once males release pollen, the degradation process speeds up and flowers fall.

When harvesting, especially if close to females, cut the plant off at the base, taking care to shake the male as little as possible. This helps prevent any accidental pollination by an unnoticed, open, male flower.

If there must be a male in the garden for breeding, keep him totally isolated from the flowering females by moving him to a sunny window or another grow room as soon as flowers are set. His ability to produce viable pollen will not be affected by the changes in environment. If growing in both vegetative and flowering rooms, simply place the blooming male in a corner of the vegetative room until he is needed in 1-4 weeks. After a month, he might start to revert back to vegetative growth. If necessary, take a clone of the male. Keep the clone going in the vegetative grow room until he is needed for pollen. Induce flowering about three weeks before the viable pollen is needed. Within 3-5 weeks, he will be full of viable pollen.

Male harvest may be prolonged by harvesting flowers with small scissors or finger nails as they appear. After plucking off male flowers, new ones will appear. The new male flowers will be ripe when the females are in full bloom. This is a very long and time consuming process and there is a good chance of missing a few male flowers.

Harvesting most of the branches, leaving only one or two pollen bearing branches works well. Since one male flower contains enough pollen to fertilize many female ovule, only one or two branches, full of male flowers, will be necessary to produce enough pollen for breeding. This method is often incorporated with moving the male into the vegetative room for rejuvenation or placing him in a sunny window.

Resin glands frost this ripe indica.

SINSEMILLA HARVEST

Sinsemilla flowers are mature from 6-12 weeks after the photoperiod has been changed to 12 hours. The best time to harvest sinsemilla is when THC production has peaked, but not yet started the degradation process. In most varieties of marijuana this peak is reached at essentially the same time. Lower flower tops that received less light might be a little slower in maturing. These varieties tend to go through 4-5 weeks of rapid bud formation before leveling off. The harvest is taken 1-3 weeks after growth slows. With most varieties of *indica*, harvest is ready all at once, in 6-8 weeks. In fact, some buds are so resinous, they appear to have been rolled in sugar!

These Thai plants were induced to flower 10 weeks ago. They flowered for 3 months before harvest.

Other varieties, most commonly *staves*, will tend to form buds at a more even rate throughout flowering, with no marked decline in growth rate. With these varieties, buds at the top of the plant may reach peak potency a few days to a couple of weeks prior to buds located on lower branches. These types may require several harvests and are usually of equatorial origin. These long season plants do not flower as quickly once flowering is induced with the 12 hour photoperiod. They take much longer to grow in- doors and could easily take as long as three months to reach peak bud formation.

There are several-ways to tell when peak potency is reached. The methods work separately or in combination with one another. Smoking, diminishing returns and scientific observation are three excellent methods used to test for peak ripeness.

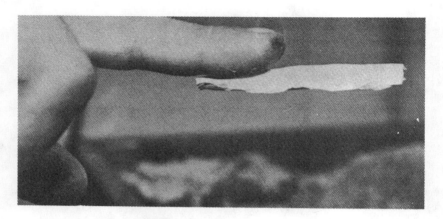

Finger is so resinous, the joint sticks.

SMOKING is by far the most delightful. Simply harvest an average bud, dry it at 200° F for 10-15 minutes and smoke it. The smoke will probably be harsh, but palatable. This should be done when you are straight, and several times throughout flowering. This method lets the high decide the best time to harvest. This method is the most fun, but the least reliable.

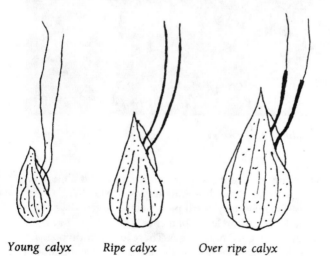

Young calyx   *Ripe calyx*   *Over ripe calyx*

DIMINISHING RETURNS is a point that is reached when the pistils on the bottom of the bud are dying (turning brown) at a faster rate than they are growing from the top of the bud. At this point, THC production has usually peaked out, and is on its way down hill. This method is the best way to tell a ripe bud with the naked eye.

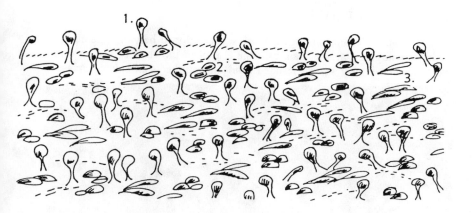

1. Capitate stalked trichomes 2. bulbous trichomes 3. stalked trichomes

30x Portable with batteries.

SCIENTIFIC OBSERVATION is achieved with the help of an inexpensive microscope (20-50 x). It is the most precise way to tell when THC production has reached its peak. Take a small, thin, resinous portion of the bud and place it under the microscope at a low magnification setting (20-50 x). A flashlight or lamp may be necessary to provide top light. The top light enables an unshadowed view of the resin glands. There are several 30x portable scopes on the market for $20-30. The portable microscopes afford a quick peek at the resin glands without harvesting the bud. Many samples may be taken in a short while.

Three kinds of glands may be seen. The glands with the knob at the top (1) (*Capitate-stalked trichomes*) are the ones that have the highest concentration of THC. These are the glands to watch. The other glands, (2) *bulbous* and (3) *stalked glands or trichomes* may also contain THC, but much less. When the *capitate-stalked trichomes* have developed a head and are still transparent, is the best time to harvest. When the glands start to turn brown and get smaller, they are starting to decompose and the THC content will go down. Check over a period of several days and check several buds from different plants to make sure the maximum amount of *capitate-stalked trichomes* are ripe for harvest.

HARVEST STEP-BY-STEP

1.   Stop all fertilization at least two weeks prior to harvest. Chemical fertilizers will give plants a chemical taste if applied too soon before harvest. Excess chemicals may also be leached from the soil the week before harvest.

This indica flower is dead ripe.

Step Two: Mist plants heavily to wash off undesirable residues that may have accumulated on plants. The bath will not affect resin production. Just make sure to wash the garden early in the day to allow excess water on leaves to dry before nightfall. This guards against fungus and bud blight. If bud mold is a real threat, dry buds with a fan.

Step Three: Harvest entire plant, or one branch at a time, by cutting near the base with clippers. Jerking roots and all creates a mess, and is unnecessary. The root system may be discarded along with used soil. The roots are of no consequence now; all of the THC is produced in the foliage.

Step Four: Harvest near the end of the day. This allows a full, sunny day for active resin production.

Step Five: It is not necessary to hang plants upside down so all the resin drains into the foliage. There is no THC potent resin to drain. However, drying the entire plant by hanging it upside down is very convenient. When stems are left intact, drying is much slower. Leaving all the larger leaves on the tops acts as a protective shield to flower buds. Tender resin glands are protected from bruises and rupture.

Pluck the large fan leaves from tops before hanging to dry. This will make final manicuring easy and faster.

6. There are many ways of harvesting. One of them is to cut each branch in- to lengths of 6-24 inches, then manicure the freshly harvested tops, cutting away all leaves with clippers or scissors. Hang the branches until dry. Once dry, cut the tops from the branches, taking special care to handle the tender tops as little as possible. This method is very easy and the one most commonly used indoors.

7. Another way is to harvest the entire plant by cutting it off at the base, then hang it upside down. Wait for it to dry before removing any fan leaves or manicuring the tops. This method is similar to most outdoor harvests, where the entire crop has to come in at the same time. A little THC may be lost using this method, since the tender tops are more susceptible to bruises and rupture once they are dry.

8. A third method of harvest starts to remove the larger leaves one or two days before actually cutting the plants down. Harvesting the large leaves early gets them out of the way. The flower covered plants are then harvested with little or no manicuring.

9. Tops are manicured after drying. Foliage not covered with resin and leaves are snipped away. Buds are removed from the main stem.

10. After manicuring, the tops are packaged in a rigid container, like a glass jar, to preserve the resin glands.

11. Budget enough time to harvest properly. To complete the harvest, beginning to end, budget at least 18 hours per pound. This would be a nice Saturday for you and a friend or several nights alone and loaded again! This time includes: harvest, manicuring and packaging everything in canning jars.

12. Go for a second crop if there is enough room, by leaving the harvested stubs of plants with a little foliage on them. Put the harvested stubs on the perimeter of the garden if starting clones. It only costs some water, fertilizer and a little bit of time. With 18 hour days, they will revert back to vegetative growth. You can leave them on the outside of the garden to get another harvest, or use them for mother plants. Remember the longer the crop stays in the grow room, the more susceptible it is to disease attack.

SEED CROPS

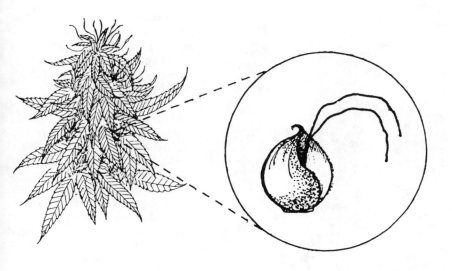

Close up of calyx (seed bract) that contains a ripe seed.

Seed Crops (or in Spanish, *con semilla,* meaning with seeds) are harvested when the seeds are a rich, dark brown. Often seeds may actually split open their containing calyx. The flowering female grows many ready, receptive calyxes until pollination occurs. Seeds are mature within 6-8 weeks. Then, all energy goes into seed production. THC content is usually of minimum importance. Harvest all sinsemilla branches. The seeded branches are ready about a week later. Seed crops can actually be left in the ground until seeds rattle in the pod. Watch out for fungus that might attack the weakening female and her cache of ripe seeds.

Pollinate only one or two branches. (See: "Breeding". The female will produce almost all unpollinated branches, sinsemilla. The sinsemilla tops are harvested when ripe and the *con semilla* part of the plant can stay in the ground until seeds are clearly mature.

When seeds are mature, remove them from the pods and store them in a cool, DRY place. The seeds are viable and ready for planting as soon as they are harvested, but they may grow sickly plants. Let the seeds dry out a few months before planting. Dry seeds will produce much healthier plants and the germination rate will be much higher.

SECOND CROPS

It is easy to have a second crop by leaving several undeveloped, lower branches and foliage on harvested plants.

In fact, a second crop is the best option for growers reaping their first harvest (See No. 2, below). Harvested branches and buds will grow new flowers or vegetative growth.

There are two basic ways to go about growing a second crop from the same plants: (1) Retain the 12 hour photoperiod and leave several undeveloped lower branches and flower buds on each plant. Branches will grow spindly flowers that will be ready in one to four weeks. This method is most productive with *cannabis sativa* that matures slowly and has a long harvest.

(2) Change photoperiod back to 18 hour days and, leave a few immature flowers, leaves and branches on each plant. Give the, harvested, leafy, buddy stubs a double dose of a high nitrogen fertilizer to help promote green, leafy growth. This will induce the harvested stubs to revert to vegetative growth in about a month. New growth will come from the flower tops and the plant will get very bushy. Let the rejuvenated plants grow until they are the desired size, about waist high, then induce flowering with 12 hour photoperiod. If second crops are allowed to get very tall, they produce light, sparse buds. They are already root-bound. When this is coupled with leggyness, sparse buds result.

This harvested plant reverted back to vegetative growth in about 30 days.

For example, a person that grew a beautiful crop of females and knew each plant by name, had to harvest. Instead of starting from seed again, the person decided to leave a few leaves and buds on the harvested stubs of the females. Vegetative growth was induced with 18 hour days after harvesting. A month later many, many clones were taken from the original favorite females. The original mothers were induced to flower about a month after the clones were taken. The clones were rooted, transplanted and moved into another room with 18 hour days. The original harvest was taken on January 1. The second harvest, was April 1! The second harvest was almost equal to the first in weight, but the buds in the second harvest were smaller. Taking clones from rejuvenated plants also diffuses hormones and stresses plants severely. A stress reaction of the clones could be premature flowering.

DRYING

After the harvest, marijuana is dried before smoking. Drying converts THC from its nonpsychoactive acid form to its psychoactive neutral form. Drying also converts 75% or more of the freshly harvested plant into water vapor and other gases.

When harvested, growth essentially stops. Major changes in the THC content will probably be degraded. Prolonged periods of light, heat (90° F), friction from fondling hands and damp, humid conditions should be avoided.

THC is produced in the leaves and flowers. Stems and roots may smell like they should be smoked, but contain few cannabanoids if any, and the resin is not very psychoactive. Doing things like boiling the roots is crazy! Growers that hang plants upside down, do so for convenience, rather than to let resin drain into the buds. Hanging plants is a labor saving way to facilitate slow, even drying. Large, moist stems may also be removed and small branches hung from the ceiling. Drying time is cut by several days.

One horticulturist that harvests 1-1.5 oz. daily uses a food preserver. The stash is dry in less than 24 hours. The preserver essentially dehydrates the tops very evenly. The smoke remains amazingly mellow.

Microwave a little if you are in a hurry. Turn the microwave on in short, weak bursts of 15-30 seconds each. Recycle until dry. The smoke is OK. It will take 10-15 minutes at 200° F when using a gas, electric or popular toaster oven. The smoke is raspy and harsh.

Food preserver dehydrates flowers.

Top yard-long colas hang to dry. Above: Smaller tops dry in a box.

Left One ounce of prime sinsemilla.

For best results, drying should be slow and should incorporate circulating, temperate (40-60°), dry air. When dried slowly, over 2-3 weeks, moisture evaporates evenly into the air, yielding uniformly dry buds with minimal THC decomposition. These buds will taste sweet and smoke smooth. Buds dried quickly, burn hot and taste harsh. Tops dried too slowly might contract fungus and/or not burn at all.

Hang tops from string near the ceiling in a dark room with an oscillating fan on the floor. Remember, light is one of the biggest enemies of drying marijuana. The tops or plants should be hung overhead. Never let the fan blow directly on the drying plants.

It is very easy to build a small drying room. Just tack some plywood together into a small room, then hang some strings across the ceiling. Another option would be to let the grow room rest while the harvest is drying within.

Hanging plants above the HID in the shadows of a grow room, while starting the next crop, is a common practice. I do not recommend it. Two different climates are required for growing and drying marijuana. Buds that are dried too hot and fast will smoke harshly. Fungus and spider mites can easily become a problem especially if ventilation is inadequate. Keep constant lookout for any signs of fungus, mold or spider mites on both drying and growing plants. Mold can ruin a great flower top in a matter of days.

Light, heat and friction are dry and drying, marijuana's biggest enemies. Ml three are major contributors to the biodegradation process. Keep dried marijuana off hot car dash boards, heat vents, etc. Friction is probably the biggest destroyer of tender THC resin glands. Baggies and fondling hands rupture many tiny resin glands every minute! To keep dried marijuana in mint condition, store it in an air tight, rigid container and place it in the refrigerator. Do not place it in the freezer, very cold temperatures can destroy the THC glands. Ordinary canning or Mason jars, allow buds to be admired as well as protected. Jars are very popular for skunk weed. The fragrance is so pungent and skunk-like, that it requires glass to contain the smell. Placing an orange or lemon peel in the jar will add aroma to the bouquet.

LEAVES dry very well in a paper bag. Just throw leaves, shake and small buds in a shopping bag and fold the top over. Place the bag in a dry, warm place, out of the way, like on top of the refrigerator or the hot water heater. Check it every few days, turning the leaves over. They should be dry in a week or two. The warmer the sack, the faster the marijuana dries, and the harsher it smokes.

Chapter 12 BREEDING

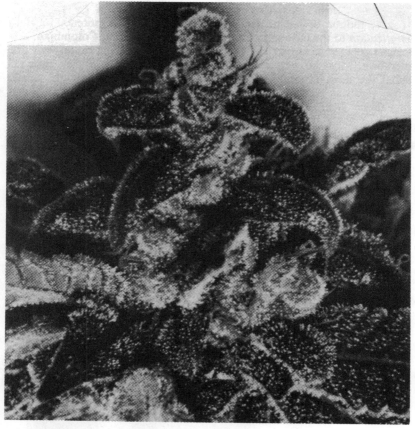

Selective breeding produced the indica above.

The purpose of this chapter is to give a basic outline of the selective, sexual propagation (breeding) of *cannabis*. For a detailed discussion of breeding, read the best book written on the subject: *Marijuana Botany* by Robert Connell Clarke, $19.95 And/Or Press 1981. It is available at many bookstores and distributors.

In *Marijuana Botany, An Advanced Study: The Propagation and Breeding of Distinctive Cannabis*, Clarke discusses, in understandable, scientific detail, genetics and breeding, as well as cloning, climate, chemistry and much more of interest to the serious breeder. *The Marijuana Grower's Guide* by Ed Rosenthal and Mel Frank, is the first classic book about growing marijuana. It has an incredible amount of information on potency, chemistry, growing and just about anything you can think of about growing marijuana. Both books are available at most bookstores, they are worth every cent of the price.

Cannabis indica seeds, that are the product of several generations of selective, indoor breeding, are highly prized for their potency and acclimatization to the indoor environment. Thai, Hawaiian, Colombian, and Mexican (*cannabis sativa*) are OK, if grown indoors for more than one generation. Most growers prefer the *indica* seeds, because they have exhibited the most favorable characteristics for indoor cultivation: squat, bushy, vigorous growth, early, sustained potency, disease resistance and heavy flower yield.

Breeding is almost a necessity in an indoor garden, since most of the seed available is from various outdoor climates, or is of questionable descent. By breeding for desirable characteristics, and acclimating plants to the indoor environment, vigorous, potent plants result. More generations per year are possible with indoor breeding. In fact, as many as 3 years or generations may easily be completed in one year indoors.

Selective breeding is simply assuming and controlling the role of Mother Nature once again. In nature, pollen is shed into the wind to randomly fertilize any receptive female. The breeder will add precision and control to this process. He or she will catch pollen from a desirable male and put it in contact with chosen female pistils.

There are two basic kinds of breeding: (1) inbred or true bred: plants of the same strain or ancestry that are crossed with one another. (2) outbred or hybrid: plants of different strains that are crossed or cross-pollinated.

Inbreeding is necessary for a pure breed to be established. This true or pure breed is necessary so common growth characteristics may be established. If the plants are not a pure breed, it will be impossible to predict the outcome of the hybrid plant. After the 5th to 6th generation, negative characteristics, like low potency, leggyness and lack of vigor tend to dominate. Inbreeding is necessary to establish a true breed, but has been shied away from after the strain has been established.

Inbreeding is used to establish a stable reference point or plant to start from. The chosen females are bred back with males of the same strain. This will establish a true breed or plants with the same growth characteristics. These plants, of known ancestry and growth characteristics will be used to breed hybrid plants.

History students will remember the inherited physical and mental problems, that plagued royal European families that inbred for generations.

The more generations that practiced inbreeding, the more physical deformities and mental deficiencies surfaced. Seeds from self-pollinated hermaphrodite plants are inbred. These inbred hermaphrodites are good plants to stay away from because they could mutate in a few generations.

OUTBREEDING or producing hybrid seed has been the norm in horticulture for many years. Farmers, breeders and *cannabis* horticulturists have found choosing parents of different strains, exhibiting exceptional, positive, dominant characteristics, will result in a super plant, also referred to as *hybrid vigor*. Yes, it is possible to cross *sativa* with *indica*. In fact, some growers swear by the cross, saying you get the best of both plants, vigor and size from the *sativa* and squat, bushy, early, potent growth from the *indica*.

This indica is the result of 8 years of indoor breeding.

Choosing from a large and varied plant stock, is the key to successful breeding. Since the origin of most seed is questionable, an accomplished breeder waits to see what kind of plant it produces, before deciding which plants to cross to form hybrid seed. There is no guarantee for a breeder, planting only a few seeds, that they will grow into vigorous plants, even if the seeds are from dynamite smoke. The breeder, growing many plants from various strains of *cannabis indica* (and/or *sativa*), will have many plants to choose from. The more seeds planted, the better the chances of getting exactly what you want.

Male pollen from hermaphrodites, having only a few male flowers on a predominately female plant, may be used to cross-pollinate another female. This method may yield as high as 75% female plants. None the less, when using hermaphrodite breeding stock, chances are increased of producing hermaphrodite seeds. Most breeders have found consistent results breeding only male and female plants of different strains.

BREEDING STEP-BY-STEP

Step One: Choose male breeding stock exhibiting desirable characteristics.

Flowering male is covered with a plastic bag.

Step Two: . One branch full of male flowers is all that will be needed, unless a large crop is desired. Other branches may be stripped of flowers to help contain pollen and guard against accidental, random pollination. The male can be isolated from the females, once flowers have developed, but not yet opened, by placing him in a sunny window or in a vegetative grow room. This will slow flower development and not hurt the male in any way.

A branch of ripe, male flowers may be cut and placed in water. It will remain healthy for several weeks. When the pollen sacks open, proceed with step three. The remaining male plant may then be cut back or harvested.

Step Three: When the pollen pods start to open, place a clean, French bread sack or baggie over the branch to collect pollen. Secure the bag at the bottom with a piece of string or wire tie. Keep the bag over the branch for several days to collect pollen.

Step Four: When enough pollen has been collected, shake remaining pollen off into the bag. Remove spent branch.

The female is now covered with the pollen filled baggie.

Step Five: Ideally, pistils should be ready for fertilization 3 to 4 weeks after the first calyx has appeared. Receptive pistils are white and fuzzy, not starting to turn brown. Cover the selected female branch that has many ripe, receptive pistils, with the pollen filled bag. Shake the bag. Does it feel good? She could kiss you at this very moment!

Step Six: Use a small paint brush to apply the pollen from the bag to the pistils if just a few seeds are desfsired from many different females. Be very careful.

Just use a little pollen on each calyx and keep it from spreading to the sinsemilla crop.

Step Seven: Leave the bag for two or three days, to ensure fertilization. Be careful not to scatter pollen on adjacent sinsemilla crop when removing the bag.

Step Eight: After fertilization, seeds will be ripe in 3-6 weeks. Harvest seeds when they split open the containing calyx or rattle in the pod.

Step Nine: Let seeds dry for 2-3 months, in a cool, dry place, before planting.

Indoor Cannabis Breeding

Robert Connell Clarke has been breeding *cannabis* for the better part of 20 years. He currently lives in Holland where *cannabis* breeding is legal.

©1992 Robert Connell Clarke
for revised *Indoor Marijuana Horticulture*
by Jorge Cervantes 1993

The breeding of improved varieties of drug *Cannabis* adds a rewarding new dimension to one of America's most rapidly growing gardening hobbies. Indoor marijuana horticulture is rapidly gaining popularity across America but only a very limited number of *Cannabis* cultivators consciously select and breed their plants in an effort to create improved varieties. Clandestine marijuana breeders secretly work to improve drug types of *Cannabis* , but the vast majority of marijuana growers practice no selection at all, and continue to use accidentally produced seeds from domestic sinsemilla, seeds from imported marijuana, or clonal material from another grower. This chapter gives a short history of drug *Cannabis* breeding, tips for indoor breeders, indoor selection criteria, and descriptions of suitable indoor varieties. A few simple breeders terms are introduced in an effort to remain contemporary with breeders of other crops.

Domestic Drug *Cannabis* Breeding

During the early 1960s marijuana cultivation came to America. Ancient cultivators gave American growers a strong start by favoring and selecting potent varieties for at least 3,000 years. At first, *Cannabis* seeds found in illicit shipments of marijuana were casually planted by inquisitive smokers. Commercial domestic marijuana cultivators were unknown. Nearly all domestically produced marijuana that lacked seeds was immature, and that which was mature, fully seeded. Tropical varieties from Colombia and Thailand rarely matured to the late floral stage before frosts killed them. However, the sub-tropical Mexican and Jamaican varieties occasionally did mature outdoors across the southern two thirds of America. Some of the tropical varieties regularly survived until maturity in coastal Southern California, Florida, the Gulf Coast, and especially Hawaii.

Since most imported marijuana was full of seeds, many exotic varieties were available. Early marijuana cultivators tried all available varieties in their search to find potent plants that would consistently mature before killing frosts. Early-maturing northern Mexican varieties were the most favored as they consistently matured at northern latitudes. The early-maturing *C. sativa* inbred line or IBL varieties of the early and mid 1970s such as 'Pollyanna' and the late-maturing 'Original Haze' resulted from crosses between earlier-maturing Mexican and Jamaican varieties and more potent but later-maturing Panamanian, Colombian, and Thai varieties.

Most early varieties were bred for outdoor growing but others were specially developed for glass houses or indoors under artificial light, where the season can be artificially extended to allow the later-maturing types

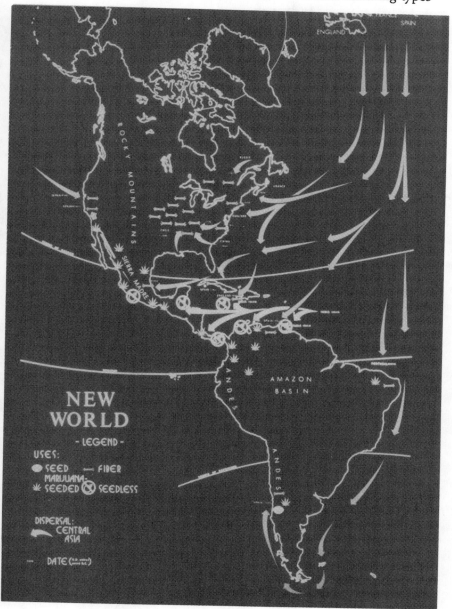

to finish. Once varieties had been perfected that would mature under these conditions, pioneering marijuana breeders selected for potency (THC content), followed by the additional aesthetic considerations of flavor, aroma, and color. Modifying adjectives such as minty, floral, spicy, fruity, sweet, purple, golden, or red were often attached to selected

varieties; and the marijuana connoisseur was born. Continued inbreeding of the original favorable hybrids resulted in some of the 'super-*sativa* s' of the 1970s such as 'Original Haze', 'Purple Haze', 'Polly', 'Eden Gold', 'Three Way', 'Maui Wowie', 'Kona Gold', and 'Big Sur Holy Weed'. These were the first domestically created Inbred Lines or IBLs of drug *Cannabis*.

During the second half of the 1970s marijuana breeders had great success with developing connoisseur *C. sativa* varieties. More potent and exotic-smelling flowers brought both greater pride and greater profit to the grower. Outdoor purple varieties gained popularity, largely following on the coattails of the extraordinary 'Purple Haze' of Central California.

Cannabis cultivators both indoors and outdoors wanted a variety with high flower yield and with short broad stature as well. The answer came in the form of an exotic new imported variety. Hashish varieties from Afghanistan provided the perfect solution. Plants of the *C. afghanica* variety, popularly referred to as 'indica' or 'hashish plant', are characteristically short and bushy with broad dark green leaves. Since *C. afghanica* varieties originate from far northern latitudes with a short growing season they nearly always mature quite early, finishing outdoors between the middle of August and the end of September. Plants often stand only 3 to 6 feet tall at maturity and produce copious resin covered flowers. *C. afghanica* varieties are used to make some of the world's finest and most potent hashish. Smoking the dried flowers provides much of the same aroma and flavor as fine hashish, so connoisseur smokers were willing to pay extra for the exotic *C. afghanica* flowers. Dozens of separate introductions of *C. afghanica* were made during the middle to late 1970s. Since the Russian-Afghan War began in 1979 many additional introductions of *C. afghanica* were made into America from northwestern Pakistan.

C. afghanica spread throughout America very rapidly. Marijuana breeders intentionally crossed *C. afghanica* with sweet tasting but late-maturing *C. sativa* varieties to produce earlier-maturing hybrids. Thai X Afghan hybrids were particularly sweet and potent. Hybrid vigor caused by dominant heterosis or the blending of different favorable dominant traits was usually evident in the early hybrids. Flower potency increased and yields were much higher although the plants rarely exceeded 10 feet in height. Soon the majority of cultivators began to grow various *C. afghanica* X *C. sativa* hybrids. From these early hybrids some true-breeding inbred line or IBL varieties were created.

Since *Cannabis* is wind pollinated, and sinsemilla is usually grown in small crowded gardens, accidental pollination by uncontrolled males often results in many seeds. Accidental seeds were much more common than intentionally produced seeds, and were rapidly and widely distributed as a contaminant in sinsemilla. Intentionally produced seeds were usually only passed along from one serious cultivator or breeder to another and their distribution was much more limited. Accidentally produced seeds containing various proportions of the introduced *C. afghanica* gene pool were grown and unintentionally crossed again and again without strict selection. Random outcrossing produced a confused hybrid condition involving several parental lines in which favorable combinations of traits were rarely reproducible. Few of the offspring of F_2 and subsequent generations appeared alike, their gene pools having been formed of randomly collected traits passed along from their assorted predecessors. As the mixed gene pools reassorted they manifested many undesirable as well as desireable characteristics. Many of the original imported varieties that were used as the original building blocks of the IBL varieties have vanished and their genes have been diluted into the massive domestic drug *Cannabis* gene pool. Although many of the favorable genes may still exist, it is nearly impossible to retrieve them in combination with other favorable traits.

By the early to mid 1980s the vast majority of all domestically produced commercial sinsemilla in America had likely received some portion of its genes from the *C. afghanica* gene pool. By 1980 it was already becoming difficult to find the pre- *C. afghanica* varieties that had been so popular only a few years earlier. By 1985 it was nearly impossible to find pure *C. sativa* varieties cultivated domestically. 'Afghani#1', 'Hindu-Kush', 'Mazar-i-Sharif' and 'Skunk Weed' were some of the more successful pure *C. afghanica* inbred line or IBL varieties. Their hybrid offspring have spread far and wide.

It might appear that *C. afghanica* hybrids were perfectly suited for domestic cultivation and received with open arms by all American *Cannabis* growers. Although the use of *C. afghanica* varieties increased nationwide throughout the mid 1980s, owing to its delayed introduction in many areas of the Mideast and Midwest; its popularity began to decline in the West and other regions where drug *Cannabis* varieties were first introduced. Accidental recombination into complex hybrids had brought out some of the less desireable traits of *C. afghanica* that had previously been hidden. Without careful selection and breeding *Cannabis* begins to turn weedy, and as natural selection takes over, drug varieties lose their vigor, taste, and potency. Low potency, slow flat dreary high, skunky acrid fecal aroma, harsh taste, and susceptibility to mold are traits that soon became associated with many *C. afghanica* X *C. sativa* hybrids.

Many sinsemilla connoisseurs felt that *C. afghanica* had not lived up to expectations. Commercial and home cultivators had quite the opposite opinion. The characteristics of *C. afghanica* such as hardy growth, rapid maturation, and tolerance to cold allowed sinsemilla to be grown outdoors in the northern tier of states from Washington to Maine. This revolutionized the domestic marijuana market by making a potent homegrown smoke possible for those living in the northern latitudes of America and widened the scope and intensity of sinsemilla cultivation in America and Europe. During the 1980s production areas spread from the epicenters of the West Coast, Hawaii, and the Ozarks into at least 20 major marijuana producing states. A little sinsemilla is still grown outdoors in each of the 50 states.

Creating new hybrid crosses between IBLs restores vigor and supplies new combinations of genes for further breeding. Serious connoisseur *Cannabis* breeders have returned to some of the older pure *C. sativa* varieties as a source of "new" genetic material for variety improvement. Breeders can enhance the flavor and potency of inbred varieties by crossing the older pure-breeding IBL varieties with highly inbred *C. afghanica* X *C. sativa* hybrids. Also breeders are constantly searching for new sources of exotic germplasm. Pure *C. afghanica* varieties are still highly prized breeding stock and new *C. afghanica* varieties from Central Asia are occasionally introduced and tested. *C. sativa* varieties from South Africa have gained favor with breeders, as they mature early but do not suffer from many of the drawbacks of *C. afghanica* such as mold susceptibility and acrid flavor. Imported South African varieties, since they come from so far south of the equator, mature in August but are often very short, not very potent, and relatively low yielding. However, persistent selection has resulted in inbred South African varieties such as 'Durban'. Crosses with inbred *C. sativa* and *C. afghanica* varieties or their hybrids are usually vigorous and early-maturing and may express the desireable *C. sativa* or *C. afghanica* traits of potency, fragrance, full flavor, and high yield within a few select individuals. These select plants are preserved through cuttings for later use as seed parents.

Since the late 1970s several breeders have worked with *C. sativa* ssp. fibrosa sect. spontanea weedy *Cannabis* varieties from Central and Eastern Europe. Most Western cultivators called these varieties "ruderalis". These weedy varieties mature in July or August which makes them desireable to use in drug *Cannabis* varieties in an attempt to hasten maturity. It is not clear whether these weedy populations are truly wild varieties or merely escapes from *Cannabis* hemp cultivation that have turned weedy. Unfortunately in either case the weedy varieties are almost devoid of THC, the hybrids are of very low potency, and consequently repeated back crosses to the high-THC parent and recurrent selections must be made to restore potency. These backcrossed lines should be well adapted to far northern latitudes but very few of them have proved to be potent enough to be accepted by sinsemilla growers.

Exotic imported varieties from India, Kashmir, Nepal, Africa, and Indonesia are occasionally used in first filial generation or F_1 hybrid crosses to enhance potency or impart particular flavors to the smoke. Since commercial shipments do not often originate in these regions, the seeds are usually collected in small numbers by travelers and are very rare compared to seeds from the major marijuana producing regions of Colombia, Mexico, Jamaica, and Thailand.

Because *Cannabis* is a difficult plant in which to fix traits through selective breeding, and only the female plants are of economic importance, it is advantageous to clone exceptional plants by rooting cuttings. Through cloning large numbers of identical select female plants can be grown. Besides circumventing the vagaries of genetic recombination, cloning can provide uniform crops of female plants in one generation, rather than through many generations of selection and breeding. No rouging of male plants is required to produce sinsemilla

as no male plants are cloned and no pollen is produced. All of the female flowers mature simultaneously and the entire field can be harvested at once. This is an obvious boon to commercial *Cannabis* cultivation.

Due to continuing governmental pressure against outdoor growers, sinsemilla growing has largely moved indoors. Halide and sodium-vapor light systems are most often set up in attics, bedrooms, or basements where space is limited. Under these circumstances there is no room for nonproductive plants and the single best clone is usually selected for all future cultivation.

C. afghanica hybrids have proved to be well adapted to indoor clonal cultivation. *C. afghanica* varieties mature quickly allowing 3-4 harvests per year and yield up to 100 grams of flowers on plants less than 3 feet tall. Many *C. sativa* varieties are often too stretchy and tall and take too long to mature. *C. afghanica* hybrids are much easier and more economical to grow than pure *C. sativa* varieties. The tops of the tallest plants, very near the lights, shade the bottom branches and prevent them from producing any flowers.

Modern indoor growing conditions often seem ill-suited for the improvement of *Cannabis* through selective breeding. Grow rooms are small in comparison to the plowed fields that are usually planted for the breeding of open-pollinated crops such as maize or *Cannabis* . Most modern indoor *Cannabis* growers use clones of select female plants for sinsemilla flower production and rarely if ever grow a male plant or even plant a seed. Commercial growers try never to have seeds in their product and have little interest in making seeds. Clones provide uniform predictable crops, harvest after harvest. Clones remain consistent and stable through dozens of clonal generations as long as they are not infected by viruses or other contagious pathogens. There are no markedly inferior plants in a mono-clonal grow room. However, since all the plants in a mono-clonal population are genetically identical to one another there are also no unique and potentially superior plants. All offspring are identical and only as good as the mother plant from which the cutting was first taken. Grow rooms represent the antithesis of breeding. They rely on asexual reproduction to provide enough vegetative cuttings to grow and mature into a crop and seeds rarely enter the picture. Female clones improve grow room performance but preclude the possibility of seed production. Breeding is no longer practiced and variety improvement ceases entirely. It is difficult to say if cloning will have a lasting effect on *Cannabis* breeding and the evolution of the cultivated *Cannabis* gene pool, but it has certainly limited variability in grow room populations.

Accelerated eradication efforts in America by state and federal law enforcement during the 1980s lowered the supply and the quality of domestically grown *Cannabis* . Shortages fueled the hyper inflation of *Cannabis* prices. The price of *Cannabis* continues to steadily rise while the quality is rarely as high as it was only a few years ago. This situation has resulted in the increase of home *Cannabis* cultivation for personal use as smokers try to provide themselves with a steady hassle-free supply

of consistently high quality *Cannabis*. The vast majority of personal grow
rooms have only one to 4 grow lights and produce just enough smoke to
satisfy the needs of the household in which they are set up.

Increased acceptance of *Cannabis* as an applicable therapeutic agent
for the treatment of the side effects of appetite loss and nausea
associated with AIDS and cancer chemotherapy is resulting in an increase
in the number of small home growing operations. The afflicted public has
learned that *Cannabis* can be effective in relieving their discomfort. It is
impossible to buy legal *Cannabis* for medical use in America so patients
are turning to their close friends for their medicine or growing their own
closet crop. As more and more patients suffering from glaucoma, AIDS,
and the nausea associated with chemotherapy decide to relieve their
discomfort by smoking *Cannabis*, many will be forced to become closet
Cannabis growers in order to medicate themselves.

Different varieties of drug *Cannabis* provide the smoker with differing
intensities and types of highs. *Cannabis* varieties also differ in their
therapeutic effect. These differences are produced both by the potency
and cannabinoid profile of the particular *Cannabis* variety as well as
variations in individual patient's physiology and mind set. Individual
Cannabis varieties specially bred for a particular potency level and
particular cannabinoid profile, tailored to the individual medical needs and
personal preferences of each patient, can be created by home *Cannabis*
breeders. This type of personal selection of the most therapeutically
effective varieties could provide each patient with the best possible
treatment for their particular condition and circumstances. For instance,
it may turn out that a less potent variety could have all the therapeutic
benefits of a more potent variety without the side effect of making the
patient 'stoned'.

Although the crowded conditions of indoor grow rooms are not ideal
for breeding *Cannabis* , the 1980s have shown us that the immediate
future for *Cannabis* and *Cannabis* breeders in America is in indoor grow
rooms under lights. Compromises have been made to circumvent law
enforcement efforts and sinsemilla is still produced. If *Cannabis* quality is
to improve, rather than remaining frozen in its present cloned state, then
improvements will have to come from the selective breeding of indoor
Cannabis crops. The illegality and high visibility of marijuana cultivation
make it preferable to limit the size of gardens and the frequency of visits
to observe the plants. This lowers the total number of potential breeding
plants the breeder will have to choose from and limits the amount of time
that can be spent with each plant. Indoor grow rooms provide the grower
with more privacy than outdoor gardens and allow the grower to
concentrate more on breeding.

All gardens and fields are finite. Even outdoor *Cannabis* gardeners
tend to make their fields small in an effort to avoid detection. Grow
rooms are bounded by walls and seem extremely finite and small. However,
in America today the total indoor space devoted to *Cannabis* cultivation

may equal or even exceed the outside area devoted to *Cannabis* cultivation.

The vast majority of progress in the breeding of improved drug *Cannabis* varieties has been made in small scale growing situations both outdoors in fields and indoors in glass houses or grow rooms. No domestic *Cannabis* breeder has ever felt as if they had enough space for breeding and conditions always seemed overcrowded and cramped. Despite the adverse conditions imposed by clandestine crowded conditions greatly improved drug *Cannabis* varieties have been created both in America and in Holland.

Dutch *Cannabis* seed companies sprang up during the middle 1980s offering seeds of predominately American sinsemilla varieties along with a few Dutch and

assorted foreign varieties. Their breeding lines were established from improved varieties collected in America and elsewhere. Except for making available a wide range of simple multi-hybrid crosses the Dutch seed companies such as the Seed Bank, Super Sativa Seed Club, and the Sensi Seed Bank have done little to improve the varieties that they initially collected. The Dutch seed companies reproduced established varieties, attempting to clean them up and make them more homogeneous, while preserving their individual character. This is always difficult with open-pollinated plants such as *Cannabis* that suffer from inbreeding depression, especially when there are only small populations to select from.

Inbreeding depression results in a loss of general health and vigor caused by an accumulation of recessive gene pairs. Some Dutch varieties have also proved to be acceptable early-maturing material for sinsemilla production outdoors under natural daylight conditions at far northern latitudes.

Service from the Dutch seed companies was at times slow. Resulting from short stocks many substitutions were made in orders. Sometimes seeds did not appear dark and fully mature because they were grown under artificial lights. To many growers the Dutch seeds seemed over priced. Despite these shortcomings, the *Cannabis* varieties offered by Dutch seed companies met with great acceptance in America. Most of the varieties offered were better than the varieties customers already had so they were satisfied. The mail order availability of improved *Cannabis* varieties coincided with the general knowledge of cloning and much of the material from the individual offspring of the Dutch seeds is still being used for sinsemilla production in America today. The Dutch seed companies that exported seed to America went out of business in 1991. *Cannabis* seeds are still available at selected coffee shops and from a few retail seed shops in Amsterdam and other Dutch cities. The cultivation of *Cannabis* for seed and the sale of *Cannabis* seed is currently legal within Holland but the importation of *Cannabis* seed into America is not allowed under American law.

Many of the original improved varieties were derived from dihybrid or polyhybrid crosses between traditionally used land races of drug *Cannabis* from such diverse origins as Afghanistan, Colombia, Jamaica, Mexico, Panama, and Thailand. The extreme potency and delicate characteristics of these initial hybrids often resulted from the heterosis condition of hybrid vigor reflecting the diverse genotypic backgrounds of the original land races incorporated into the hybrids. Today it is nearly impossible to acquire many of the original land races available during the 1970s and modern breeders must often rely on collections of select domestic inbred lines derived from these original polyhybrid crosses. In some ways the breeder's task is easier because many previous breeders have already made improvements that will benefit future breeding programs. There is no reason to repeat other breeder's work. However, it may also be impossible to undo some of the unfavorable combinations made by earlier breeders whose priorities in breeding may have differed from the priorities of the current breeding project. Even if parts of the original gene pools have been carried over into the hybrid offspring, individual genes have surely been lost. It is a tragedy that many of the original varieties are lost forever. The initial easy hybrids relied on the basic genetic building blocks of the land races and can no longer be made. However, it is more important now than ever to preserve what does remain of the original diverse drug *Cannabis* gene pool and use it to develop new and better varieties that meet our current criteria for satisfying smoke and other *Cannabis* products. Further improvement will be another leg in the long uphill climb to higher quality *Cannabis* , and as always it will be well worth the effort.

Breeding Tips

Indoor grow rooms offer several advantages over outdoor gardens. Grow rooms offer easy access and encourage frequent visits especially when the grow room is conveniently located in the grower's home. Monitoring of male plants for pollen dispersal and females for pistil ripeness and seed maturity requires frequent visits to inspect the plants. This is often nearly impossible in clandestine outdoor gardens where privacy is lacking and visits must be kept to a minimum if detection is to be avoided. Inside a grow room there is a much lower chance of stray pollination from an unselected source than there is in an outdoor garden. Filters can be used to cover the intake vents and then no pollen or dust can enter the grow room.

Usually varieties that perform well under artificial lights will also perform well outside or in a glass house under natural sunlight. The converse does not hold true nearly as often. Varieties that perform well outside often prove to be a disappointment when grown under artificial light. This explains much of the general success experienced by breeders who have been forced to breed under artificial light conditions. Their varieties have often proved to be acceptable for both indoor and outdoor cultivation. However, there are few varieties that are superior for both indoor and outdoor applications and most varieties perform best with the same growing conditions under which they were selected and bred.

Cannabis is not a particularly straightforward plant to breed although it produces copious quantities of both pollen and seed. The life history of *Cannabis* presents several obstacles to improvement by selective breeding. Individual *Cannabis* plants are usually either all male or all female and thus individual plants are usually incapable of selfing. Selfing is the most effective means of fixing desirable traits, since the selected genes are more likely to be represented in both the pollen and the ovule if they come from the same plant. In *Cannabis* breeding, the genes controlling a selected trait must be present in two separate individuals, one male pollen parent and one female seed parent. The psychoactive resin of *Cannabis* is only produced by female plants. This makes it very difficult to recognize potentially favorable traits in male parents, especially when these traits must ultimately be expressed in the female offspring. All *Cannabis* varieties are wind-pollinated and inter-cross freely. Perspective female seed parents must be isolated from all male plants to avoid stray pollinations until they are to be pollinated with a select male.

The actual strategy for pollinating enough flowers to provide sufficient seed without seeding the remainder of the plants and spoiling the sinsemilla crop can be structured in several ways. The simplest way to make seed is to supply one select pollen source (one male clone or seedling) inside a grow room with a variety of female clones or seedlings as seed parents. This situation is analogous to leaving only the best male plant in a field to pollinate many of the best female plants. Each female parent will provide a different set of offspring from each cross but the male parent will be the same in each case. Cloning offers indoor growers an added advantage because very small female plants can be produced in very little space that are fully ripe and receptive for pollination and seed production yet large enough to produce sufficient seed for future breeding. More variety of seed parents can be grown on a smaller area. This offers a wider genetic base for selection and increases the number of potentially excellent crosses that a breeder can make.

Each female clone will differ in its ability to make favorable gene combinations with any given male clone. This is the female clone's Specific Combining Ability or SCA. If the percentage of favorable offspring resulting from a specific cross is high, then the SCA of the individual cross is high. If an individual clone is crossed with many other clones, and is found to produce high percentages of favorable offspring when crossed with a variety of mates, then it has a high General Combining Ability or GCA. Parents that show high SCA in specific crosses, and especially high GCA in many crosses, are preserved by cloning and are highly valued for further breeding. A clone's GCA is a measure of its reliability as a parent and GCA can only be measured by repeated crossing with a wide variety of other clones. Determining a clones GCA requires much space in the grow room. If only 5 female clones are tested with 5 male clones then 25 crosses must be made. At least 10 female plants should be grown from each cross for evaluation. This means over 500 seedlings must be started to produce 250 females.

The ultimate breeding system would provide an individual isolated grow room for each male pollen parent. Many different female clones could be grown in each room and only one male used in each room to pollinate all of the female clones within. If a reliable male parent is used, common pollination by one male is an especially good way to test a large number of female clones for their crossability. During the early stages of a breeding project, if a male must be used that has not been test crossed with various females, then it is advisable to use an open-pollinated imported variety with favorable vegetative and floral characteristics, or better yet an improved vigorous inbred line such as 'Skunk#1', 'Early Girl', 'California Orange', etc. This increases the chances that a vigorous male is chosen rather than an inbred male that could produce inferior weak offspring.

Multiple pollen sources can be used within a common grow room without contamination of neighboring plants if certain precautions are taken. The most efficient way to perform multiple crosses within one grow room, is to think ahead when the grow room is filled, and remember to make an additional set of both male and female clones for each batch of seeds. In other words for every cross that is to be made with a certain clone, a separate cutting of that clone is provided for each pollen and seed parent. If the grower wishes to cross one female clone with many different pollen sources then enough cuttings are made at the start so that one cutting may be pollinated by each different pollen source. As the female clones become ripe they are removed individually from the common grow room and pollinated with a single pollen source.

The pollen is either collected from selected males, dried, and stored in a deep freezer until use or a ripe male plant that is shedding pollen is introduced from another grow room. If the female plant is artificially pollinated with stored pollen it is then left outside the common grow room for 3 days, allowing time for the pollen to either germinate and initiate seed formation, or die so that it will not be able to accidentally pollinate other plants. After 3 days the female seed plant is sprayed with water to kill remaining pollen and returned to the common grow room. If a living male plant is used for the pollen source, then the male and female plants are left together in isolation until the male releases its pollen. If the male is already shedding pollen then it is only necessary to dust the female plant with pollen by shaking the male plant over it. The male plant can be returned to its grow room immediately. If pollination is successful within 2 days the female stigmatic hairs will wither slightly and darken in color indicating that they have been fertilized. Then the female plant is rinsed with a spray of water to kill remaining pollen and returned to the common grow room. The remainder of the clones within the common grow room remain completely seedless and later serve as perfect controls when comparing the virtues of each variety.

If an insufficient number of individual female clones are available for individual seed parents, and larger female plants with branches are available, then individual branches can be bag pollinated (see *Marijuana Botany* by Robert C. Clarke, And/Or Press: Berkeley). Stray pollinations can be very dangerous within the confines of a grow room. Great care must be taken to avoid accidental pollination. It is safest to make pollinations individually outside the grow room. The major advantage to producing larger sized plants indoors is that they ripen more properly than small plants and more fully express their genetic potential. This makes them easier to evaluate in terms of their general worth. Comparative selections can be made between small individuals of the same population but larger plants are required to judge a variety's general worth.

If male clones are to be used as a direct pollen source, it is advisable to induce them to flower two weeks later than the female seed clones for early-maturing varieties, and 4 weeks later than the female seed clones for late-maturing varieties. Otherwise the males will mature and shed their pollen before the female stigmas are ripe and receptive. Often it is easier to flower the males well ahead of the females and store the pollen for a short time until the females are receptive. Pollen can be stored in a cool dry place for several weeks without much loss of viability. If pollen is to be stored for longer it should be placed in paper envelopes in a cool dark place and dried with desiccant. The dry pollen is then placed in a sealed container with additional desiccant and stored in a deep freezer. Many of the pollen grains will die upon defrosting, but if several grams of pollen were frozen, enough of the pollen grains will still be alive to pollinate many plants. It is best to defrost pollen inside a refrigerated sealed container containing a desiccant or to administer the pollen to the female plants while it is still frozen as it will not have time to defrost, condense moisture, and clump together making it more difficult to spread around. The simplest way to keep a viable pollen bank is to keep multiple clones of each male in the vegetative state and flower them as they are needed for pollen production.

Male parents should be selected from the most consistent lines expressing favorable traits. Once individual male plants have been selected, clones of each should be preserved until the SCA and GCA of each has been determined through crosses with several female clones. Male plants are difficult to judge based on their visible traits alone since they do not produce flowers that elaborate THC containing resins. Once a male plant with high specific combining ability is selected it becomes a very valuable addition to the breeders available gene pool.

Seeding female plants hastens their maturity by one or two weeks but the seeds must be given time to fully mature. In the end it takes almost as much time to produce good seed as good sinsemilla.

Large late-maturing plants that are growing in the Spring on a natural light cycle can be cloned as soon as they are old enough to have slightly woody stems and long before they flower naturally. If the rooted cuttings are transferred to a grow room set at an inductive photoperiod of 12 hours of darkness then they will flower and reveal their sex long before the mother plant from which they were taken. If they are females they will continue to flower and when the small clone matures it will give a hint of what the large plant will be like when it matures properly.

It is a fairly simple proposition to select two parents from varieties with favorable characteristics, cross them, and select a few offspring that exhibit most of the favorable characteristics from each parental variety. If these unique combinations are cloned then the improved hybrid clones are preserved for future cultivation with a minimum of work. However, it is much more difficult and involved to undertake the breeding of a stable IBL from an F_1 hybrid cross. This takes years of careful selection and grow outs of large number of offspring for evaluation.

A simple analogy can be made with colored flowers. If a 'pink' flower is the goal of a flower breeding program then a 'red' variety might be crossed with a 'white' variety. Almost all of the F_1 offspring will be 'pink', but how 'pink' are they? Upon careful observation the most 'pink' F_1 individuals can be selected and cloned. However, when the select F_1 hybrid 'pink' offspring are crossed to each other, their F_2 offspring will show great diversity. Some will be varying shades of 'pink', but many of the offspring will be more 'red' or 'white' than 'pink'. Here is where a breeder's work really begins in an effort to produce a true-breeding 'pink' IBL variety rather than simply selecting and cloning the best 'pink' individuals. Parents must be selected that have a high level of 'pinkness' and pass their 'pinkness' on to future generations. These individuals are said to have a high General Combining Ability or GCA.

Selection from huge populations is a luxury rarely afforded to drug *Cannabis* breeders. 'Original Skunk#1' is one of the only drug *Cannabis* varieties that has been repeatedly selected for many years from large grow outs due to its widespread use as a commercial variety.

Favorable Characteristics for Indoor Varieties

General Vigor

Parental plants for the production of seed should be strong and vigorous. Weak plants may harbor genetic deficiencies that interfere with their proper growth. Strong vigorous plants are less likely to conceal genetic weaknesses that may later cause problems. Rapid growth and rich green foliage are signs of vigor.

Potency

The potency of a drug *Cannabis* variety is its single most important attribute. If a variety is not potent enough then the smoker will have to consume too much plant material in an effort to get high and will not be satisfied. Potent *Cannabis* is high in the psychoactive cannabinoid compound Tetrahydrocannabinol or THC. THC content is controlled by simple inheritance. When a high-THC variety is crossed with a low-THC variety, the F_1 hybrid offspring are relatively uniform in THC content, and the percentage of THC is approximately intermediate between the two parental varieties.

The simplest way an indoor grower can create different hybrids is to cross two diverse gene pools and select only a few of the best offspring. These select plants are cloned by making cuttings and then the clones are multiplied and grown out for production use. The first breeding step of creating F_1 hybrids has been taken. The improvement process need not stop here. At the very least the best F_1 plants should be inter crossed with one another and the best plants from the second inbred or F_2 generation cloned for production use. This allows one more generation of selection and allows the genes from the two parental lines to recombine into additional different combinations that may prove acceptable as clonal material. To ensure success thousands of F_2 offspring should be grown for selection. However, many advances have been made selecting from F_2 populations of only a few dozen plants. There are no substitutes for close scrutiny and harsh selection. When a very good plant is found, whether it is male or female, a cutting should be made, grown on under a vegetative photoperiod, and serially cloned so its gene pool is preserved for later breeding experiments. The decision to continue improving an already acceptable variety through continuing selective breeding, or to cease selection and preserve the unique products of genetic recombination through cloning, is up to the individual breeder.

Backcross techniques are effective in creating more potent varieties and in improving or rejuvenating depressed inbred lines. Increases in THC content can be made by crossing an existing low potency but otherwise favorable parental or P_1 variety with a more potent P_1 variety that may not have other favorable characteristics, such as early maturation or short stature, but is high in THC. Individual female F_1 offspring are backcrossed to select males of the original favorable P_1 variety to produce the first backcross or BC_1 generation. The best female plants in the BC_1 population are selected for gross phenotype and potency and are backcrossed to males of the original favorable P_1 variety producing the second backcross or BC_2 generation. The females of the BC_2 generation are selected and backcrossed to the P_1 males as in the BC_1 generation to make the third backcross or $BC3$ generation. This backcross scheme is repeated until the offspring closely resemble the original P_1 variety but with significantly higher THC percentage and more potency.

Another way to increase THC content is by constant inbreeding selection within the same variety to create a more potent inbred line or IBL. An IBL is created by continually selecting brother and sister plants from the same initial parental cross and using them as parents for the next generation. Potency is increased by selecting the most potent offspring of the F_1 generation and crossing them amongst themselves to give the F_2 generation. The F_2 plants are once again selected for potency and the most potent plants are used as parents for the $F3$ generation.

However, constant inbreeding often results in a situation known as inbreeding depression that causes a loss of health and vigor in the offspring. The inbred offspring could be very high in THC but so weak that they could not survive long enough to mature properly.

Many currently popular *Cannabis* varieties were selected from polyhybrid gene pools resulting from broad crosses between drug *Cannabis* land races of various origins. From these diverse F_1 hybrid gene pools relatively true-breeding IBL varieties were established and used for further breeding. Some IBL varieties such as 'Skunk#1' have been constantly improved through intense selection and inbreeding for over 10 years without many signs of inbreeding depression. This has been possible because these IBL varieties were initially based on and selected from an extremely broad hybrid gene pool and inbreeding depression has had less influence. It is very difficult to prevent inbreeding depression without using a wide range of parental plants in each generation. This often proves difficult within the confines of a home grow room.

Backcrossing and inbreeding are techniques that can be used for fixing many favorable traits and should be considered in the breeding of *Cannabis* varieties for any purpose.

Resin Content

One of the most important determinants of potency is the amount of resin on the surface of the female flowers. The majority of THC is synthesized and accumulated in the resin glands. Hashish is made from the resin glands of *Cannabis*. Plants that elaborate many resin glands are usually more potent than those with only a few resin glands. Parents are selected from lines that produce large amounts of resin glands on both the bracts and the associated leaves.

Flower to Leaf Ratio

The bract surrounding each individual *Cannabis* flower contains the majority of the THC containing resin glands. Bracts contain far more resin glands than even small leaves. Therefore the most potent floral clusters are those with the highest number of flowers and the fewest number of leaves, or a high flower to leaf ratio. Pure *C. sativa* IBL varieties and *C. sativa* X *C. afghanica* hybrid varieties usually have higher flower to leaf ratios than pure-breeding *C. afghanica* IBL varieties. Some IBL pure *C. sativa* varieties such as 'Original Haze' produce sparse stretchy floral clusters but they also have a high flower to leaf ratio.

Large Floral Clusters

Large floral clusters are important because the larger the floral clusters, the more individual female flowers they contain, the more surface they have for the elaboration of resin glands, and the more stash the grower gets to smoke. The size of the flowers is largely determined by the number of flowers that are produced within each floral cluster along the stem. It is not enough for a plant to merely produce many floral clusters. Each floral cluster must contain many individual resin-covered flowers.

Quality of High

The quality of the marijuana high varies considerably between different varieties of *Cannabis*. Some are characterized as sedative while others are considered mentally stimulating. 'Afghani#1' and 'Hindu Kush' are both considered sleep inducing. 'Original Haze' is one of the most mentally stimulating varieties. All 3 can be extremely potent if they are grown to maturity but they always differ in the quality of the high. Conscious drug *Cannabis* breeders will choose the particular types of highs they prefer and make selections accordingly.

Therapeutic Effects

Variations in the quality of the high may result from variations in the cannabinoid profile of each variety. Although THC is the primary psychoactive cannabinoid it is not the only cannabinoid. Several other cannabinoids are psychologically or physiologically active and could modify the effects of THC. As *Cannabis* becomes accepted as a therapeutic agent for the relief of symptoms associated with cancer and AIDS chemotherapy and the treatment of assorted other medical conditions it is likely that certain varieties will prove to be more efficacious for the relief of specific medical conditions than others. This is an important consideration and deserves the attention of *Cannabis* breeders.

Taste and Aroma

One of the greatest pleasures of smoking *Cannabis* comes from the variety in flavor and aroma of the flowers and their smoke. The aroma of fresh plants is very consistent between varieties and even beginning growers have little trouble discerning a 'Skunk#1' from an 'Afghani#1' or an 'Original Haze'. Each has a very distinctive aroma and the aromas tend to blend when the distinct varieties are crossed. A rich earthy hash-like 'Afghani#1' crossed with a minty sweet Thai variety often produces offspring that are rich and sweet expressing flavor characteristics of both parents. The flavors of some varieties are so distinct that they can be detected at first sniff even when they make up one quarter or less of the hybrid offspring's genetics.

At the same time breeding *Cannabis* for flavor and aroma can be illusive and frustrating. Over one hundred different aromatic terpenoid flavoring ingredients have been isolated from *Cannabis*. If we assume that at least 30 different aromatic terpenoids are found in any one plant, that there is likely at least one gene controlling the synthesis of each of the terpenoid compounds, and the amount of each produced; then there are obviously myriad gene combinations that can influence the flavor and aroma of *Cannabis*. Although some flavor combinations of individual varieties persist in crosses, it is often very difficult to reproduce the flavor of a variety exactly, due to the large number of potential combinations involved in any single cross. Inbreeding has proved to be the most effective way to preserve a desirable varietal flavor and taste but inbreeding can lead to a loss of potency and vigor.

Short Stature
Short stature is vital in indoor varieties grown from seed that must be short enough when mature to be within the penetration of the grow lights. The use of clones allows very short pieces of female branches to be flowered and the resultant mature plants are very short. The height of the plant is largely determined by the distance along the stem between flowers, and the length of time the clone continues to grow vegetatively after an inductive photoperiod is started before it begins to form flowers. The farther apart the flowers are, the taller and more stretched the plants will be. The longer a clone remains vegetative the taller it will grow. Shorter plants are plants that begin to form flowers at close spacing along the stem immediately following a change to a flowering 12 hour photoperiod. Plants should be selected for dense flowers and an immediate response to flowering photoperiod.

Early Maturation
Early maturation is of value because the faster a plant matures the earlier it can be harvested and the sooner the grow room can be used for the next crop. Varieties that mature quickly allow less time for attack by mold, mites, and other pests. Early maturation should not be confused with early flowering.

Mold and Mite Resistance
The two most devastating pests of indoor *Cannabis* crops are gray molds and spider mites. Mold and spider mites can cause epidemic destruction of indoor *Cannabis* crops especially when the crop is grown from only one clone. Environmental controls for gray molds and environmental as well as biological controls for spider mites have proved to be the most effective preventive controls of these pests. Of course the most effective preventive control would be to breed resistant varieties for use along with proper environmental controls as crops in indoor grow rooms. Varieties with inherited resistance to these pests are sorely needed.

Suitable Indoor Varieties

'Afghani#1'
'Afghani#1' is an IBL variety originally developed during the late 1970s by Cultivator's Choice from an imported *C. afghanica* hashish variety. 'Afghani#1' is a dark green broad-leaf variety of medium height and produces coarse heavy buds that are covered with resin at maturity. 'Afghani#1' is a fairly leafy variety but the small leaflets around the

flowers develop plenty of resin. The aroma and taste are thick, greasy, and medicinal and occasionally acrid and unpleasant. 'Afghani#1' is one of the most potent varieties available and produces a very physical, sedative, and almost narcotic effect. 'Afghani#1' requires 8-9 weeks to mature under a 12 hour photoperiod.

'Big Bud'
'Big Bud' is a relatively unstabilized *C. sativa* X *C. afghanica* hybrid variety. 'Big Bud' was originally developed in the Portland Oregon area as a clone for indoor sinsemilla production and was multiplied and distributed through Dutch seed companies. 'Big Bud' is best known for its high yield especially when it is grown closely packed under high intensity lights. The medium to dark green floral clusters are large and dense with a high resin content. Yield, length of maturation, and potency are variable because 'Big Bud' has never been stabilized through inbreeding. Approximately 25% of the females will be very high-yielding but late-maturing and approximately 25% of these will be potent. Since half of the seeds produce male plants this means that 32 seeds are required simply to assure an even chance of getting one high-yielding and potent plant. If further combinations of traits such as flavor and aroma are desired then many offspring should be grown and tested. This type of selection of future parental material from rough polyhybrid varieties often proves unfeasible within the confines of a small grow room. It is more economical in terms of population size and grow room capacity to rely on IBL varieties such as 'Original Skunk#1' for parental material for breeding experiments.

'California Orange'
'California Orange' is a stabilized *C. sativa* X *C. afghanica* hybrid variety of medium height and yield developed by Cultivator's Choice. The medium green medium broad-leaf plants produce copious resin even on the surface of the small leaflets. Some individuals have a pronounced citrus aroma and flavor. 'California Orange' is very potent with a fairly clear high. 'California Orange' requires 8-10 weeks to mature under 12 hour photoperiod.

'Early Girl'
'Early Girl' is another *C. sativa* X *C. afghanica* hybrid variety developed for over 10 years by Cultivators Choice. In this case the variety tends 90% towards the *C. afghanica* side and the *C. sativa* contribution is almost entirely masked. Although this hybrid has been stabilized through persistent inbreeding, the offspring continue to show considerable diversity. The dark green small to medium height broad-leaf plants produce a moderate yield of acrid hashish-tasting flowers of fairly high potency and physical high. The great advantage of 'Early Girl' is that it requires only 7-9 weeks of 12 hour photoperiod to mature completely. 'Early Girl' also tends to grow in a tall slender column and is well adapted to close spacing in indoor grow rooms.

'Early Pearl'

'Early Pearl' is a stabilized early-maturing hybrid variety originally developed for outdoor cultivation in the American Midwest that also performs very well under lights. 'Early Pearl' originates from a hybrid cross between 'Early Girl' and the stabilized *C. sativa* variety 'Polly' from the Sierra Foothills of California. Further inbreeding has led to a relatively stable variety. 'Early Pearl' is an early-maturing *C. sativa* -dominated *C. sativa* X *C. afghanica* hybrid variety that produces very resiny, sweet, and potent flowers. 'Early Pearl' usually requires only 6-8 weeks of 12 hour photoperiod to completely mature.

'Hindu-Kush'

'Hindu-Kush' is a true-breeding *C. afghanica* IBL variety commonly used for indoor cultivation and as parental material for hybrid crosses. 'Hindu-Kush' plants are short with dense leafy flowers and produce resin over much of their leaf surface. The flowers are rather coarse with an often strongly acrid earthy aroma and flavor that reminds one of primo Afghani hashish. 'Hindu-Kush' usually requires 8-10 weeks of 12 hour photoperiod to mature.

'Northern Lights'

'Northern Lights' is a stabilized *C. sativa* X *C. afghanica* hybrid variety that was developed in the late 1970s near Seattle, Washington. The Northwest of America was the center of indoor sinsemilla production and indoor *Cannabis* breeding. Due to the poor weather associated with this region sinsemilla cultivators have long resorted to growing *Cannabis* inside under lights long before growers in other more temperate regions of America. 'Northern Lights' has been highly regarded for many years throughout the Northwest and was multiplied and distributed by Dutch seed companies. The variety was inbred and selected for short early-maturing plants with large floral clusters and resembles its *C. afghanica* parentage most closely. 'Northern Lights' has been preserved much as it originally was through inbreeding without any marked improvements other than hybridization with other established varieties. 'Northern Lights' is a dark green fairly short variety with leafy but very resiny floral clusters and requires 8-10 weeks of 12 hour photoperiod to mature completely. 'Northern Lights' has won many awards at the *High Times* magazine harvest festivals in Amsterdam.

'Original Haze'

'Original Haze' is a pure-breeding stabilized IBL developed from a pure *C. sativa* polyhybrid created from predominately Mexican and Colombian varieties along with some South Indian and Thai varieties. 'Original Haze' started as a magical mix of the most exotic *C. sativa* varieties available in California in the early 1970s. Some of the early types were lost but through diligent selection and inbreeding Cultivator's Choice preserved the essence of the variety in their 'Original Haze'. 'Original Haze' produces tall sparse light green plants with narrow leaflets and numerous thin flowers. When grown from seed it is not suitable for indoor production but small clones can be flowered and the resultant mature plants will be of manageable size. The flowers are oily with a spicy sweet and sour aroma. 'Original Haze' plants can be very potent and almost always have a clear, awake, energetic high. 'Original Haze' takes 12-16 weeks to mature under a 12 hour photoperiod. 'Original Haze' has been inbred for 20 years. Approximately 75% of the plants are female and 10-20% of these plants are very special. The remainder are only so-so. Although 'Original Haze' is troublesome to grow indoors under lights it makes excellent breeding material and is well worth the extra trouble.

'Original Skunk#1'

'Original Skunk#1' is a relatively true-breeding *C. sativa* X *C. afghanica* IBL polyhybrid with a heavy tendency towards its *C. sativa* parentage. 'Original Skunk#1' was originally developed by Cultivator's Choice in the late 1970s for outdoor and glass house cultivation. It has also proved to produce excellent sinsemilla indoors under lights. 'Original Skunk#1' is a medium green and medium broad-leaf variety of medium height that produces large long floral clusters with very few leaves. The yield per square foot of 'Original Skunk#1' grown densely packed and strongly lighted can approach 40 grams of dry flowers. The flowers have a strong sweet and sour aroma and the taste is full-bodied and satisfying. The high is powerful and fairly stimulating. 'Original Skunk#1' requires 8-11 weeks of 12 hour photoperiod to mature completely.

The true-breeding nature of 'Original Skunk#1' has helped spread the reputation it has earned at harvest festivals in both America and Holland. 'Original Skunk#1' makes an excellent choice for male breeding material. It was selected from 50 different *C. sativa* X *C. afghanica* F_1 hybrid crosses primarily for its consistent true-breeding qualities in a broad range of crosses. 'Original Skunk#1' is an IBL that came from a naturally combining hybrid selected for its crossability and true-breeding qualities, rather than a forced hybrid made in an attempt to blend two previously selected individual varieties with specific desireable characteristics. In other words 'Original Skunk#1' has been selected for its naturally high GCA. Simply crossing a select 'Original Skunk#1' with almost any other drug variety will improve it. If a grower has a variety that has certain desireable characteristics but lacks potency or yield, it is possible to cross it with an 'Original Skunk#1', and then select offspring combining the sought after characteristics of the original variety with the many additional attributes of 'Original Skunk#1'. For example a hybrid cross between the inbred 'Original Haze' and 'Skunk#1' will restore the potency of the 'Original Haze' and make it a more compact and manageable size while preserving its unique varietal flavor and high. An 'Original Skunk#1'

X 'Original Haze' F_1 hybrid developed by Cultivator's Choice and grown by Dutch Passion seed company recently won first prize at the 1992 *High Times* magazine Harvest Festival in Amsterdam. 'Original Skunk#1' has certainly earned its reputation as the benchmark standard of the sinsemilla industry.

Many of these highly bred *Cannabis* varieties occasionally produce male flowers at the tips of female branches near the end of maturation due to environmental stress during flowering. These male flowers rarely produce viable pollen, and even when they do there are rarely any viable stigmas remaining to be pollinated on the neighboring female plants.

These unique recombinations of genes have lived on as relatively true-breeding varieties and are suitable for hybridization. New varieties are developed each year in an effort to create better sinsemilla. Improved varieties of *Cannabis* can be created by using the varieties readily available from Dutch seed companies for the past few years. Seeds of improved drug *Cannabis* varieties are only sold legally within Holland by Dutch seed companies. True-breeding varieties such as 'Original Skunk#1' are most valuable as breeding material. Many polyhybrid varieties are also available from a variety of parental lines. They may be fine plants and good for cloning for sinsemilla production, but because they do not breed true, they are not as useful in breeding programs as the inbred true-breeding varieties listed above. It is advisable to create unique hybrids from the available IBL varieties rather than relying on other breeders for these simple dihybrid crosses. Individual hybrids are only easily and reliably reproduced by cloning. True-breeding hybrid varieties that grow reliably from seed can only be created through diligent selective breeding. This is a long and challenging project.

Recently *Cannabis* has begun to receive the attention it deserves as a valuable medicinal plant, as well as a valuable fiber and seed crop, rather than merely as a social and law enforcement problem. The potency and other desireable qualities of drug *Cannabis* varieties were improved by selective breeding throughout the 1980s despite the restrictions imposed by worldwide laws prohibiting *Cannabis* cultivation. We should expect this trend to continue throughout the end of the 20th century and beyond. Whatever the individual goals of the *Cannabis* breeder, and whichever *Cannabis* varieties are available, *Cannabis* breeding will prove to be a truly rewarding experience for many advanced home growers. There are few experiences so satisfying as helping to improve such a valuable plant as *Cannabis*. Good Luck!

SECTION III

CASE STUDIES

Andrew

Andrew is reasonably intelligent, takes what he does seriously, a fanatic about cleanliness, and has had vegetable/marijuana gardens for the past four years. Last year, the neighborhood kids ripped-off his garden in early September. This year, Andy decided to undermine their efforts and grow an indoor crop.

It was early July. Andy decided to take some cuttings from the 10, four month old, *cannabis indica* plants, growing among the tomatoes in his garden. He did not know which plants were male or female. "Cloning for Sex" would give Andy the answer. With a pair of scissors, he took two, 4-inch cuttings from each plant, labeling each parent plant and corresponding clone. The clones were rooted in 4-inch pots of fine vermiculite. Andy used Dip-N-Grow as a root inducing hormone and watered with a 1/2 solution of UpStart to ease the shock and prevent wilt. Each 4-inch pot, containing a clone, was covered with a plastic baggie. The baggie was held in place by a rubber- band around the 4-inch pot. The 20 pots were then placed on a large cookie sheet to help contain the run-off water.

Andy put the cookie sheet in a window facing south that gets filtered sun. Every night, when he got home from work, Andy inspected the rooting clones, before covering them with a light-tight cardboard box to maintain a 12 hour photoperiod.

The clones looked good, with leaves always stretching out horizontally in search of light. The clones were watered twice the first week, by pouring water in the cookie tray and letting the vermiculite absorb it. The excess water remained in the tray.

The end of the 8th day, the clones were wilted and looked sick. Andy removed all the excess water from the cookie sheet. Within three days, most of the clones looked healthy, but 6 still looked sick. He never let the excess water remain in the tray again. The plastic baggie humidity tents were enough to maintain moist conditions and minimal watering was necessary.

Near the end of the 4th week, there were 18 healthy clones. The leaf tips were turning yellow and white roots grew from the drain holes. He pulled one of the clones out of the vermiculite. Sure enough, the subterranean stem was now a mass of succulent roots.

The clones were also showing definite male and female flowers. Even with the 2 dead clones, Andy was able to tell that he had 5 female plants. All the males were dried and smoked. The females were transplanted into 1 gallon pots and returned to the window sill. The 12 hour photoperiod was maintained for another 6 weeks. Andy harvested 1 1/2 ounces of nice tops from the small females.

Fifty cuttings were taken from the 5 known females and rooted as before, using Dip-N-Gro. This time the clones were given 18 hours of fluorescent light.

After three weeks of rooting the clones, Andy started preparing his spare 10 x 12-foot bedroom. The furniture was removed and the bedroom thoroughly cleaned, before painting everything (walls, ceiling and doors) flat white. The floor was covered with a 14 x 18-foot painters drop cloth, curling the edges up about 6 inches around the walls. This formed a large, protective tray for the excess water. He purchased 50, one gallon pots at a yard sale, potting soil and Ra-Pid-Gro from the nursery. He already had Up-Start and Dip-N-Grow from the first clone crop. Andy also bought a 1000 watt super metal halide, with a 4-foot reflective hood, remote ballast and 24 hour timer.

Andy mounted a hook, attached to a butterfly bolt, in the center of the room. He did not need to find a 2 x 4 rafter. An old swag lamp chain was used to adjust the height of the HID. One link of the chain was attached to the ceiling hook, another link, at the desired elevation, attached to the HID lamp.

The 50, well rooted clones, were transplanted into one gallon pots. An inch of gravel was placed in the bottom of each pot, before filling it with rich potting soil. The clones were watered with 1/2 solution of Up-Start, before and after transplanting. The 50, gallon clones, were huddled closely together in a circle, 36 inches under the lamp. The HID was moved 6 inches away from the recently transplanted clones, three days later.

One month later, the 3-inch clones were 12-16 inches tall. The lamp was moved progressively higher and the gallon pots moved into a larger circle. Now, the clones took up about half of the room and had bushed out beyond the sides of their restricting pots. Andy carefully transplanted the near rootbound clones into 6 gallon pots.

Three weeks later, the entire profile of the garden had elevated. The tallest plant was 30 inches and the shortest 24 inches. The 40, 6 gallon clones were using over 15 gallons of water per week. 10, sickly clones, were jerked, yielding more space and pacifying smoke.

Some of the clones used more water than others. Andy was having a difficult time deciding how much water to give them. He solved the problem by purchasing a moisture meter and experimenting.

Andy ran a hose from the nearby laundry room sine. The hose was attached to a watering wand with an on/off valve.

Fertilization started three weeks after the transplant to 6 gallon pots, and was continued on a weekly basis. A 1/2 solution of Ra-Pid-Gro was used throughout flowering.

With two months of vegetative growth, (two months after clones had rooted) the plants were about 4 feet tall. Some long branches were pruned off, so the garden had an even profile.

The only ventilation system in the grow room was an open door. The larger leaves were yellowing and continued to die throughout their lifespan. Andy noticed the leaves were not crisp and robust like the marijuana leaves in his veggie garden. They were limp, with curled down edges.

He cut the light from 18 to 12 hours per day, inducing visible signs of flowering in two weeks. Vegetative growth slowed, stems elongated about 9 inches, leaves yellowed faster, and flowers started to emerge.

By the end of the 8th week of 12 hour days, the entire house stunk of weed. The flowers glistened with resin. The pistils at the bottom of the buds were dying about as fast as they were growing from the top. Andy harvested the entire garden with a pair of garden clippers and hung the harvest upside down on the basement clothesline. The high quality marijuana was dry 3 weeks later. The harvest weighed in at 7 ounces of resin coated, manicured tops, and 11 ounces of leaf.

Andy spent a touch over $375 on the entire project (crop #2 he only spent $200) and learned a lot. He learned to clone and gained hands-on experience in indoor, HID horticulture. Andy's second crop was cloned from the same outdoor plants (before they got ripped-off). Little changed, except soil, the addition of an exhaust fan and using a high bloom fertilizer during f lowering. Yield #2 was: 15 ounces of primo tops and 14 ounces of leaf.

Bob

Bob has been a stony for many years. He has always loved smoking 4 pot and paid for it, rather than paying attention to how it was grown. Bob is a bit cheap and a slob, maintaining a not-so-clean living environment. He heard about HID lamps on a radio advertisement and has a friend who has a friend that sells Bob dynamite sinsemilla, grown in his basement.

Bob got his tax refund check back March 1. Instead of buying marijuana or going on a blow like last year, he decided to invest in a metal halide lamp. After a 10 minute indoctrination session at the local halide store, Bob left with a standard, 1000 watt, metal halide lamp and remote ballast.

Excited with his new investment, Bob wanted to see it in action as soon as possible. He hung the lamp by a clothes hanger from a rafter, 7 feet high in the cold (40-60° F), filthy garage, attached to his home. There was no functioning electrical outlet nearby. He used a 50-foot extension cord to carry electricity the 15 feet from the nearest indoor outlet. The extension cord was very hot most of the time. After a week, it go so hot, a fuse blew. Bob just replaced the 20 amp fuse and kept replacing it throughout the growing season.

He could see sparks of electricity as he plugged the system in. Bob thought he did not have enough money to buy a timer, containing the safe on/off switch. Within 5 minutes, the lamp was up to full intensity. Bob was impressed!

He dug some dirt (mostly clay) outdoors, threw it into 12, old, sun-bleached, 5 gallon, plastic pots that had cracked across the bottom. The cracks supplied fair drainage. Bob plated over a thousand Colombian, Mexican and Hawaiian seeds from 1/2-1 inch deep in the dozen containers. Three weeks later, there were about 500 leggy, crowded, seedlings, along with a menagerie of weeds. Rather than thinning them out so they had room to grow, Bob figured, the more plants, the more smoke.

The crowded seedlings did amazingly well for the first two months, considering the lamp was so far away, the compacted, acidic, clay soil, and the temperature was 40-60° most of the time. Ventilation was wonderful, since there were many holes in the walls to let the wind howl. The nice, old neighbor lady told Bob to turn off the light in the garage to conserve electricity, as well.

Bob ran out of smoke, so he picked about 200 leggy plants. The best thing he could have done! Now, there was room for the remaining plants to grow. The 200, spindly plants, yielded 2 ounces of low quality marijuana. None the less, Bob got a buzz, accompanied by a pounding headache.

The garden was looking bad and Bob did not know what to do. While watching a TV gardening show, he learned how fertilizer really does make plants grow better. Bob bought some houseplant food, not noticing it was high-acid, African Violet food (high in P and low in N). The directions said feed monthly. Since the sickly garden had not been fertilized for three months, Bob applied the fertilizer triple strength. The plants got super green, then about a week later, the leaves contorted into all kinds of shapes. About 150 of the 300 remaining plants up and died. The rest looked sick.

Bob, being a bit frustrated and chagrined, returned to the halide store for some advice. They told him of his negligence, and if he wanted to save his crop and get any smoke at all, he better leach the soil with soapy water and induce flowering, before he killed the rest of the garden!

Bob bought a timer, set it for 12 hours and plugged it into the system. In a couple of weeks, he was able to spot the males. They were jerked and smoked.

It was July and the outdoor bug population was growing exponentially. By the time he noticed the aphids, spider mites and mealy bugs, they were well established and launching an all out assault on the sickly garden.

This time, Bob went to the nursery and asked for a spray to kill bugs in his veggie garden. He bought SEVIN, in powder form, to dust the infested plants. SEVIN was the cheapest route, as he did not have to buy a spray bottle! Bob dusted the plants, tops of leaves only, four times during the next month. A few bugs died.

Seven weeks after inducing flowering, Bob harvested 75 sickly plants, yielding 4 ounces of fair tops and 6 ounces of leaves.

Bob was super bummed out. He spent over $250 on all this shit to grow marijuana, when he could have bought all the smoke he painstakingly grew for $250. He traded his HID system for $100 worth of smoke. Bob spent $300, grew over $250 worth of marijuana and sold the HID system for $100 worth of smoke, for a net profit of $50.

If you are dumber than Bob, you may want to think twice before investing in a HID system.

Chester & Claire

Chester works for a computer software manufacturer. He has a good income and over the years has developed a connoisseurs taste for fine *cannabis*. Chester is not a gardener, but Claire, his wife, loves horticulture and has a house full of lush, green plants. A friend of theirs had been growing marijuana in his basement for 6 months, with excellent results. Chester and Claire decided to try it.

Chet took the $1000 he was going to put in his IRA account and purchased a super metal halide, H.P. sodium, all the tools listed in Chapter l, soilless mix, Peters fertilizer (Pete-Lite Special 20-10-20 and Blossom Booster 10-30-20), CO_2 enrichment system, Up-Start and several books.

Chester installed an exhaust fan to pull air out of an empty, 10 x 10-foot basement room that had recently been sheet rocked. The concrete floor was graded and equipped with a working drain. He hung the lamp on a chain, attached to a hook in the rafter, 8 feet above.

He planted 3 seeds, in each of 30, one gallon pots of soilless mix, labeling each pot as to believed origin of seed, mostly *indica*. The planted seeds were watered with 1/2 solution of Up-Start. Chester placed a large, flat sheet of translucent plastic over the pots. He set the lamp 36 inches above the covered pots and set the timer on an 18 hour daylight cycle. Three days later, the first sprouts were seen above the soil. The plastic cover was removed. Within a week, there were over 70 new seedlings.

Meanwhile, Chet had figured out how to use the CO_2 enrichment system so it provided the optimum (.15%) CO_2 level and hooked it up. The exhaust fan was set on a timer, to run for 20 minutes just before the CO_2 was injected into the grow room. A small oscillating fan ran continuously to keep the heavy, CO_2 rich air circulated.

One entire Saturday, Chester and Claire spent visiting the four retail nurseries in town. They looked over the entire plant stock and garden products, reading the labels on many fertilizers, fungicides and insecticides. They also spoke to several nurserypeople about vegetable gardening in containers. It was then Chet decided to build large planter boxes mounted on wheels.

After some experimentation, including overfertilization and leaching, Chester and Claire established the necessary fertilization program for the soilless mix. They added 1/4 solution Peters: Pete-Lite Special (20-10-20) with each watering.

The grow room was kept about 85° F with 50% humidity. The seedlings grew from 15-18 feet the first month, thanks to the near perfect conditions and CO_2 enrichment.

Chester and Claire were unexpectedly called out of town for a week. Upon their return, they found the garden over crowded and in need of water. More important, was that many plants had an infestation of spider mites, contracted from the beautiful houseplants. Many of the seedlings were near death.

Chester was in a panic, but cool Claire noticed that some of the *indica* plants had not been attacked by the mites. Chester and Claire talked it over, it was a tough decision. They decided to give all the infested plants to a friend, so he could grow them outdoors (he later got ripped-off). With the sickies gone, there were only 30, mite resistant plants left The entire grow room, garden and all the houseplants were sprayed 3 times at 10 day intervals with pyrethrum. All the miserable mites were eradicated!

The garden looked bare. Energy levels were very low after the surprise mite attack. Chester kept busy by building four 2 x 2-foot x 18-inch planters. The 30, large, *indica* seedlings were transplanted. Two weeks later, a friend remarked: "You can't even tell over half the garden was devastated by those little bastards." The growth was phenomenal. By the end of the fourth month, the lamp was at full, 8-foot elevation and the walls could hardly be seen.

Chester took down the halide and mounted it in the center of one side of the room. The H.P. sodium was mounted in the center of the other side of the ceiling. This more than doubled the light intensity in the small room. The H.P. provided much more red to stimulate floral hormones. The lamp timer was set as 12 hours and the fertilizer changed to Peters Blossom Booster (10-30-20).

After 8 weeks of flowering, Chet and Claire harvested 25 ounces of connoisseurs quality marijuana and who cares about the leaves! They were able to deposit the $1000 into the IRA account before the annual deadline.

Chester and Claire were so pleased with their first crop, they wanted to start another. The only drawback was, they did not want to wait 6 months for seeds to grow.

Their friend, Dan, had 24 extra, 4 week old clones. They had recently been rooted and were ready for transplanting. Dan had only one grow room. He was ready to induce another crop of mature, two month old clones, to flower, but he did not want the young, 4 week old clones to flower.

Chester and Dan smoked a joint of the biggest terminal bud in Chester's garden. After many hours of rambling discussion about the pleasures and perils of indoor, HID horticulture, they concluded with a fair shake for both of them.

Dan induced flowering of the mature, two month old clones in his garden, and gave Chester the 24, 4 week old clones. Chester grew the 24 clones in his grow room for 6 weeks. He then rooted two clones (using Dip-N-Gro) from each of the 24 clones Dan gave him. Chester returned the 48 new clones to Dan, after Dan's crop was harvested. Chester got 24 clones, when he needed them, Dan traded 24 clones, he did not need, for 48 clones lie did need.

CALENDAR & CHECKLIST

A calendar helps people remember what to prepare for and a regular checklist adds necessary routine to the process. The calendar outlines the life cycle of the plant semi-monthly for 4 months. Four months is the average life cycle of a clone. It notes major points of interest during each stage in life. The weekly checklist consists of a few things that must be done every week to ensure a successful crop. Page numbers that follow each description tell where to find specific information in the text.

Please read over and consider each and every point on the calendar while growing your crop. When you have finished each item on the checklist, check it off. Remember, you are MOTHER NATURE and you create the climate!

In general, a person should spend at least 10 minutes per day, per lamp to have a well cared for and productive garden. This is enough time to complete all the stuff in the weekly calendar. Do not let the time bum you out, it will be fun and easy work. Much of gardening is simply watching and paying attention. It takes time to have a decent and productive garden. If using CO_2 enrichment or hydroponics, allow 20 minutes per day for maintenance.

Large chunks of time will be spent setting up the grow room and harvesting. These are not included in the 10 or 20 minutes per day. If you feel that 10 or 20 minutes daily are not enough, and you want to spend more time, by all means do! It will be fun!

WEEKLY CHECKLIST

* Check the following to see if they function properly:

* Air ventilation

* Air circulation

* Humidity - 40-50%

* Temperature, day - 70-75: night - 50-60

* Soil moisture (dry pockets) water as needed

* Cultivate soil surface

* Check pH

* Rotate plants

* Check for spider mites under leaves

* Check for fungi

* Check for nutrient deficiencies

* Regular fertilization schedule

* Check HID system for excessive heat at plug-i.n, timer, ballast and near the ceiling

* Clean-up!

* Clean-up!

* Clean-up!

* Check walls and ceiling for mold

* Move lamp up, 2-12 inches above plants

CALENDAR

The calendar starts on January 1, and is only four months long. Two months vegetative growth and two months flowering. Since this is an indoor calendar, you may start it any day of the year you want, no mater which direction the wind is blowing, or what the weatherman says.

If the garden is full of clones grown with CO_2 enrichment or hydroponically, the, calendar could move up one to three weeks, depending on how fast the garden grows. Remember, light intensity substantially diminishes over 4 feet away from the bulb.

January (1) First Week

Take and root clones. They should root in 1-4 weeks.
Sow seeds, make sure they are warm for speedy germination
Mix dolomite lime into soil before planting
Prepare grow room. Read: "Setting up the Grow Room" and "Setting up the Lamp".
Set timer for 18 hour days and 6 hour nights

January (5-10) Second Week

Make sure the room is perfect before bringing in the plants.

Move in rooted clones or sprouted seedlings, place 24-36" under HID

Keep soil surface moist

Fertilize seedlings, they have a supply of nutrients to last them the first two or three weeks of life.

First fertilization if using soilless mix. Use an ALL PURPOSE fertilizer. Start regular fertilization schedule.

Special care should be given to soil moisture, damping-off or dry soil pockets could stunt plants now!

February (1) Fourth Week

Plants should be about 6-12 inches tall.

First fertilization, if using potting soil, with an All Purpose chemical fertilizer or Organic Tea.

Start regular supplemental fertilization program

Move HID 6-12 inches from month old seedlings, clones should be able to take more intense light sooner.

Thin and transplant seedlings into larger pots

Irrigation is less frequent now.

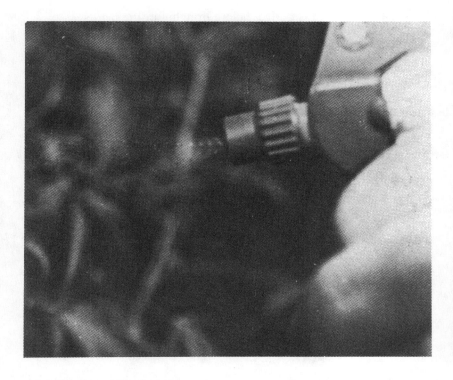

February (15) Sixth Week

Plants should be 12-24 inches tall, continue to look good, with broad, firm, green leaves.

No leaves should be yellowing yet. If they are, fine tune the weekly checklist.

Overwatering is sometimes a problem now. Check the soil with a moisture meter.

Increased circulation and ventilation are now essential.

Mist the garden with water to create rain

A magnesium deficiency could show up now, if no fine dolomite lime was added to growing medium.

Supplemental trace element mix should be applied now.

March (1) Eighth Week

The plants are two months old and may be anywhere from 20-36 inches tail. They should be stocky and very bushy. If they are bigger and healthier, you are doing the right stuff!

Take clones for the next crop!

If there are any leaves yellowing and dying, fine tune the weekly check list.

Air circulation, ventilation and relative humidity are very important now!

Leach soil to wash away any excess residues in the soil.

Female clone crops may be given 12 hours of light to induce flowering

If inducing flowering, change to super bloom fertilizer

Seedlings only two months old, should be given another month of growth before flowering is induced

Cloning for sex may now be practiced

Soil will dry out rapidly now, watch for dry soil pockets!

Magnesium deficiencies that have not surfaced, might show up now; treat with Epsom salt

Bend and tie plants over that ‚are too tall, giving the garden an even profile.

Prune plants that are shadowing other plants (optional)

If you planted enough plants, the room should be ready for a second lamp. Most growers use a 1000 watt HP sodium or a 1000 watt phosphor coated halide. Adding another lamp now will substantially increase harvest.

Leaves really begin to yellow now. If many leaves are yellowing, fine tune the checklist.

After fine tuning checklist, remove yellowing leaves only if they are clearly going to die.

Garden might still be using quite a bit of water, make sure to check it daily if needed.

March (15) Tenth Week

The tops should elongate, making the gardens profile about 6-12 inches taller than two weeks ago and showing few or no signs of much vegetative growth.

Males showing their sex should be removed or saved in another room for breeding. Females might show a few white hairs (pistils)

Continue fertilizing with a high bloom fertilizer

Older leaves may start to drop a little faster, due to decreased nitrogen in the super bloom fertilizer or if only a HP sodium lamp is used

Check all the critical factors listed in the checklist.

April (1) twelfth week

Branches, now finished with the elongation process, should be as tall as they are going to get. The only change will be in growth of more and heavier calyxes on the flower buds.

This is the time of peak THC production. During the next one to four weeks, the tops will double in size and potency!

Continue to water as needed and feed super bloom fertilizer t-Females sex should be fully evident now

Bud blight or mold could become a problem. Constant scrutiny is a must! It shows up overnight, Watch Out!

Give the garden a good bath to wash off any unwanted chemical or organic residues that may have accumulated on foliage

Last chance for spraying and fertilizing if you plan to harvest within two weeks. If there are any nutrient, fungi or insect disorders, this is the last chance you will have to use sprays to combat them.

April (15) Fourteenth Week

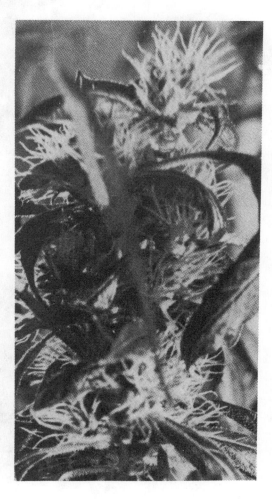

Buds should be oozing with resin by now

Some shade leaf yellowing is normal.

Indica and early maturing buds will be close to ready or ripe now.

Harvest if ready.

Water as needed, using a water meter to , check moisture level.

Water stress only during last few days before harvest.

No insecticides!

No fungicides

No fertilizer!

Check for bud blight or bud mold.

Check weekly checklist.

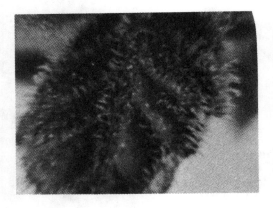

May (l) sixteenth week

Everything should be ready for harvest by now. If it is not, consider growing an earlier maturing strain of marijuana,

Harvest now or within a couple of weeks. Thai takes up to 6 weeks longer to flower!

THC content is on its way downhill now!

Let "Seed Crops" go until the seeds are big and healthy, before harvesting.

Move in rooted clones for next crop

GLOSSARY

This GLOSSARY contains many very simple and some not so simple words in the context of their usage in this book. Many examples are given to promote good indoor horticultural practices.

ABSORB - to draw or take in: Rootlets ABSORB water and nutrients.

AC (ALTERNATING CURRENT) - An electric current that reverses its direction at regularly occurring intervals. Homes have AC.

ACID - a sour substance: An ACID or sour soil has a low pH. ACTIVE - a hydroponic system that ACTIVELY moves the nutrient solution

ADOBE - heavy clay soil, not suitable for container gardening

AERATION - to supply soil and roots with air or oxygen

AEROPONICS - growing plants by misting roots suspended in air

AGGREGATE - medium, usually gravel, that is all nearly the same size, and used for the inert hydroponic medium.

ALKALINE - refers to soil with a high pH: Any pH over 7 is considered ALKALINE. ALL PURPOSE (GENERAL PURPOSE) FERTILIZER - A balanced blend of N-P-K: ALL

PURPOSE FERTILIZER is used by most growers in the vegetative growth stage. AMENDMENT, SOIL - to change soil texture by adding organic or mineral substances

AMPERE (AMP) - the unit used to measure the strength of an electric current: A 20 AMP circuit

is overloaded when drawing more than 17 amps.

ANNUAL - a plant that normally completes its entire life cycle in one year or less: Marijuana is an ANNUAL.

APHID - small insect of various colors: APHIDS suck the juices from plants. ARC - luminous discharge of electricity (light) between two electrodes ARC TUBE - container for luminous gasses and houses the arc ATTACK - to assail: Bugs and fungus ATTACK the garden.

AUXIN - classification of plant hormones: AUXINS are responsible for foliage and root elongation.

BACTERIA - very small, one celled plants, that have no chlorophyll

BALLAST - A stabilizing unit that regulates the flow of electricity and starts a HID lamp. BANDIT - Jerk that jerks other peoples marijuana.

BAT GUANO - Bat manure, high in phosphorus (P): BAT GUANO is the organic super bloom fertilizer.

BEND - alter a branches growth by tying it down

BENEFICIAL INSECT - A good insect that eats bad marijuana munching insects.

BIODEGRADABLE - to decompose

or break down through natural bacterial action:
Substances made of organic matter are BIODEGRADABLE. BIOLOGY - the study of physical life and living matter: Botany is a branch of BIOLOGY. BIOSYNTHESIS - the production of a chemical compound by a plant BLEACH - Ordinary laundry BLEACH is used in a mild water solution as a soil fungicide. BLOOD MEAL - high N organic fertilizer, made from dried blood: Dogs love BLOOD MEAL!
BLOOM - to yield flowers
BLOSSOM BOOSTER - fertilizer high in phosphorus P that increases flower yield
BOLT - term used to describe a plant that is severely root bound and starved for light. The plant will grow straight up or BOLT.
BONE MEAL - organic fertilizer high in P: BONE MEAL is mixed in soil to stimulate root growth of clones and seedlings.
BONSAI - a very short or dwarfed marijuana plant BOTANY - the science and study of plant life
BRANCH - a secondary or lateral stem growing BREAKER BOX - electrical circuit box having on/off switches rather than fuses
BREATHE - Roots draw in or BREATHE oxygen, stomata draw in or BREATHE CO_2. BREAK DOWN - to BIODEGRADE
BREED - to sexually propagate marijuana under controlled circumstances
BUD - a small stem on a branch containing thick rows of calyxes
BUD BLIGHT - a withering condition that attacks flower buds
BUFFER - a substance that reduces the shock and cushions against

fluctuations. Many fertilizers contain BUFFER agents.
BUG - tiny creature that eats or sucks juice from marijuana
BULB - I. the outer glass envelope or jacket that protects the arc tube of a HID lamp 2. clove or BULB of garlic.
BULBOUS TRICHOME - spherical shaped resin producing plant hair with no stalk BURN - 1. leaf tips that turn dark from excess fertilizer and/or salt BURN 2. Foliage that gets to close to a hot HID will BURN BUSHY - a plant having dense foliage
CALYX - the pod harboring female ovule and two protruding pistils, seed pod CANNABANOID - a hydrocarbon unique to *cannabis*
CANNABIS - scientific name for marijuana specifying genus
CAPITATE-STALKED TRICHOME - resin producing plant hair, high in THC content CAPTAN - commercial wettable powder fungicide.
CAPTAN stops soil and foliage fungus.
CARBON DIOXIDE ($^.2$ CO_2) - a colorless, odorless, tasteless gas in the air necessary for plant life
CARBOHYDRATE - neutral compound of carbon, hydrogen and oxygen: Sugar, starch and cellulose ~e CARBOHYDRATES.
CAUSTIC - a substance that destroys, kills or eats away by chemical activity CBD - cannabidiol: CBD usually prolongs the high.
CBN - cannabinol
CELL - the base structural unit that plants are made of: CELLS contain a nucleus, membrane, and chloroplasts

CELLULOSE - a complex carbohydrate that stiffens a plant: Tough stems contain stiff CELLULOSE.

CENTIGRADE - a scale for measuring temperature where 100 is the boiling point of water and 0 is the freezing point of water.

CFM - Cubic Feet per Minute

CHAIN - used as an adjustable hanger for a HID lamp CHELATE - combining nutrients in an atomic ring that is easy for plant to absorb

CHEMICAL - substance of or relating to chemistry: CHEMICAL fertilizers are loosely *synthetic*.

CHLOROPHYLL - the green photosynthetic matter of plants: CHLOROPHYLL is found in the chloroplasts of a cell.

CHLORINE - chemical used in water systems

CHLOROSIS - the condition of a sick plant with yellowing leaves due to inadequate formation of chlorophyll: CHLOROSIS is caused by a nutrient deficiency, usually iron or in- balanced pH.

CIRCUIT - a circular route traveled by electricity

CLAY - soil made of very fine organic and mineral particles: CLAY is not suitable for container gardening.

CLEAN - to rid of dirt, germs and debris: ALL GROW ROOMS SHOULD BE CLEAN. CLIMATE - the average condition of the weather in a grow room or outdoors CLIPPERS - heavy duty scissors used in horticulture to trim, prune, or harvest plants CLONE - 1. a rooted cutting of a plant 2. asexual propagation CO_2 ENRICHMENT - adding CO_2 to the atmosphere of a grow room to speed growth

COLA - Spanish and American slang word for a marijuana flower top: COLA, in Spanish, actually means *TAIL*.

COLD - temperatures below 50° F

COLOR SPECTRUM - the band of colors (measured in nm) emitted by a light source

COLOR TRACER - A coloring agent that is added to many commercial fertilizers so the horticulturist knows there is fertilizer in the solution. Peters has a blue COLOR TRACER.

COMPACTION - soil condition that results from tightly packed soil: COMPACTED soil allows for marginal aeration and root penetration.

COMPANION PLANTING - planting garlic, marigolds, etc. along with marijuana to discourage insect infestations

COMPOST - mixture of decayed organic matter, high in nutrients: COMPOST must be at least one year old. When to young, decomposition uses N, after sufficient decomposition, COMPOST releases N.

CON SEMILLA - Spanish meaning: *WITH SEEDS:* A seed crop is CON SEMILLA. CONTAINER - pot or planter having drainage holes: A CONTAINER contains a growing medium.

CONTROL - to regulate and influence all factors contributing to healthy marijuana growth COPPER - one of the trace elements necessary for plant life CORE - Many times the transformer in the ballast is referred to as a CORE.

COTYLEDON - seed leaves, first leaves that appear on a plant COTTONSEED MEAL - acidic organic fertilizer and soil amendment high in nitrogen

CREEPER - marijuana high in CBD having psychoactive qualities that sneak up on smoker: The CREEPER high usually lasts longer.

CROP - the total of plants grown and harvested: John used CO_2 enrichment and harvested a bumper CROP.

CROSS-POLLINATE - pollination of two plants having different ancestry

CRYSTAL - I. Appearance resin has when found on foliage 2. Fertilizers many times come in soluble CRYSTALS.

CUBIC FOOT - volume measurement in feet: Width X length X height = CUBIC FEET.

CULTIVATE - to encourage plant growth by controlling growth inducing factors

CURE - 1. slow drying process that makes marijuana more pleasant and palatable to smoke 2. to make a sick plant healthy

CUTTING - I. growing tip cut from a parent plant for asexual propagation 2. clone 3. slip

DAMPING-OFF - fungus disease that attacks young seedlings and clones causing stem to rot at base: Overwatering is the main cause of DAMPING-OFF. DC (DIRECT CURRENT) - an electric current that only flows in *one* direction

DEATH - end of life and resin production DECOMPOSE - to rot or decay etc., through organic chemical change DEHUMIDIFY - to remove the moisture from air

DEHYDRATE - to remove water from foliage

DEPLETE - to exhaust soil of nutrients, making in infertile: Once a soil is *used* it is DEPLETED.

DESICCATE - to cause to dry up. Safer's Insecticidal Soap DESICCATES its victims.

DETERGENT - liquid soap concentrate used: l. as a wetting agent for sprays and water 2. pesticide, NOTE: DETERGENT must be totally organic to be safe for plants. DIAZINON - commercial insecticide that kills aphids, mealy bugs and white flies

DIOECIOUS - plants having distinct male and female plants

DIP-N-GROW - liquid root hormone: DIP-N-GROW is one of the best product on the market.

DIRECTIONS - guidance or supervision of an act: Always read DIRECTIONS before acting.

DIRT - I. filthy or soiling substance 2. soil from back yard generally not suited for container gardening.

DISEASE RESISTANT - robust plant that seldom is attacked by disease: *Indica* is very DISEASE RESISTANT.

DOLOMITE LIME - pulverized limestone high in calcium and magnesium, used to raise and balance soil pH: DOLOMITE LIME is slow release and maintains a constant soil pH.

DOME - the part of the HID outer bulb opposite the neck and threads

DOME SUPPORT - the spring like brackets that mount the arc tube within the outer envelope DOPE - I. slang word for *cannabis* 2. person that does not read directions before deciding what to do: Hey DOPE, read the directions!

DOSE - amount of fertilizer, insecticide, etc., given to a plant, usually in a water solution

DRAINAGE - to empty soil of excess water: Good DRAINAGE: water passes through soil evenly promoting plant growth, BAD DRAINAGE: water stands in soil, actually drowning roots.

DRIP LINE - a line around a plant directly under its outermost branch tips: Roots seldom grow beyond the DRIP LINE.

DRIP SYSTEM - very efficient watering system that employs a main hose with small water emitters. Water is metered out the emitters, one drop at a time.

DRY ICE - cold, white substance formed when CO_2 is compressed and cooled: DRY ICE changes into CO_2 gas at room temperatures.

DRY SOIL POCKET - small portion of soil that remains dry after watering: DRY SOIL POCKETS may be remedied by adding a wetting agent (soap) to water and/or waiting 15 minutes between waterings.

DRY WELL - drain hole, filled with rocks

ELECTRODE - a conductor used to establish electrical arc or contact with non-metallic part of circuit

ELONGATE - to grow in length: Cannabis ELONGATES from 3 to a foot when flowering is induced

ENCARISA FORMOSA - a parasitic wasp that preys on whiteflies

ENVELOPE - outer protective bulb or jacket of a lamp

ENVIRONMENT - everything that surrounds and governs a plants life

EPSOM SALTS - hydrated, magnesium sulfate in the form of white crystalline salt: EPSOM SALTS add magnesium to soil.

EQUINOX - when sun crosses the equator and day and night are each 12 hours long: The EQUINOX happens twice a year.

EVAPORATE - to convert liquid into vapor: Much water EVAPORATES into the atmosphere of a grow room.

EXHAUST FAN - a fan that PULLS air OUT of the grow room: An EXHAUST FAN is very efficient.

EXTENSION CORD - extra electrical cord that must be 14 gauge or larger (i.e. 12 or 10 gauge) FAN LEAVES - large, fan-like marijuana leaves: FAN LEAVES are usually low in potency. FAN, OSCILLATING - a fan that turns back and forth FEED - to fertilize FEMALE - pistilate, ovule, seed producing FERTILIZE - 1. to apply fertilizer (nutrients) to roots and foliage 2. to impregnate (unite) male pollen with female ovule.

FERTILIZER BURN - overfertilization, first leaf tips burn (turn brown) then leaves curl FISH EMULSION - fish particles suspended in a liquid: FISH EMULSION is high in organic nitrogen.

FISH FERTILIZER - organic fertilizer made from fish, high in N: FISH FERTILIZER stinks like year old fish.

FIXTURE - electrical fitting used to hold electric components

FLAT - a 18" x 24" x 3" deep container, with good drainage, used to start seedlings or clones FLAT WHITE - very reflective, whitest, white paint available

FLUORESCENT LAMP - electric lamp using a tube coated with fluorescent material has low lumen and heat output: A FLUORESCENT LAMP is excellent for rooting cuttings.

FLOWER - blossom, a mass of calyxes on a stem, top or bud

FOLIAGE - the leaves, or more general, the green part of a plant

FOLIAR FEED - misting fertilizer solution which is absorbed by the foliage

FONDLE - to handle, showing affection: Excessive FONDLING will bruise and rupture tender THC resin glands.

FOOD - 1. nutrients, fertilizer is plant food. 2. Carbohydrates, sugar and starches are FOODS produced by plants.

FOOT-CANDLE - f.c. One f.c. is equal to the amount of light that falls on one square foot of surface located one foot away from one candle.

FRESH AIR - clean, *new* air from outdoors: FRESH AIR is necessary for a garden to do well. FRESH SOIL - potting soil that has not been *used*

FRITTED - to fuse or embed nutrients with a glass compound. FRITTED Trace Elements (PTE) are long lasting and do not leach out easily.

FUNGICIDE - product that destroys or inhibits fungus

FUNGUS - a *lower* plant lacking chlorophyll that may attack green plants: Mold, rust, mildew, mushrooms and bacteria are FUNGI.

FUSE - An electrical safety device consisting of a fusible metal that MELTS and interrupts the circuit when overloaded.

FUSE BOX - electrical circuit box containing circuits controlled by fuses

GPM - Gallons Per Minute

GARDENING - cultivating a garden

GENERAL PURPOSE FERTILIZER - See: ALL PURPOSE FERTILIZER

GENE - part of a chromosome that influences the development and the potency of a plant: GENES are inherited through sexual propagation.

GENETIC MAKE-UP - the genes inherited from parent plants: GENETIC MAKE-UP is the most important factor dictating vigor and potency.

GLANDULAR TRICHOME - resin secreting plant hair

GRAVEL - soilless medium used in many *active recovery* hydroponic systems GREEN LACEWING - insect that preys on mealy bugs

GUANO - dung from birds, high in organic nutrients: Sea bird GUANO is noted for being high in nitrogen (N).

HALIDE - binary compound of a halogen(s) with an electropositive element(s)

HALOGEN - any of the elements fluorine, chorine, bromine, iodine and astatine existing in a free state: HALOGENS are in the arc the arc tube of a halide lamp.

HEMP - fibrous *cannabis* low in THC, used to make rope and give people who smoke it a headache

HERMAPHRODITE - one plant having both male and female flowers: The breeding of HERMAPHRODITES are hard to control.

HERTZ (Hz) - a unit of a frequency that cycles one time each second: A home with a 60 HERTZ AC current, cycles 60 times per second.

HID - High Intensity Discharge

HONEYDEW - a sticky honey-like substance secreted onto foliage by aphids, scale, and mealy bugs

HOOD - the reflective cover of a HID lamp: A large, white HOOD is very reflective.

HOR - The abbreviation stamped on some HID bulbs meaning they may be burned in a HORIZONTAL position.

HORIZONTAL - parallel to the horizon

HORMONE - chemical substance that controls the growth and development of a plant. Root inducing HORMONES help clones root.

HORTICULTURE - the science and art of growing plants

HOSE BIB - water outlet containing an on/off valve

HOSTILE ENVIRONMENT - environment that is unfriendly and inhospitable to disease and conducive to plant growth

HOT - temperature over 90° F.

HUMIDITY (RELATIVE) - ratio between the amount of moisture in the air and the greatest amount of moisture the air could hold at the same temperature

HUMUS - dark, fertile, partially decomposed, plant or animal matter: HUMUS forms the organic portion of the soil.

HYBRID - an offspring from two plants of different breeds, variety or genetic make-up HYDRATED LIME - instantly soluble lime, used to raise or lower pH

HYDROGEN - light, colorless, odorless gas: HYDROGEN combines with OXYGEN to form water.

HYDROPONICS - growing plants in nutrient solutions without soil

HYGROMETER - instrument for measuring relative humidity in the atmosphere: A HYGROMETER will save time, frustration and money.

I-LINE - metal halide HID lamp manufactured by Sylvania: Made for use in some mercury vapor ballasts.

INBRED - (true breed) offspring of plants of the same breed or ancestry

INCANDESCENT LAMP - electric lamp having a filament that gives off light and heat: An INCANDESCENT LAMP is best used as a heat source.

INDUCE, INDUCTIVE - to effect, cause or influence via stimulation Flowering is INDUCED via a 12 hour photoperiod.

INERT - a substance that will not chemically react. INERT growing mediums make it easy to control the chemistry of the nutrient solution.

INFESTATION - condition resulting from many bugs or fungus attacking plants INHIBIT - to restrain, stunt or hold back from free and spontaneous growth

INSECT - small invertebrate animal: Aphids, mealy bugs and spider mites are INSECTS.

INSECTICIDE - a product that kills or inhibits insects

INTENSITY - the magnitude of light energy per unit: INTENSITY diminishes the further away from the source.

IRON - one of the trace elements essential to plant life

JACKET - protective outer bulb or envelope of lamp

JIFFY 7 PELLET - compressed peat moss wrapped in an expandable plastic casing. When moistened, a JIFFY 7 PELLET expands into a small pot that is used to start seeds or clones.

KILL - to put a plant to death via negligence or harvest

KILOWATT HOUR - measure of electricity used per hour: A 1000 watt HID uses one kilowatt per hour.

LACEWING -insect that preys on

LADY BUG - orange spotted beetle that preys on aphids and other insects (not MITES): LADY BUGS are attracted to bright light BUZZZZZZZ...POP!

LAMP - a device that produces light and heat

LEACH - to dissolve or wash out soluble components of soil by heavy watering LEADER - See: MERISTEM

LEAF - thin, broad outgrowth from stem that manufactures food

LEAF CURL - leaf that is curled due to overwatering, overfertilization, lack of Mg, insect or fungus damage or negative tropism

LEAFLET - small immature leaf

LEGGY - plant that is abnormally tall, with sparse foliage: LEGGYNESS is usually caused from lack of light.

LIFE CYCLE - a series of growth stages through which *cannabis* must pass in its natural lifetime: The stages are seed, seedling, vegetative and floral.

LIGHT BALANCER - a device that moves a lamp back and forth across the ceiling of a grow room to provide more *balanced* light.

LIME - used in the form of DOLOMITE or HYDRATED LIME to raise and/or stabilize soil pH

LIMP LEAVES - Leaves that are lacking in vitality, strength and firmness: Lack of ventilation or poor growing conditions usually cause LIMP LEAVES.

LITMUS PAPER - chemically sensitive paper used for testing pH

LOAM - organic soil mixture of crumbly clay, silt and sand

LOW PRESSURE SODIUM LAMP -

LUCALOX - High Pressure Sodium lamp produced by General Electric

LUMALUX - High Pressure Sodium lamp produced by Sylvania

LUMEN - measurement of light output: One LUMEN is equal to the amount of light emitted by one candle that falls on one square feet of surface located one feet away from one candle.

MACRO-NUTRIENT - one or all of the *Primary Nutrients* N-P-K or the *Secondary Nutrients* Mg and Ca

MALATHION - commercial insecticide, kills about all insects, except for spider mites MALE - staminate, pollen producing

MANICURE - trim leaves and large stems from buds with scissors or fine pruners MANUAL REMOVAL (of insects) - is with a quick squish of the fingers or set of sponges (more civilized)

MANURE - cow shit, rabbit shit, chicken shit, etc. used as an organic fertilizer and soil amendment: MANURE must be thoroughly composted and free of acid salts to be a good fertilizer.

MARIJUANA - illegal drug ingested for its THC content

MASON JAR - canning jar used to seal in freshness and protect delicate resin glands on *colas*

MEALY BUG - small, round, whitish, shell-like insect that lives in colonies, infesting gardens

MEAN - average throughout life: HID's are rated in MEAN lumens.

MEASURING CUP - a vessel with incremental measurements in ounces, cubic centimeters (cc), tablespoons, etc.: A MEASURING CUP is necessary in all gardens.

MERCURY VAPOR LAMP - outdated and oldest member of the HID family MERISTEM - tip of a plant or central leader

MICRO-NUTRIENTS - also referred to as TRACE ELEMENTS, including S, Fe, Mn, B, Mb, Zn and Cu.

MILLIMETER - .04 inch

MILORGANITE - processed sewage sludge: MILORGANITE not acceptable for indoor marijuana cultivation, yuck!

MIRACLE-GRO - commercial soluble fertilizer

MIST - to manufacture rain with the help of a spray bottle

MITE, SPIDER - the indoor horticulturists most hated enemy! A microscopic spider (in a broader sense INSECT) that may be white, red, or two spotted. MITES live on leaf undersides and suck the tender leaves dry of life giving fluids.

MIX - to thoroughly combine and blend soils and amendments: Liquids, crystals and wettable powders are MIXED.

MOISTURE METER - fantastic electronic devise that measures the exact moisture content of soil at any given point.

MONOCHROMATIC - producing only one color: LP sodium lamps are MONOCHROMATIC.

MOTHER NATURE - the vast outdoors and all she holds: The indoor horticulturist assumes the role of MOTHER NATURE.

MOTHER PLANT - female marijuana plant that is used for cutting (cloning) stock: A MOTHER PLANT maybe grown from seed or be a clone.

MULCH - a protective covering of organic compost, old leaves, etc.: Indoors, MULCH keeps soil too moist, and possible fungus could result.

MANOMETER - .000001 meter, N.M. is used as a scale to measure electromagnetic wavelengths of light: Color and light spectrums are expressed in NANOMETERS (NM).

NECROSIS - localized death of a plant part NECK - tubular glass end of the HID bulb, attached to the threads NITROGEN (N) - essential element to plant growth. One of the 3 major nutrients.

NON-RECOVERY - hydroponic system that does not recover nutrient solution once applied

NURSERY - gardening store that sells many of the things indoor marijuana horticulturists need: A NURSERY is a great place to gather information.

NURSERY-PERSON - person that, if knowledgeable, can be a wealth of information: All indoor horticulturists should have a NURSERY-PERSON buddy.

NUTRIENT - plant food, essential elements N-P-K, secondary and trace elements fundamental to plant life

OHM's LAW - a law that expresses the strength of an electric current: Volts X Amperes = Watts.

OPTIMUM - I. the most favorable condition for growth 2. peak production ORGANIC - made of, derived from or related to living organisms OUTBRED - see hybrid OVERFERTILIZE - trying to hard, overdosing plants with supplemental fertilizer OVERLOAD - load to excess: A 20 amp circuit drawing 17 amps is OVERLOADED.

OVERWATER - keeping soil so wet, that no oxygen can get to roots: OVERWATERING will drown roots and eventually kill a plant.

OVULE - found within the calyx, and contains all the female genes: When fertilized, an OVULE will grow into a seed.

OXYGEN - tasteless, colorless element, necessary in soil to sustain plant life PARASITE - organism that lives on or in another *host* organism: Fungus is a PARASITE. PASSIVE - hydroponic system that moves the nutrient solution PASSIVELY through absorption or capillary action

PEAK - highest level, greatest degree, maximum

PEAT - partially decomposed vegetation (usually moss) with show decay due to extreme moisture and cold.

PEAT PELLET - See: JIFFY-7

PERENNIAL - a plant, such as a tree or shrub that completes its life cycle over several years PERLITE - 1. sand or volcanic glass, expanded by heat, holds water and nutrients on its many irregular surfaces. 2. mineral soil amendment PEST - bug, fungus, bandit, or anything detrimental to marijuana

PETERS FERTILIZER - high quality soluble fertilizer used by many professional nurseries and horticulturists: Available in many N-P-K, secondary and trace element formulas.

pH - a scale from 1-14 that measures a growing mediums (or anything's) acid to alkaline balance: *Cannabis* grows best in a 6.5 to 8 pH range.

pH TESTER - electronic instrument or chemical used to find where soil or water is on the pH scale

PHOSPHOR COATING - internal bulb coating that diffuses light and is responsible for various color outputs

PHOSPHORUS (P) - one of the three macro-nutrients that promotes root and flower growth

PHOTOPERIOD - the relationship between the length of light and dark, in a 24 hour period

PHOTOSYNTHESIS - the building of chemical compounds (carbohydrates) from light energy, water and CO_2

PHOTOTROPISM - the specific movement of a plant part towards a light source PIGMENT - The substance in paint or anything that absorbs light, producing (reflecting) the same color as the PIGMENT.

PISTILS - small pair of fuzzy white hairs extending from top of calyx: PISTILS catch pollen and channel it into contact with the ovule for fertilization.

PLANT - 1. a living, stationary being, that produces green chlorophyll through photosynthesis 2. to sew or place in the earth for growth PLANTER - large soil container used to grow plants in

PLUG (IN) - to establish an electrical circuit by inserting PLUG: There are two types of 110 volt PLUGS, 2-prong and GROUNDED 3-prong. Safety requires use of the 3-prong PLUG.

POLLEN - fine, yellow, dust-like microspores containing male genes POLLEN SACK - male flower containing POLLEN.

POD (SEED) - a dry calyx containing a mature or maturing seed

POT - I. container for growing medium 2. American slang word for marijuana POTASSIUM (K) - one of the 3 macro-nutrients necessary for plant life POT BOUND - root system that is BOUND, stifled or inhibited from normal growth, by the confines of a container

POTENT - marijuana rich in THC that provides a desirable psychoactive effect POTTING SOIL - sterile soil, usually purchased in bags. Most POTTING SOILS have the proper texture, pH and nutrient content for indoor horticulture. POWER SURGE - interruption or change in flow of electricity PREDATOR - beneficial bug or parasite that hunts down and devours harmful insects.

PREVENT - to keep bugs and fungus from attacking garden by creating a hostile environment PRIMARY NUTRIENTS - N-P-K

PRIMO - American slang word for potent, top quality *cannabis* (PRIMO means COUSIN in Spanish)

PROPAGATE - l. SEXUAL PROPAGATION - to produce a seed by breeding a male and female plant 2. ASEXUAL PROPAGATION - to produce a plant by cloning

PRUNE - to alter the shape and growth pattern of a plant by cutting stems and shoots PUMICE - lightweight volcanic rock, full of air and water holding cavities: PUMICE is a mineral soil amendment.

PVC PIPE - plastic pipe that is easy to work with, readily available and used to pipe water into a grow room or make a watering wand.

PYRETHRUM - natural insecticide made from the blossoms of various chrysanthemums:

PYRETHRUM is the most effective natural spider mite exterminator. RA-PID-GRO - commercial soluble fertilizer, available in MULTI-USE 23-19-17 formula RAZOR BLADE - used to make fine, precision cut, when taking cuttings RECOVERY - hydroponic system that RECOVERS the nutrient solution and recycles it REFLECT - to throw back light. Flat white REFLECTS the optimum amount of light.

REJUVENATE - A mature plant, having completed its life cycle (flowering) that is stimulated by a new 18 hour photoperiod, to REJUVENATE or produce *new* vegetative growth. RESIN GLANDS - tiny pores that secrete resin

RINSE - to wash thoroughly with tepid water, to mist

RIP-OFF - jerk that steals marijuana, bandit

ROOT - 1. the tender light and air sensitive underground part of a plant: ROOTS function to absorb water and nutrients as well as anchor a plant in the ground. 2. to ROOT a cutting or clone

ROOT BOUND - see POT BOUND

ROOT HORMONE - root inducing substance

ROOTONE F - powder, root inducing hormone with fungicide

SAFER INSECTICIDAL SOAP - Insecticidal soap: Controls just about all bad bugs including the hated and feared SPIDER MITE.

SALT - crystalline compound that results from improper pH or toxic build-up of fertilizer.

SALT will burn plants, preventing them from absorbing nutrients SAND - heavy soil amendment: Coarse SAND is excellent for rooting cuttings.

SCALE - 1. tiny, round, shell-like insects, that affix themselves to plants, live in colonies and infest crops 2. an instrument of measurement.

SEAL-A-MEAL - air tight sealer for plastic baggies used to SEAL in freshness of pungent marijuana

SECONDARY NUTRIENTS -calcium (Ca) and magnesium (Mg)

SEED - the mature, fertilized, ovule of a pistilate plant, containing a protective shell, embryo and supply of food: A SEED will germinate and grow, given heat and moisture.

SHAKE - Bunk, lower growth or least potent portion of harvest. Many times SHAKE is flaked or powder-like and used for cooking.

SHORT CIRCUIT - condition that results when wires cross and form a circuit. A SHORT CIRCUIT will blow fuses.

SINSEMILLA - two Spanish words : SIN = WITHOUT, SEMILLA = SEED, combined into one word by Americans: SINSEMILLA describes flowering female *cannabis,* that has not been fertilized.

SMOKE - I. marijuana 2. polluting substance

SOAP - 1. cleaning agent 2. wetting agent 3. insecticide. All SOAP used in horticulture, should be biodegradable

SOCKET - threaded, wired holder for a bulb

SODIUM VAPOR (HP) - High pressure Sodium HID lamp

SOILLESS MIX - a growing medium, made up of mineral particles such as vermiculite, perlite, sand, pumice, etc. NOTE: Organic moss is many times a component of SOILLESS MIX.

SOLUBLE - able to be dissolved in water

SOLUTION - 1. mixing a solid or liquid with water to form a SOLUTION 2. answer to a problem

SPHAGNUM MOSS - moss grown in Canada used for soil amendment: SPHAGNUM MOSS is normally decomposed into moss peat.

SPORE - seed-like offspring of a fungus

SPROUT - I. a recently germinated seed 2. small new growth of leaf or stem SPONGE ROCK - light, mineral, soil amendment

SQUARE FEET (SQUARE FEET) - length X width

STAGNANT - motionless air or water: Water must be drained and not become STAGNANT for healthy marijuana growth.

STAMINATE - male, pollen producing

STARCH - complex carbohydrate: STARCH is manufactured and stored food.

STERILIZE - to make super clean by removing dirt germs and bacteria

STRAIN - l. ancestry, lineage, phenotype, a particular type of marijuana having the same characteristics. 2. to abuse a plant by withholding nutrients, water, etc.

STROBOSCOPIC EFFECT - a quick pulsating or flashing of a lamp

STRESS - a physical or chemical factor that causes extra exertion by plants: A STRESSED plant will not grow as well as a NON-STRESSED plant.

STUNT - dwarf, to slow or inhibit growth: A STUNTED plant will take a long time (forever) to resume normal growth.

STOMATA - small mouth-like or nose-like openings on leaf underside, responsible for transpiration and many other life functions: The millions of

STOMATA, must be kept very clean to function properly.

SULFUR - one of the trace elements essential to plant life

SUGAR - food product of a plant

SUPER BLOOM - a common name for fertilizer high in phosphorus (P), that promotes flower formation and growth

SWINGLE - METALARC SWINGLE by Sylvania is designed to work in SOME mercury vapor ballasts. A SWINGLE lamp produces substantially fewer lumens than the standard metal halide.

SYNTHESIS - the production of a substance, such as chlorophyll, by uniting light energy, elements or chemical compounds

SUMP - a reservoir or receptacle that serves as a drain or receptacle for hydroponic nutrient solutions

TAP ROOT - the main or primary root that grows from the seed: Lateral roots will branch off the TAP ROOT.

TEFLON TAPE - tape that is extremely useful to help seal all kinds of pipe joints. 1 like TEFLON TAPE better than putty.

TEPID WATER - warm 70-80° F water Always use TEPID WATER around plants to facilitate chemical processes and ease shock.

TERMINAL BUD - bud at the growing end of the main stem

THC - tetrahydrocannabinol

THERMOSTAT - a device for regulating temperature: A THERMOSTAT may control a heater, furnace or vent fan.

THIN - to cull or weed out weak, slow growing seedlings

THRIP - a small sucking insect detrimental to marijuana

TIMER - an electrical device for regulating photoperiod, fan, etc.: A TIMER IS A MUST IN ALL GROW ROOMS.

TOP - the flower buds

TOXIC LIFE - the amount of time a pesticide or fungicide remains *active* or *live* TRANSFORMER - a devise in the ballast that transforms electric current from one voltage to another.

TRANSPIRE - to give off water vapor and by products via the stomata

TRANSPLANT - to traumatically uproot a plant and root ball, and plant it in *new* soil TRAUMA - injury suffered during cloning, transplanting or abuse TRELLIS - a frame of small boards (lattice) that trains or supports plants TRIM - to cut growing tips, maintaining an even garden profile TRUE BREED - see INBRED

TUNGSTEN - a heavy, hard metal with a high melting point that conducts electricity well: TUNGSTEN is used for a filament in tungsten halogen lamps.

ULTRAVIOLET - light with very short wavelengths, out of the visible spectrum UNALUX - High Pressure Sodium lamp manufactured by Sylvania for use in SOME mercury vapor ballasts

UP-START - Ortho product that contains 3-I 0-3, Vitamin B_1, and root inducing hormones UP-START is excellent for use with seedlings, clones and transplants to ease *shock*

VARIETY - strain, phenotype (see strain)

VEGETATIVE - growth stage in which marijuana rapidly produces new growth and green chlorophyll

VENT - an opening such as a window or door that allows the circulation of fresh air VENTILATION - circulation of fresh air, fundamental to healthy indoor garden An exhaust fan creates excellent VENTILATION.

VERMICULITE - mica processed and expanded by heat. VERMICULITE is a good soil amendment and medium for rooting cuttings.

VERTICAL - up and down

VITAMIN B_1 - VITAMIN that is absorbed by tender root hairs, easing transplant wilt and shock

WEED - l) slang word for marijuana in the U.S. 2) any undesirable plant. One persons WEED is another persons flower!

WETTING AGENT - a compound that reduces the droplet size and lowers the surface tension of the water, making it wetter. Liquid concentrate dish soap is a good WETTING AGENT if it is biodegradable.

WHITE FLY - a small, white, moth-like marijuana muncher

WICK - a *passive* hydroponic system using a WICK suspended in the nutrient solution, the nutrients pass up the WICK and are absorbed by the medium and roots

WIRE TIES - Paper coated WIRE TIES are excellent for tying down or training plants. YIELD - the product or harvest of a garden

ZINC - an essential trace element

INDEX

Air 29, 152-171; temperature 147-148,
    158-161, 164, 214; humidity 148, 158,
    161, 164, 176; ventilation 35, 154-156,
    159-160, 241; circulation 35, 154-156,
    176, 189, 241
Alcohol, methyl 166; rubbing 174, 219
Algae 140
Aluminum foil 50, 79
Amperes (amps) 59, 72-79, 80, 86
Annual plants 23, 67, 107, 195, 223
Aphids 187, 282 Appliances 86
Arc tube 56-58, 68-69
Aspirin 94
Attic 33, 160, 170

Backdrafts 157
Ballast 55, 57, 59, 80, 85, 158, 160, 163;
    about 58-59; kits 58, 70; halide 66; HP
    sodium 70; fluorescent 73, 76; LP sodium
    72; looping 55
Bandits 28,30,280
Bacillus thruingiensis 178
Basements 32, 33, 96, 159, 191, 280-281,
    283
Bees 183, 189
Bending 218-221
Bleach 145
Blood meal 125
Bloom See: Flower and flowering
Bolting 215
Bone meal 125-126
Boron 118-123,131
Branches 43, 208-209, 211, 215, 218,
    220-221, 225, 232, 239, 249
Breaker box 82, 86
Breaker switch 82
Breeding 209, 225, 244-275
Buffing 140, 149
Buds See: Flowers and flowering
Bugs See: Insects
Bulbs 57, 63, 66, 69 about 77
Burn, light 41 fertilizer 114
Butane 165, 167-168

Calcium 95, 87, 114, 118-123, 131, 149;
    disorders 137
Calcium carbonate 87, 143
Calcium hypochlorite 145
Calcium nitrate 87
Calyx 223, 225-226, 239, 249
Cannabis 26 28, 30, 32, 38-39, 93, 107,
    120, 123, 162, 175, 189, 218, 222,
    223,250-275 also see: indica and sativa
Capacitor 57-58
Carbohydrates 24,37, 154, 209
Carbon 118

Carbon dioxide (CO2) 29, 153-171, 283-
    284; 24 production of 165-170 24
Cellulose 24
Chain 35, 85,279, 283
Charcoal 175
Checklist 288
Chimney 157, 170-171
Chlorine 114, 147
Chlorophyll 37, 72, 75, 118-119, 160, 190,
    205, 221, 223 24
Chlorosis 35
Clay soils 90
Clean and cleaning 35, 154-155, 174-175,
    177, 190, 198,236,278
Clones and cloning 29, 33, 73, 98, 118,
    131, 132, 141, 160, 163, 191-192, 206-
    214, 221, 230, 278-279
Cloning for sex 73, 209-211, 279 Cola 225
    Also See Flowers and Flowering
Cold weather 28-29, 159
Color spectrum 28, 38, 60, 72,73-75
Color tracer 93 Companion planting 175,
    177
Compost 92, 102-103, 123, 165
Containers 55, 89, 105-111, 208, 215-216
Copper 118-123, 131
Copper oleate 191
Copper sulfate 87
Core 58-59, also See: Transformer
Cottonseed meal 125 Cuttings See: Clones
    and cloning
Cutworms 92, 103

DEA 10-12
Damping-off 191-192, 202-203
Dehumidify 29, 163, 191 Dirt 101, 104,
    281
Diatomaceous Earth 178
Disease 103, 161, 174, 175, 208;
    prevention 174-176; control 177 - 195
Drainage 90, 98, 106, 110, 140, 147, 192,
    279, 281
Drip line 89, 107
Drip system 118
Dropcloth 35
Dry ice 165
Dry well 110
Drying 230, 232-241, 249

Eggs 93, 177,183-184,186
Electricity about 77-84; circuits 82, 86, 88;
    consumption 82-84; cost 32, 224; current
    59; ground 59, 77-79, 87, 149; meters
    84; overload 78, 86-87; power surge 63,
    68, 86
Electricians 82

Electrodes 57-58, 63, 77
Epsom salts 137, 149
Equinox 39
Ethylene 165
Exhaust fan See: Fan Extension cord 80, 87, 281

Fan leaves 44, 230, 241
Fan, exhaust or vent, 35, 59, 85, 154-156, 160,171-173, 193, 283 circulation 156, 194, 241, 284
Faucet 35, 133
Female 25,29, 31, 39, 201, 203-206, 209, 215, 222-223, 225-228, 245 25
Fermentation 165
Fertilizers 113-138, 146, 236, 280, 282-283; "push" concept 98-99, 133
Fertilization See: Pollination
Filament 56, 70-71 Fire 52,58,60,77,79,87
Fish emulsion 131
Flowers and flowering 25,29, 31, 39-40, 61, 67, 115, 118, 120, 125, 164, 200, 207, 209,220,280
Fluorescent lamps 28, 56, 73-77, 164, 209, 214
Flushing See: Leaching
Foliar feeding 120,131,134-136,149,95, 209
Foot-candle 42
Fortified mix 119
Fungus 92, 96, 103, 106, 114-115, 123, 161, 174, 190-195, 201-202, 236, 239; control 191-191; foliar 191, 193-194; soil born 191-192; mold 156, 176, 194,236,241,283
Fungicide 87, 191-195, 202
Furnace 29, 35, 159
Fuse 59, 77, 79, 87, 281
Fuse box 79-80, 86-87

Garlic 175
Genes 201-202, 223
General Electric (GE) 61-62, 66
Generators 84-84
Germination 23,26114, 118, 120, 200, 202-203
Gnats 189
Gradual release fertilizer 120-123
Gravel 140-141, 143, 148
Greenhouses 164, 165, 183
Growbags 105, 118
Grow rooms 148-149, 156-157, 159, 164-166, 170, 189, 203-208, 224; about 32; construction 32-36
Growth rate 28, 31, 38-40, 43-44, 51-55, 89, 93-95, 105-109, 118, -123, 132, 138-141, 158, 163, 164, 176, 200, 205, 214, 221, 285-288
Growing mediums, See: Soil and Soilless mix
Guano, bat 56, 125-131 sea 131

Halogen 71-72

Harvest 29, 108, 148, 154, 205, 225,230-240
Harvest sun 28, 67, 224, 282
Heat 59, 85, 103, 159
Heat vent 35, 159
Heat tape 97, 160
Hermaphrodites 87, 201, 222, 227-228,245-246
Hertz (HZ) 80
HID (High Intensity Discharge) Lamps 28, 37, 56-57, 60, 160, 163, 164, 188, 198, 201, 207-209, 279-281; restarting 63, 68
Honeydew 187
Hoods, reflective 45-52-50, 279
"Hor" 64
Hormone, floral (auxins) 220-221, 224
Horticulture 23,26,35, 132, 140,183, 215, 220, 224, 245, 280, 283
Hose (water) 117-118, 280; dryer (air) 157, 170-171
Hose bib See: Faucet
Humidifier 163
Humidistats 163, 171
Humidity 29, 35, 147, 158, 161-162, 191-191, 193; tent 115, 160, 214, 279
Hydrochloric acid 145 Hydrogen 118
Hydroponics 75-94, 87, 139-152; active 141; passive 141; recovery 148-152; water leaks 157
Hygrometer 35, 162, 193

Incandescent Lamps 56, 69-71, 160, 214
Indica 201, 207, 232, 245-249, 278, 284
Insects 30, 40, 43, 103, 161, 174-189; prevention 174-177; control 177-189
Insecticides 174-177, 185-189, 195, 282, 284
Ion, negative generator and deionizer 170
Iron 118-123, 131; deficiency 138
Irrigation See: Watering

Jiffy 7 pellet 101

Kerosene 159-160, 166
Kilowatt (KW) 82-84
Kilowatt hour 80

Lady bugs 183, 188
Lamps See: specific lamp name
Larva See: Eggs
Law 7-21,28,32,82
Lawyer 12-21
Leaching 30, 95, 110, 114, 120, 133-138, 145, 149, 209, 211, 236, 282
Lead 149
Leaf mold 123, also See: Fungus
Leaves 24,44, 113, 118, 154, 186, 188, 198, 201, 207, 221, 224, 230,241
Leggyness 43,51,107,149,203,215
Life cycle 22-26,38-40, 200, 205, 222, 227-228

Life of lamp; metal halide 63, 65-66; HP
    Sodium 69-70; LP Sodium 73; fluorescent
    77
Light 28, 37-42, 67, 224, 282, intensity
    41-45, 50-51; reflection of 35, 45-50
Light balancers 33, 46, 51-55, 60
Lime, calic 87; dolomite 95-97, 99,
    104,123, 133; hydrated 96-87, 99, 104;
    quicklime 87
Lime sprays 191
Limestone 143
Litmus paper 93
Low Pressure (LP) Sodium 55-56,72-73
Lumen 42, 61, 66
Lumen-per-watt 55-56, 61, 71-72

Macro-nutrients 118-128,146, 205,209,
    223,282-283
Magnesium 114, 118-123, 131, 149;
    disorders 137
Magnifying glass 184, 235
Male 26,31, 201, 209-214, 225, 227-228,
    231-232, 249
Manganese 118-123, 131
Manicuring 232-239
Manure 92,102,123-131
Marijuana 24,26,28-31, 35, 89, 92-93, 87,
    110, 114-116, 118, 120, 131, 133, 128-
    136, 145-147, 158, 164, 170, 175, 184,
    186, 200-201, 205, 207, 209-209, 220,
    222, 227-230, 232, 236, 241, 280, 282
Mealy Bugs 188, 282
Measuring cup and spoons 198
Mercury vapor lamps 56, 61
Meristem 221
Metal halide lamps 61-66 also See: HID
    lamps
Micronutrients 114, 118-123, 131, 146;
    disorders 138
Microscope 235
Milorganite 131
Misting 183, 198, 214, 236
Mites See: Spider Mites Miticide 181-183,
    185, 187, 182-189
Mixing 93, 95-96, 98, 110, 132, 196
Moisture meter 115-116, 280 Mold 156,
    158, 176, 194; of buds 194,236,241
Molybdenum 118-123, 131
Monochromatic 72-73
Mother Nature 27, 30, 35, 85, 116, 123,
    128, 153, 163, 174, 221, 227, 245
Mother plant 206, 207-214, 240
Mushroom compost 98
Mylar, reflective 46

N-P-K See: macronutrients
Natural gas 160, 165-168
Natural sprays 172
Nicotine sulfate 180 189
Nitric acid 87
Nitrogen 92, 102, 118-136, 146, 205, 209,
    212, 223, 282-283; disorders 128-136
Nodes 212, 218

Nursery 30, 92, 93, 97-98, 101, 107-131,
    165, 191, 218, 279, 284
Nurseryperson 120, 183, 191, 196, 214,
    284
Nutrient solution 140, 147-148, 151
Nutrients 113, 118-131, 132, 134,139;
    disorders 128-138, 149,208

Odor abatement 170
OHM's Law 59, 80
Oil spray 172, 183-186
Organic amendments 92; fertilizer 123131,
    134; tea 131, 146
Outdoor gardening 20-30, 38, 43, 95,110,
    153, 187, 201
Outlet, electrical 80-82, 86,
Over-fertilization 119, 134, 149,
    281-282
Over-watering 116, 191-192, 203
Ovule 222-223, 225
Oxygen 37, 90, 116, 118, 139-140,149,
    153, 175

PCB's 76
Parasites 183, 187
Parent plant 209-211, 223, 278
Peat moss 93, 100, 123
Peat pellets 101
Perlite 91, 98-100, 104
Pesticides See: Insecticides and
    Miticides
PH 91, 93-95, 87-99, 114-134, 143, 146-
    149; pH testers 93-95
Phosphor coating 56, 61, 77
Phosphorus 118-136, 205, 209, 212, 223,
    282-283; disorders 128-136
Photoperiod 29, 38-39, 88, 200, 205, 211,
    225, 232-233, 240, 278-279
Photosynthesis 24, 37, 72, 75, 113, 118,
    154, 160, 164
Phototropism 38
Pigment 50
Pilot light 166
Pinch back 219
Pinesol 190, 194
Pistil 223-224,225, 249,280
Planter box 109, 218, 284
Planting 31, 111, 214, 278, 281, 283, 291
Plastic See: Visqueen
Plug-in 77, 82, 87-88,281
Pollen and pollination 19, 200, 222-224,
    227, 231, 239, 245-249 26
Police 7-21,28,32,82
Pot bound See: Root bound
Potash See: Potassium Potassium 118-136,
    205, 209, 223, 282-283; disorders 128-
    136
Potassium hydroxide 87, 147
Potency See: THC
Pots See: Containers
Predatory insects 183, 185, 187,182-189
Primary nutrients See: macronutrients
Propagation 201, 223; asexual 206-207;
    sexual 201, 223, 249

Propane 160, 166-167
Pruning 218-221, 280
Psychometer See: Hygrometer
Pulleys 85
Pumice 91, 98, 142
Pumps 146-148, 151; jackrabbit 195

Rain 153-155 also See: Misting
Raised beds 110, 125
Reflective light 46-51
Rejuvenation 207, 230-232, 237-240
Reservoir 147-148, 149
Resin 225, 232-235, 241-280
Resin glands 163, 234-235, 241
Respirator 183, 198
Ripeness 233-235
Rockwool 143-145
Root bound 107-109, 131, 134, 215
Root cubes 101, 152, 192, 202, 212, 214-215
Root hairs 107, 113-116 24
Root rot 106
Rooting hormones 131, 209-209, 214
Roots 24,89, 107-111, 119, 139-140, 145, 149, 153, 162-163, 200, 202-206
Rules of Thumb 6,43-44,57,77,79, 96-87, 98, 106, 108, 114-116, 133,146-147, 149, 155, 161, 163, 164, 170, 177

Salt 93-96,114,134,136,143,146
Sand 98,100,115,123,192,215
Sativa 40, 43, 201, 233, 240, 245-249, 281
Scale 188-189
Seaweed 131
Second crops 230, 240
Secondary nutrinets 119 also See: macronutrients
Security 7-21, 28,32,82
Seed 152, 201-202, 207, 223, 245-249 23
Seed bract See: Calyx
Seed crops 239
Seedling 35, 101, 118, 120, 163, 191, 200-201, 203, 282 23

Sevin 189, 282
Sex 26,31, 205-206, 209- 211, 222, 225
Sex reversal 227-228
Shade 44-45, 51, 109
Shock electrical 82; transplant 215
Short circuit 80
Short crop 108
Side lighting 51, 55
Silicon 163
Sinsemilla 26,31, 102, 131, 206, 226-227, 232-235, 239, 249
Peak potency 233-235
Siphon 148
Smell See: Odor
Smoking 233
Sodium hydrochlorite 145
Sodium Hydroxide 87, 147
Sodium (HP) lamps 66-70, 209, 224

Sodium (LP) lamps 72-73 Soil 111, 118, 175, 192, 203; amendments 90-94; texture 90, 175; acid 95, 128; alkaline 95, 128; potting soil 95, 87-98; soil mixes 101; temperature 97, 103, 110, 133; pH 91,93-95,87-99,114-134, 143;compaction 102, 104, 175
Soilless mix 98-99, 120-124,192,284; for hydroponics 140-145
Solarizing 102-103
Spacing of plants 45 also See: Light Balancers
Spider mites 162, 181, 184-186, 282, 284
Sprays and spraying 155, 179-182 185-189, 191-195, 198, 208
Sprayers 195-209
Stadium method 45
Staminate 218 also See: Male
Stem 25,26, 113, 118, 182, 201
Sterilizing 145
Stigma See: Pistil
Stippling 184, 186
Stomata 24,113, 119, 154-158, 162, 172, 198
Strain See: Variety
Stress, temperature 93, 198; from cloning 209; from abuse 221, 224, 228-230, 236
Stroboscopic effect 66
Sugar 113, 119, 154
Sulfur (S) 114, 118-123, 131; disorders 138
Sulfur dioxide 165
Sulfur sprays 191
Sun and sunlight 38, 52, 60, 181, 183, 223-224
Sylvania 61-62, 66

Teflon tape 149
Temperature 147, 193 also See: Soil or Air
Terminal bud 24,253
THC 164, 201, 207, 225-226,230-232,236, 241
Thermometer 158
Thermostat 159-160, 171
Thinning 111, 203
Thrips 188
Timers 29, 57,59,85-86, 88, 151, 166, 171, 281, 283-284
Tools 35-36
Toxic life 181-186, 198
Trace elements See: Micro Nutrients
Transformer 58, 72, 76,
Transpiration 113-114, 116, 162, 193, 205
Transplanting 98, 107, 109, 131, 152, 203, 215-217, 280, 284 shock 101, 131, 152, 215-217
Trellis 109, 218
Trial 14-21
Tungsten Halogen 71-72
Ultraviolet light 61; protective goggles 56

Underwatering 116

VHO See: Fluorescent lamps

Variety of *cannabis* 201-202, 225,239-246
Vegetative growth 38, 67, 115, 118, 200,
     205, 209, 249, 280
Ventilation 114, 116, 128, 193, 280-281
     also See: Fan
Vermiculite 91-92, 98-100, 114-115, 143,
     192, 215
Vigor See: Growth rate
Vinegar 87
Visgueen 35, 50, 103
Vitamin B$_1$ 131, 152, 214, 215-217 Volt
     59,80
Voltage, line 57; drop of 80

Wasps 183, 189
Water and watering 35, 90, 113-118, 159,
     203, 215-216, 230, 280; pH 95, 114;
     temperature 114, 149; application 132,
     147-148, 152, 280; evaporation 147-148,
     156; wnad 35
Water Table 110
Watts 80
Watthour 80
Watts-per-square-foot 42
Westinghouse 61-62, 66, 72, 75
Wetting agent 116-117
White paint 45, 50-50, 279
Whiteflies 186
Whitewash 50, 190-191, 208 34
Wind 28, 155, 282 also See: Air
Wind burn 35,149
Window 171-171
Wire electrical 79-80
Wire ties 218
Wood ashes 125
Worm castings 104, 123-131

Yeast 165
Yield 44, 245

Zinc 118-123, 131,282